W9-BCK-401

# THE AIDE IN EARLY CHILDHOOD EDUCATION

# THE AIDE IN EARLY CHILDHOOD EDUCATION

**VIVIAN EDMISTON TODD**
CURRICULUM CONSULTANT

WITH CONTRIBUTING AUTHOR
**GEORGENNIE H. HUNTER**
KINDERGARTEN TEACHER



THE MACMILLAN COMPANY
NEW YORK

COLLIER-MACMILLAN LIMITED
LONDON

Printed in the United States of America



The Macmillan Company
866 Third Avenue, New York, New York 10022

Collier-Macmillan Canada, Ltd., Toronto, Ontario

Library of Congress catalog card number: 70-190673

Printing: 2 3 4 5 6 7 8 Year: 3 4 5 6 7 8

# PREFACE

Parents, teenage siblings, grandparents, and others interested in working with a child are essential parts of his early environment. As aides, these people augment the effectiveness of the teacher who guides the learning of children. As volunteers or employees, working either at school or at home, aides to early childhood education are now recognized as important elements not only in the education of preschool and primary grade groups but in the out-of-school lives of children.

All who are involved in the education of young children benefit by the work of aides. The child who has a richer learning experience because of an aide will reap the benefits throughout the rest of his life. The child's home, his school, and his community will benefit when an aide helps him to be a happier member of an educational group and a more competent individual at his age level. The teacher who has an aide can have the satisfaction of seeing greater accomplishment of the children's group.

An aide benefits not only the children and their teacher but also himself by helping to guide the learning of young children. An aide can increase his understanding of the learning process and of human relationships. If the aide is a teen-ager, he can preview the role of parent; if he is a parent, he can improve his effectiveness in that role; and if he is an older friend or relative, the aide can have the satisfaction of being of service to the young as they find their way into the social order.

The aide has a unique function in linking school and community for the good of the children. The parent, teen-ager, or other aide who takes time to help young children on the school playground or in the classroom is a visible reminder of the importance of community support for, and involvement in, the school.

*The Aide in Early Childhood Education* was written as a handbook for parents as well as for other aides who guide the learning of young children. It emphasizes the ability of a child to learn through experience and assumes the importance of the child becoming increasingly able to utilize such skills as the following:

1. To perceive meaningfully—especially to observe with accuracy and to interpret accurately.
2. To conceptualize—especially to form useful concepts, to link concepts to experience, to link concepts in useful generalizations, and to apply concepts with satisfaction.
3. To read—especially to link experience with words heard, spoken, or written, to link memories and imaginings with words, and to link words with words and other symbols.

An aide has an important role in facilitating the development of such skills in each child. He is an important and welcome addition to the teaching team.

In selecting what is useful for an aide to learn in the early childhood field, the authors made these assumptions:

1. An aide learns inductively by observing how children react to situations and by considering such observations as feedback on the guidance provided for the children.

2. An aide needs to know various learning activities in common use by teachers and how to supplement these activities effectively. The aide cannot work effectively with children in a vacuum.

3. The teacher and others who guide the development of an aide are familiar with pertinent concepts developed in such books as *The Years Before School* by Todd and Heffernan.[1]

The preparation of this manuscript involved the cooperation of many people and of many institutions, too many to list individually. However, the continuing interest and assistance of the Bruce M. Purvine and Clyde E. Osborne families and of the following institutions should be acknowledged: Long Beach Day Nursery; Long Beach Unified School District; Long Beach Public Library, Boys and Girls Department; California State University at Long Beach; Fallbrook Union School District; San Diego County Library, Fallbrook Branch; and Oceanside Union Elementary School District.

Two poems by Barbara McBride (Mrs. Laurence McBride) and a story by Marion Hager were written for this book. Chapter 6 was reviewed by Dr. Marina Krause, and Chapter 7 was reviewed by Dr. Doris Tabor, both of the Department of Elementary Education, California State University, Long Beach. For these contributions, the authors wish to express their appreciation.

Although it is possible to acknowledge personal indebtedness in the specific activity of manuscript preparation, it is not possible even to be aware of the authors' infinite indebtedness to those who have contributed to the conceptualization from which a manuscript is written. The book makes available, for instance, some current versions of unpublished poems and stories from the lore of early childhood education.

The book also entails applications of linkage as presented by Ronald G. Havelock.[2] Linkage theory offered the simple role of "knowledge conveyor" that is so suitable to the paraprofessional and helped in clarification of the teacher roles: diagnostician, consultant, leader, and so on, in addition to the fun-of-learning-conveyor and knowledge-conveyor roles that are shared with the aide.

V. E. T.
G. H. H.

[1] Vivian Edmiston Todd and Helen Heffernan, *The Years Before School*. New York: The Macmillan Company, 1970.

[2] Ronald G. Havelock, *Planning for Innovation Through Dissemination and Utilization of Knowledge* (Ann Arbor, Michigan: Center for Research on Utilization of Scientific Knowledge, 1969). (ERIC: ED 015 535.)

# TABLE OF CONTENTS

# THE AIDE IN EARLY CHILDHOOD EDUCATION

# WHAT AN AIDE DOES

The basic role of an aide is to increase the likelihood that each young child will acquire basic concepts and skills of learning and of good citizenship more quickly and more completely than he would otherwise. An aide works with young children individually and in groups of two or three. An aide may be a teen-ager, a parent, or a grandparent helpfully guiding a preschool child or a primary school child to explore his home environment. Or he may be a person walking through a neighborhood at the moment when the young children who live there need help to get their pet kitten down from a low limb of a tree. The aide may also be a student who takes advantage of an opportunity to participate in a Project Tutor and thus comes to work with a child informally but more or less regularly. Or he may be enrolled in a college or high school class that provides its students with field experience in preschool or primary grades. In short, the aide may be a person of any age over ten or twelve who works with one or more young children, inside or outside of a classroom.

What an aide does depends somewhat on the situation in which he works with young children. If he is in a classroom, he has the guidance of the teacher in charge of the classroom in fitting into carefully planned learning situations. If he is in a child's home, the aide works within limits set by the expectations of the parents. But in both the classroom and the child's home, and in neighborhood situations, the aide is basically working in terms of what the child needs to learn, and in terms of building a child's self-confidence and love of learning.

In guiding child learning, an aide begins by establishing rapport with the child. Just being near a child day after day leads to the development of rapport. If during that time occasions arise for the child to get help from the aide directly and personally, rapport develops more rapidly. As an aide sees that the child has materials he needs to work with at the time that he reaches for them, feelings of mutual confidence develop. A child quickly accepts a person who helps him if he needs assistance, helps him obtain juice, milk, or water when he is thirsty, helps him see or learn something new, or in other ways helps him solve his problems and enjoy new experiences.

Whether aides are volunteers or paid assistants, what they do depends on what assistance the teacher desires and what needs the children have at the time.

### An Aide to an Early Childhood Group

When an early childhood group of children has an aide as well as a teacher, it has a better chance of having an educational experience rather than a child-care experience. With one or more aides, a group is more likely to move smoothly through the activities planned for the day. Furthermore, aides can make the difference between a day that is tiring to both teacher and children and a day that is a happy learning experience.

The first national survey of Head Start programs showed that in over 80 per cent of the school systems having such programs, parents were serving as teacher aides.[1] Furthermore, the study revealed that over 6 per cent of the school systems were using work-experience programs; over 25 per cent, Neighborhood Youth Corps; over 4 per cent, Vista Volunteers; and over 9 per cent, Work-Study programs to increase the adult personnel for the programs. Aides of various kinds are an integral part of Head Start, Home Start, and other early childhood groups.

### A Paraprofessional

An aide in early childhood education works with professional educators as a paraprofessional. If an aide is associated with a classroom teacher, he enlarges the effectiveness of the classroom teacher in guiding the learning of each child in the class. If an aide is associated with a school faculty as a Playground Aide, he makes it possible for members of the faculty to have "an unhampered duty-free period for lunch" or a "coffee break" during a recess period for the children.[2] If an aide is associated with one or two parents, or with a school system, with responsibility for guiding learning of an individual child, he enables the parents and school system to be more effective in their respective roles. An NEA Research Division sample survey of the nation's public-school teachers . . . revealed that one classroom teacher in four had the support of a teacher aide in his classroom assign-

[1] "Head Start in the Public Schools, 1966–1967," NEA *Research Bulletin*, XLVI, 1 (March 1968), 3–8.

[2] "Teacher Supervision of Lunch Periods," NEA *Research Bulletin*, XLV, 3 (October 1967), 72–74.

ment.[3] The survey reported that most teachers have secretarial assistance, and 46 per cent received assistance with lunch duty from teacher aides. But about 26 per cent of the teachers receive assistance from aides in instruction of small groups, preparation of instructional resources, classroom environment, and instruction of individuals. The fact that a significant increase has taken place in the percentage of teachers reporting assistance in the classroom by one or more paraprofessionals suggests that further demand for aides can be expected.[4]

Paraprofessionals in early childhood education include those who take care of attendance records, health records, or other records useful to the fiscal, medical, or other agencies that interlock with the school; those who have responsibility for the care of school facilities on a daily basis or on an occasional basis; and those who observe the teacher as an early step in their preparation for professional, paraprofessional, or parental responsibility. Each of these auxiliaries to the teacher should have some understanding of the aide's function in helping the teacher to guide the development of children. Anyone working in proximity to the teacher should enhance the relationship of teacher and children, and if necessary, he should also be able to enrich the learning of the children through momentary or extended functioning as an aide.

Like an aide, any other paraprofessional comes into the children's group through an introduction or explanation by the teacher. "Miss Jones will be taking pictures of our playground this morning," the teacher may say. "We can help her by playing just as we usually do, and letting her do her work with her camera. Before she starts her work, she is going to talk with us now for a few minutes." Miss Jones then holds her unloaded camera while each child has an opportunity to begin feeling at home with picture taking.

## AN AIDE TO A TEACHER

### Responsibility of a Group Aide

An aide to an early childhood group is often spoken of as a Teacher's Aide. The teacher has the responsibility of creating an environment that is favorable to pupil development, for planning and directing learning experiences for the children, and for identifying group objectives and helping the children attain them. She assesses the needs of the group and plans and teaches in terms of those needs. At the same time, the teacher diagnoses the individual needs of the children and guides individual child development within the group experiences.

[3] "Teacher Aides in the Public Schools," NEA *Research Bulletin,* XLVIII, 1 (March 1970), 11–12.
[4] Ibid.

An aide is likewise concerned with meeting individual and group needs and helping each child to develop in terms of them. Both the teacher and the aide must guide pupil learning in ways that will build the self-confidence of each pupil. As long as the aide reinforces and extrapolates what the teacher does, he helps pupils learn. But if the aide worked at variance with the teacher, he would confuse pupils and interfere with their learning and with their pleasure in it. For the good of the pupils, the aide to a group must indeed be an aide to the teacher.

The title Teacher's Aide emphasizes the fact that a classroom aide works closely with the teacher who is in charge of a group of children. At all times an aide should be alert to help the teacher guide the learning of the children. Because the role of an aide depends on that of the teacher, a close look at what an aide does and what a teacher does will clarify the relationship between their two roles.

In a preschool or a primary grade group, the teacher has the primary responsibility of guiding the learning of the children. The aides have secondary responsibility. The teacher is always in charge of the group of children, but she may work with part of the group and have an aide work with another part. Or she may work with the whole group with the help of an aide. In an emergency the teacher may even turn over the responsibility for the entire group to the aide for a few minutes. The teacher is providing cues to help an aide know whatever she thinks is important for the children to do at any particular time. Thus the aide is able to follow the teacher's cues and to do his part in guiding the learning of the children.

### Planning the Educational Program

In guiding the learning of a group of children, the teacher plans a program of activities for them. She is able to do this because she has spent years studying and thinking about how children learn, and what is important for them to learn through a sequence of activities. The teacher plans the entire school year and makes detailed lesson plans for units within that general plan. Each day she thinks of what is especially important for the children to do that day and shares her daily lesson plan as well as the unit plans with her aides. Thus the aides and teacher are thinking along the same lines about the learning activities for the children. The primary responsibility for these plans rests with the teacher, but the aides are also responsible for them. An aide must also have the plans clearly in mind if he is to help carry them out effectively.

A good educational program for a group of children starts with a definition of what the children need to learn. The children should be different at the end of the program from what they were at its beginning. Educators often classify these objectives or expected changes into three major domains, namely:

TEACHER AND AIDE DISCUSS OBJECTIVES AND PLANS.

1. The affective domain including objectives such as the following:
   a. The child will believe that. . . .
   b. The child will become increasingly interested in. . . .
   c. The child will appreciate. . . .
   d. The child will value. . . .
2. The conative or psychomotor domain, including objectives such as the following:
   a. The child will respond when he hears his name.
   b. The child will help to put away what he used.
   c. The child will read a sign aloud pronouncing each word.
   d. The child will write a list of words legibly.
   e. The child will add a three-line column of numerals accurately.
   f. The child will jump rope thirty times without missing.
3. The cognitive domain, including objectives such as the following:
   a. The child will recall from memory. . . .
   b. The child will understand the similarity between . . . and. . . .

c. The child will know the Pledge of Allegiance.
d. The child will understand the concept of. . . .[5]

The teacher of a group of children plans the children's learning activities in order for them to achieve the objectives suitable for the group. She plans classroom experiences and study trips that will help the children develop new interests. She thinks of questions to discuss so that the children will develop the values they need. As the teacher plans new learning experiences for the children, she also plans to have a review of earlier experiences and continued practice as needed by the children. With an aide to help children reinforce what they have been learning, the teacher has much broader scope in guiding the children's learning.

The children in a classroom group will develop new interests; they will begin to form new beliefs and to become more firm about beliefs they have formed earlier. In addition to such expected changes in the affective domain are changes in the children's conative domain—changes expected in their skills and habits. They will be able, for instance, to balance themselves on only one foot when previously they were able only to do so on both feet. Or they will be able to write both their first and their last names using capital and small letters. They will begin to notice the birds that sometimes visit the school playground, read stories written at a more advanced level of difficulty than they could before, or read and enjoy stories that were formerly of no interest to them. If these changes in both the affective and conative domains are clear in the minds of each aide as well as the teacher, teacher and aides can then work as a team to guide the learning of children.

Aides as well as teacher need to have in mind each day the two or three main ideas that are to be emphasized that day. If this is the day that the lawn is to be mowed, then an aide can help the teacher guide the children to develop the concept of growth. Perhaps the teacher has talked with the children about the fact that grass grows and needs to be cut, and the fact that hair grows and is cut by those who like it to be short. Then on the grounds an aide can help the children observe not only new growth, but also trees that have been pollarded and bushes that have been pruned to guide their growth as people want it to be, and can reinforce the concept of growth in these and other ways. Knowing the concepts to be developed through the teacher's lesson plans for the day, the aides can think about supplementing the teacher's plans for the whole group by planning additional learning experiences for individuals as well as small groups of children.

[5] D. R. Krathwohl, B. S. Bloom, and B. B. Masia, *Taxonomy of Educational Objectives* (New York: David McKay Co., Inc., 1964).

In general, knowing the importance of his work in reinforcing the work of the teacher to guide the learning of children, an aide makes sure that he knows the changes that a teacher expects to occur in the children in his charge. Then he plans to supplement daily lesson plans that the teacher prepares. Each day the aide can reinforce, elaborate, and enrich the planned learning experience for as many of the children as possible.

An aide can help the teacher make plans if he asks questions about what might fit into the learning activities for the group as a whole, or for certain individual children. For instance, an aide who knows how to play a guitar may ask about bringing his guitar to play when the children are singing. He may explain, "The children on our block like to sing while I play my guitar." The teacher may feel that such enrichment will be appropriate later or that some of the children are indeed ready to have the guitar accompany their music. No matter what the teacher's decision is, the aide will better understand whatever plans are worked out for guiding the children's singing.

In general, an aide must let the teacher know what responsibility he is eager to assume. Maybe he has noticed that a child has been awkardly trying to perform on the horizontal bar at the playground, and has figured out how to help the child learn the stunt. "Will it be all right if I help Tom on the horizontal bar today?" the aide may ask. Then a plan can be worked out with the teacher so that the aide will not be needed at some other place during the time he is helping Tom. It is easy for an aide to take increased responsibility if he plans with the teacher how the aide's new responsibilities will fit into the total educational program for the children.

Ideally, an aide is in a flexible situation in which roles and duties are worked out between teacher and aide. As they work together, and as the aide becomes more skilled and confident, their relationship is modified as seems desirable.

### Carrying Out the Educational Program

The teacher of a preschool or primary school group of children is often fortunate enough to have one or more aides to help guide the learning of the children. The teacher depends on the aides to reinforce concepts and beliefs that she has developed with the children and to provide additional practice with building desirable skills and habits.

The teacher also depends on aides to help her while she is working with the children to develop concepts and the generalizations that tie the concepts together. She anticipates the props she will need to work with and has them all at hand, but she may suddenly realize that the children are ready for a new, related experience, or that they need to have a different approach to understanding an important concept. If she needs some more material, the teacher can often enlist the help of an aide in procuring it. An aide who is familiar with the teacher's educational materials can quickly find what is required.

Throughout the entire school day, both aides and teacher continuously guide the children as they learn from their group experience how to function as sovereign citizens within a democratic group. Each child is free to initiate and carry on constructive learning experiences as long as he does not interfere with the rights of others to do likewise. For instance, in a free-play situation a child can make use of a toy that another child was using and has now discarded, but he is not free to take a toy that another child is using at that time. He can ask, "May I have it next?" and arrange to have the toy to use a few minutes later. An aide, like a teacher, guides children to learn respect for the rights of others and for their own rights. For instance, he often encourages a child to say to a more aggressive one, "I'm using this. You get another."

Aides as well as teacher help children to learn to use words in controlling their environment. The child who pushes another child out of his way in order to get where he wants to go learns to keep his hands to himself and to ask for what he wants. At the crucial moment, an aide is there to give him the pattern of speech that he needs to use, for instance "May I have it next?" to replace grabbing.

Like teachers, aides encourage children to try out their ideas within the limits of physical safety. An aide on the playground encourages a child to take a turn on a climber, but also teaches the child to make a wide circle around the swings to get to it. At the carpenter's bench, an aide makes as few suggestions as possible but is ready to make the comment that encourages the child or enables him to have a successful work experience.

Aides, like teachers, are invaluable in sharing the achievement of a child. "I did it!" the child exclaims, and the aide is right there to share the excitement of accomplishment, to reinforce the child's self-confidence, and to help him to set additional goals that are feasible for him to reach. Helping each child to develop a genuine sense of his own worth may, in the final analysis, be the major contribution that an aide makes to the children in a group. An additional adult who is sensitive to the needs of children increases the likelihood of all of the children building genuine self-confidence.

The teacher knows what is to be expected of her group of children and of each child in it. She identifies the learning problems that each child encounters and diagnoses his needs. By using feedback about what individual children and the group as a whole are learning, she plans subsequent learning experiences for them. She can plan fuller living and learning activities for the children if she can supplement her own activities with those she suggests for one or more of her aides.

An aide can depend on the teacher's planning in terms of how children mature and develop through sequences and varieties of experience. The teacher has had years of college study as well as years of experience with guiding the learning of children. Her comments and suggestions merit careful attention.

An aide helps a teacher to carry out the educational program for a group in many ways. These include reinforcing in pupils:

1. Learning concepts and generalizations.
2. Functioning in a group democratically.
3. Substituting words for physical problem solving.
4. Perceiving cues to new kinds of behavior.
5. Responding to the cues appropriately.
6. Enjoying experimentation.
7. Developing self-confidence.
8. Appreciating good health and nutrition.
9. Learning to get along with others.
10. Learning to move with a group.
11. Enjoying learning.
12. Widening interests joyously.

The aide often makes it possible for children to experience pleasure in what they learn. "I like this," the aide says with sincerity, and the children echo, "Like this!" Such pleasure is an integral part of an environment that is favorable to learning. The happy child learns.

### Helping the Deviate Learner

An aide is indispensable in helping the deviate learner. While the teacher is guiding the learning of the group of children, the aide is available to help guide the child who is not learning at the same pace as the remainder of the group. With a fast learner or one experienced in what is being learned, an aide can introduce a supplementary experience. With a slow learner who is falling behind the group, an aide can provide the additional cues that enable the slow learner to move ahead more rapidly. With the child who loses interest in the group activity, an aide can set up some familiar activity that provides a change of pace for him, if necessary in another setting. Thus the aide makes it possible for the group to be guided by the teacher without the interruption that would otherwise be necessitated by attending to a particular learning problem of a child in the group.

Recognition of this important function of an aide has led to his exploitation in some instances through increasing the number of children working with a single teacher. To enlarge the size of a group of children by adding a teacher 's aide, however, is a misuse of an aide. An aide helps to increase the learning of the children through the increased interaction of children with their teacher. The interaction of children with an aide is an important supplement to interaction of children with their teacher but should never be a substitute for it.

### Preparing and Maintaining a Setting for Learning

An aide has an important role to play in setting the stage for learning activities. He arrives at school before the children and, with the teacher, creates for them a learning environment that arouses their curiosity and entices them to reexplore familiar learning activities. Throughout the school day the aide anticipates each learning activity the teacher will guide and readies the materials and the setting that are needed for it. As the new activity is started, the aide makes sure that the materials that were an integral part of the previous learning activity are cleared away. In doing this, an aide enlists the help of any child who has finished an activity and is looking around to see what to do next.

### Avoiding Interference with Learning

In addition to helping children to learn under the guidance of their teacher, an aide must also be careful to avoid interfering with their learning. An aide who is more concerned about himself than about the children is likely to ask the teacher what he should do rather than observe what the children are learning, what materials or help, if any, are needed, and what he can do quietly and unobtrusively to help the teacher. The self-conscious aide will do well to stand quietly by as an observer until he can see helpful things to do and can talk with the teacher outside of the children's time with her to validate his thinking about being helpful.

In general, the wise aide keeps in mind that the teacher is guiding the learning of the children, and that the role of the aide is to facilitate the interaction of the children with their teacher. The aide helps to build the relationship between the children and their teacher. He does not let his relationships with the children interfere with their relationships to their teacher. He may supplement that relationship, but at no time and in no way should he interfere with it.

## AN AIDE AT SCHOOL

### Daily Routine

A group of young children needs to be able to anticipate with confidence that tomorrow will be like today. The child wants the next school day to be somewhat similar in structure to the day that preceded it. Routine gives stability to the lives of the children, and the well-educated teacher carefully plans the nature of that routine, and the various activities that accompany it. She may communicate the basic schedule to the aides by giving them a card or a sheet of paper with a list of the time intervals for that day, and the kinds of activities occurring in each interval. Or the teacher may prefer to use several basic schedules, and to tell the aides each day what is to be their schedule for that day.

Usually an aide begins his school day at least half an hour before the children are expected to arrive. The teacher may arrive at the same time as the aide or earlier. If teacher and aide have not yet discussed the plans for the day, they should do so. Then the aide takes responsibility for setting up at least part of the equipment that the children will need as soon as they arrive—outdoor equipment as well as indoor equipment and supplies.

The basic routines of the aide are those that are essential to support the activities of the teacher in guiding the learning of the children. Prior to each activity, the aide sees that the teacher will have at hand whatever she needs, such as sets of materials each child will need for a craft activity. During the activity, the aide is near enough to fetch quickly any item that may have been overlooked. It is important for the teacher and the children to interact continuously without interruption during a learning activity for the group. After the activity is completed and the children have put away materials and moved on to another activity, the aide quickly returns the equipment to the place where it is kept and rearranges the furniture for subsequent activity.

The aide, as a person who is less involved with the children, is often the person who can make sure that the sandbox toys are back in the sandbox and are not lying in a dangerous place or forgotten under a swing. He can see that the paintings of the day went home with each artist, that the books are returned to the library table, and that what has been used has been put away at the end of the day.

An aide, like the teacher is prepared to cheerfully help an individual child clean up spilled milk, or whatever other mess the child may make.

The last activity of the school day for children and aides is putting away the equipment. When the teacher says that it is time to clean up, the aide helps to guide the children in getting the tricycles, wagons, and other vehicles into their garage, and the swing seats and other removable parts of outer equipment into storage. Soon the outdoor play area is safe from passers-by whose physical weight could break equipment made for children but not for heavier people.

When the last child has helped put away indoor equipment and has left for the day, the aide finishes whatever cleaning and putting away needs to be done. If facilities are used only for the young children, putting away equipment can mean arranging it for them to use the next day. If, however, facilities are shared with grown-up or other groups, the aide sees that all of the equipment is put away so that it may be set up the next day. If the aide cleans hand prints from the surfaces at the conclusion of each day, they will always look nice.

### Fitting into Plans for a Day

An aide quickly learns the schedule of the early childhood group and the facilities and equipment that the group will be using. Thus he prepares to guide the children to develop the routine that is an integral part of a day in an early childhood group. At the same time the aide prepares to help with the variations that are likewise an important part of each day. With group and individual activities varying from day to day, an aide is ready to help children quickly to procure the materials that they want to use in each learning activity.

### Enriching Plans for Each Month

The activities of a children's group change from season to season, and from month to month within each season. The aide is eager to see what objectives a teacher has for the children, what learning experiences she plans as a means of bringing about expected changes in the children, and what kinds of feedback she uses as a basis for her day-to-day planning. Then the aide can plan how to help the children anticipate and later recapitulate the learning experiences. The aide observes the critical elements in each learning experience and helps individuals and small groups of children to have similar additional experiences as well as the opportunity to remember, repeat, and talk about the original experience.

### Guiding Perception

An aide, like a teacher, is always alert to guide a pupil in observing his environment. If a black, woolly caterpillar is briefly visible on a twig, an aide helps the pupils near him note its beauty, watch its movement, and think about factors associated with it. "Do you think it is looking for food?" he may ask, and then point out the holes in the leaf the caterpillar is on.

An aide may be the adult at hand when a child runs his finger over a sharp edge and then sees blood on his finger. The aide is prepared to calmly help the child understand that the edge was sharp enough to cut through his skin, and to help him link his observation of blood with a perception of his need to get an adhesive bandage for it.

### Conceptualization

Knowing the great number of times a young child needs to see one kind of object before he builds a generalized concept of the object, an aide enriches a child's day with opportunities to conceptualize. For instance, if the teacher has worked with the group learning to understand the concept of *ten,* an aide will help individuals and small groups to read books and bulletin board displays that picture ten dogs or ten other objects, to see that two hands have ten fingers, to take ten steps, to clap ten times, and to formulate the idea of *ten* in as many different situations as the day can afford.

### Encouraging Creativity

An aide also has an important role in encouraging individuals and small groups in creative expression of concepts that they formulate. Children who have enjoyed walking through multicolored leaves and have gathered especially attractive ones may want to use number concepts to count them, craft skills to make a leaf collage, or verbal skills to make a rhyme or a song or a story about the leaves. An aide is ready to help children in such creative activities.

### Guiding Children into Other Learning Skills

Keeping in mind the importance of having skills with which to learn, an aide is alert to help children develop additional interest in them and to build perception and conceptualization in relation to school subjects. An aide helps a child observe the letter that starts the sign naming the street as well as the rainbow that appears in the sky.

### Helping with an Emergency

An aide is helpful at any time but he is indispensable whenever an emergency occurs. If two children have both claimed a toy, or if a child has skinned his knee, or some other unexpected event has occurred, at least one child will need individual help at the same time that the audience group needs guidance in learning how to react to the emergency. The teacher has to depend upon an aide to assume one of these helper roles while she assumes the other.

### Working with an Individual or a Small Group

When the teacher is working with children in a large group, often one or more individuals are not relating to the large group. Perhaps a child is suddenly feverish and needs to be taken to the school nurse. Perhaps a child or two has interests different from those of the large group and needs encouragement to go to another place. Perhaps a child needs to rest by himself or to go to the bathroom. In short, when an aide is available to identify and provide for individual needs, they can be taken care of without interrupting the teacher-centered activity.

### Preparing for Future Activities

When children are all busy with constructive activities, an aide can work with materials that need to be processed for a later activity. If he knows children will be engaged in craft activities following juice time, an aide in a preschool group makes sure that all the materials are prepared in sufficient amounts so that each child will have what he needs to work with as soon as he is ready to begin. This anticipation of the next event in the children's day means that the aide is often thinking ahead while the teacher is actively engaged in working with the children. His skill in doing so can make the difference between a skeleton program and an enriched one.

## HOW AN AIDE GUIDES CHILD LEARNING

| AREA OF LEARNING | BEHAVIORAL OBJECTIVE FOR CHILD | SPECIFIC CHILD BEHAVIOR |
|---|---|---|
| Physical | Child maintains control | Child identifies and satisfies physical needs (e.g. learns when to go to toilet)<br>Seeks activity and rest as needed |
| | AIDE HELPS CHILD RECOGNIZE AND SATISFY HIS NEEDS | AIDE ASKS CHILD ABOUT HIS PHYSICAL NEEDS (e.g. on a hot day, asks, "Are you thirsty? Do you need a drink?") |
| Social | Child interacts happily with peers and adults | Child observes results of his own actions and modifies what he does next time (e.g. notes that Sue cries when he takes the toy she was using. Next time asks Sue for the toy.) |
| | AIDE HELPS MAINTAIN EQUAL RIGHTS FOR ALL | AIDE ASKS QUESTIONS TO AID PERCEPTION (e.g. "Is Sue unhappy?")<br>AIDE SUGGESTS MORE SATISFYING ACTION (e.g. "Another time ask Sue if you can have the next turn with the truck.") |
| Emotional | Child releases emotions in a socially acceptable way | Child finds satisfaction in constructive physical outlets for his emotions (e.g. eagerly gets ready for new activity. Cleans up what he spills.) |
| | AIDE HELPS CHILD FIND CONSTRUCTIVE ACTIVITIES | AIDE ALTERNATES SEDENTARY AND PHYSICAL ACTIVITIES.<br>AIDE HELPS CHILD PREPARE FOR AND DO CONSTRUCTIVE ACTIVITIES (e.g. washing, punching a bag, listening to music)<br>AIDE CALMLY AND CASUALLY HELPS CHILD CLEAN UP AND PLAN HOW TO AVOID MESSES |

| | | Doing | Remembering | Thinking |
|---|---|---|---|---|
| Intellectual | Child links experience with words<br>Child thinks with words | During experience child actively perceives and conceptualizes accurately | Child recalls experience with words and later sentences.<br>With more experience, child needs fewer multisensory cues. | Child links words with experience and memories, orally and with print.<br>Child organizes and reorganizes concepts, and formulates generalizations. |
| | AS LINKING AGENT, AIDE HELPS CHILD LINK EXPERIENCE WITH WORDS | AIDE GUIDES PERCEPTION: GIVES CHILD LABELS FOR WHAT HE OBSERVES<br>AIDE GUIDES FORMULATION OF ACCURATE CONCEPTS AND GENERALIZATIONS<br>HE POINTS OUT RELATIONSHIPS AS WELL AS ATTRIBUTES | WITH PANTOMIME, 2- AND 3-DIMENSIONAL REPRESENTATIONS (e.g. models, cutouts, pictures), AIDE GUIDES RECALL OF EXPERIENCE WITH CONCEPTS AND GENERALIZATIONS | AIDE ENCOURAGES THINKING AT EVERY OPPORTUNITY<br>AIDE PROVIDES SPOKEN AND PRINTED WORDS AS PART OF EXPERIENCE OR RECALL OF IT |

## STRATEGIES AND TACTICS

The way an aide guides child learning can be thought about within different theoretical frameworks. One such framework is suggested in the examples of the chart entitled "How an Aide Guides Child Learning." It classifies child learning into four areas: physical, social, emotional, and intellectual. Within each of these primary areas of child development, curriculum specialists identify sequences of behavior to be expected in a child.

These expected forms of behavior are the objectives that teachers have in mind as they guide children. These objectives can be stated in general terms as shown in the second column, or in specific terms as illustrated in the third column. A teacher becomes proficient in stating objectives at any level of specificity, and in moving back and forth among various levels of specificity. In planning with an aide, the teacher uses specific behavioral objectives so that an aide will know precisely what to do with the children. But the teacher also helps the aide to see that the specific behavioral objectives fit into larger and more general goals.

The teacher and aide can use the chart as illustrated by thinking about the first entry—"Child maintains control." With preschool children developing control of their bladders, the aide as well as the teacher notes when a child is clutching himself in the genital area. The aide responds to the cue by saying, "Let's go to the bathroom," and by helping the child move in that direction.

An aide soon learns to respond to a great many cues by which individual children show their needs. The aide can develop a list of these cues to discuss with the teacher and to use with the children.

In guiding learning, an aide makes use of objectives as well as a variety of strategies and tactics. These are based on psychological and educational research just as the more extensive strategies and tactics used by an early childhood teacher are. They are designed to help each child to develop confidence in himself and assurance in meeting both new and familiar situations.

### Strategy: Enrich Environment

An aide, like a teacher, is primarily helping a child develop through interaction with his social and physical environment. As the child interacts with other people, he learns that he is an important person and that others are important too. And as the child interacts with the natural environment and the man-made artifacts within it, he sees that he is able to use it to accomplish what he wants. Thus the child gains self-confidence and self-assurance.

It is also important for an aide as well as a teacher to help each child learn better how to learn. The child actively explores what is at hand and learns in the process. An aide encourages constructive learning experiences and enlarges what a child learns from them by calling attention to what the child might overlook. The aide gives short and timely explanations that help a child build concepts and see relations among those concepts he has already formed.

AN AIDE ENCOURAGES CONSTRUCTIVE LEARNING ACTIVITIES.

A child learns better when a beloved aide or teacher is part of the learning situation. Pleasantness facilitates learning, and the aide as well as a teacher can enrich a situation by adding the emotional component that raises an ordinary experience to the level of real pleasure. What a child passes by without noticing is what an aide can make into an exciting learning experience. An unnoticed dead leaf on the edge of the walk, for instance, may have a sow bug under it and may lead to fascinating biological concepts.

**Strategy: Keep Environment Safe**

The primary strategy of an aide is to help a child move toward constructive learning experiences and away from what interferes with learning. Limits of physical safety are kept in mind by an aide as well as a teacher. Is the play area free from broken glass, nails, and other sharp objects that can cut small fingers? Is each child learning to stay clear of moving objects such as children on tricycles or on swings?

An aide is careful to see that he does not use with a child those remarks that cut off learning experiences:

"No."
"That's none of your business."

"Stupid! Don't do that!"
"You'll hurt yourself."
"That won't work."

**Strategy: Expect Learning**

An aide, like a teacher, is realistic about the fact that every normal child can and does learn what his associates expect him to learn. An aide expects learning and tries to guide each child to learn at a pace that is congenial to him. Furthermore, a wise aide firmly believes what he often tells a child and his playmates: "Tommy will learn when he is ready."

When an aide talks with adults, he avoids negative labels that detract from the encouragement of learning:

"He's a slow learner who won't get much out of it."
"He's a 'D' student."
"He has a low IQ."
"He's from a family that never does much."
"His older brothers and sisters are drop-outs, and he probably will be one too."

**Strategy: Develop Concepts Out of Experience**

Providing young children with firsthand experience through expensive study trips may be of limited value unless the children are guided in developing the basic concepts and generalizations that warranted the study trip. An aide can make it more certain that each child will observe the new situation and will learn the new terms that enable him to perceive and talk about what he is observing. By talking with each child in his care and listening to his response, an aide can make sure that the child has accurately developed important concepts and generalizations, and is thus prepared to recall them accurately later.

The importance of guiding children to perceive and conceptualize through their experience cannot be overly emphasized. Left to his own devices, a child may see three puzzle pieces simply as something to pick up and throw. But with the help of an aide he may be guided to put the pieces together to make the figure of a boy with a head, a sweater, and trousers, to identify the color of the hat, the sweater, and the trousers, to count the number of pieces, or to show another child how to solve a puzzle. In short, an aide in addition to a teacher can help a child observe and think about certain aspects of his environment. Furthermore, the aide who guides a child to abstract essential elements from his firsthand experience is able to help the child recall what he perceived and to use elements abstracted from that experience as a basis for creative expression through craft and art media.

### Strategy: Encourage Creative Expression

An aide makes it possible for more children to express themselves creatively more frequently. Such creative expression thrives on adult appreciation. "See what I made," and "Watch me," call for adult attention and response. These expressions of creativity are likely to disappear in an unresponsive environment or in an overly directive one that emphasizes conformity.

## LINKING AGENT

In guiding the intellectual development of a child, an aide is an agent who helps the child to accurately link his experience with words. Later the child can use the words to communicate that experience and related experiences to the people around him. Suppose, for example, that an aide wants a child to understand and appreciate the concept of *roundness*. The aide procures various round objects, perhaps a round orange for a snack, various sizes of round balls to play with out-of-doors, a global map of the world, and other round objects to work with indoors, and makes them an integral part of the child's environment. Then the aide talks to the child as the child uses the round objects, calling his attention to the round appearance of the object as he uses it and linking each new experience to previous experiences with roundness. "It's round like an orange," the aide may say.

From time to time, the aide gets feedback on whether the child has learned the concept of roundness. The aid may show the child an orange and a ball and ask, "How are they alike?" If the child replies that both are round, the aide can then go on to less obvious examples of roundness than total spheres. He may point out that the doorknob is round, and that wheels on an automobile are round. In such ways, the aide helps the child link together what he perceives to be round with the word *round*.

An aide also helps a child to build linkages between objects and their representations. An orange is linked with a picture of a plate of oranges and with a round piece of orange felt placed on a flannel board. Roundness in reality is linked with pictured roundness as the child experiences it through sight, touch, and kinesthetic responses to flannel board cut-outs. If the child is interested in printed words, the aide includes experience with printed words in the environment of the child and encourages him to work with the printed word, perhaps putting it as a label on a round object or a representation of it, perhaps printing the word himself, perhaps saying the word when he looks at it—in short, helping the child to build additional skills as he is willing to.

An aide reinforces linkages that the teacher builds. The aide keeps informed about those linkages the children are to learn and makes every effort to provide additional experience for them so that each linkage will be made accurately and rapidly.

## COLLECTING AND PREPARING MATERIALS

The aide is an agent to help children abstract from their experience and link together concepts and generalizations. Children need to link words with experience, and later to link these with printed as well as with spoken words. To help the children do this, an aide needs to have two- and three-dimensional representations of people, animals, and objects in the life of a child. An aide prepares for a role of supplementing the teacher as a linking agent by collecting models of familiar things which should illustrate rhyming words and simple words beginning with a single consonant. Objects to collect in miniature include:

1. A furry mouse, a tiny house.
2. A teddy bear, a chair.
3. Dolls to represent a family.
4. A boat, a car, and other common objects.
5. Farm animals.
6. Zoo animals.
7. Pets.
8. Doll dishes.

All models must be durable so that a great many hands can feel and work with them each term. The more realistic each model, the more useful it is to young children.

An aide also helps the teacher cut from old magazines pictures of objects in the lives of the children, or things to be introduced to extend their experience imaginatively. Under the teacher's direction the aide will prepare these models for use with the children in keeping with the pictures that the teacher has prepared.

Like the teacher, an aide prepares a felt or flannel board for his own use, and makes cut-outs to parallel and supplement those being used by the teacher. Often when the teacher has introduced a story or a lesson to the children with her flannel board, she leaves the flannel board with its cut-outs for the children to continue using. They talk about the ideas presented and are inspired to create paintings or cut-outs for their families at home, or to use the flannel board to retell the story to their classmates. Meanwhile, an aide may need to use a flannel board to go over the story with children who want to hear it again, or with children who want to enlarge the experience with the addition of printed words or numerals. It is important for an aide to have at least one dark-colored and one light-colored flannel board (e.g., a black one and a light blue or green one) as a contrasting background for the cut-outs.

To make a flannel board, use a rectangle of lightweight wallboard (e.g., Celotex or Masonite), plywood, or pine board as a base. Approximately two by three feet is a size suitable for displaying a few cut-outs. Across the face of the board, stretch rough textured material, perhaps good quality flannel cloth. Be sure it is smooth and without wrinkles. Its edges can be tacked on the back side of the base by using a stapler that has been spread open, and can then be covered over neatly with masking or other sticking tape.

A portable flannel board is made by hinging together two identical flannel boards (e.g., eighteen inches by twenty-four inches) to make a folding one. For the aide on the playground, a good-sized piece of flannel can be kept in a pocket and unrolled to make a visual picture of how a game is played.

At school, individual flannel boards are easily made to fit the work space of a child (e.g., fifteen inches by eighteen inches). Heavy cardboard is a suitable base for making these boards. Depending upon the achievement of the children he is working with, the aide finds it useful to have cut-outs for each child in a small group, as follows:

1. Prepare pictures as cut-outs to help a child to see relationships between familiar articles, for instance: (a) a baby, a cradle; (b) shoes, socks; (c) bread, butter; (d) a brush, a comb; (e) a knife, a fork; (f) a hat, a coat.
2. From construction paper prepare cut-outs to encourage children to identify shapes and sizes, and later to compare and contrast them, for instance as: (a) large and small, (b) thick and thin, (c) tall and short, (d) wide and narrow, (e) big and tiny.
3. Prepare cut-outs from felt or construction paper to encourage children to create designs: two sizes of: (a) squares, rectangles, triangles, circles; (b) strips, double-length strips, double-width strips.
4. To help children to learn to name colors and count objects, prepare cut-outs of the same object or shape in different colors (e.g., Christmas trees, Easter eggs, caps).
5. To guide children to learn to sort and count, add and take away, prepare numeral cut-outs in sets from 1 through 5, and from 6 through 10. From felt material prepare sets of objects to be counted (e.g., green trees, apples, colored eggs, boys, girls, hearts, pumpkins) and printed words (e.g., one, two, boys, girls).[6]
6. To encourage children to create flannel board pictures from felt cut-outs, prepare large shallow boxes with a cover, the inside of

[6] These items can be purchased commercially.

which is a flannel board. In each box the collection of felt pieces for cut-outs can include: (a) green strips for grass; (b) blue strips for sky; (c) white or gray pieces for clouds; (d) green pieces for trees; (e) brown pieces for tree trunks; (f) disks for sun, balloons, balls, wheels, etc.; (g) smaller disks for fruit and flowers; (h) triangles for sails on boats; (i) rectangles of a variety of sizes for houses, windows, wagons, etc.; (j) flesh-colored ovals for faces; (k) pieces for shirts, skirts, slacks, etc.

7. To encourage children to print and use labels with felt cut-outs, include paper, marking pen, and sandpaper squares with which to have the labels adhere to the flannel board.

In building a collection of useful materials, an aide finds it desirable to have seats for a small group of children. Small pieces of carpeting, perhaps carpet samples or remnants left from carpeting a room, are easily portable and are delightful to the sight and touch of a child. A child can select a color he enjoys and can put his seat as close to his beloved aide as he wishes. Meanwhile the aide can work with happy children either indoors seated comfortably on the floor or outdoors undisturbed by inquisitive ants or crawling insects.

In his reference card file an aide can include not only annotated references to useful children's books, records, parent education books, and professional books in early childhood education, but also recipes that are used frequently in work with young children, for instance, a good recipe for play dough. Here is such a recipe that an aide can make, either by himself first thing in the morning, or later when one or two children are eager to help.

PLAY DOUGH

1. *Measure* ingredients and mix them together:
   a. Three cups of flour.
   b. One cup of salt.
   c. One cup of water.
2. For sensory appeal, *mix* into them:
   a. Peppermint extract (for fragrance).
   b. Food color (for eye appeal).
   c. Water (for feel).

## GETTING STARTED AS AN AIDE

An aide comes into an ongoing system. Even though the system is starting to function at the beginning of a new school term, it already exists in the minds of the people who have been part of it previously. An aide begins his work by starting to build an accurate map of the system. As long as the aide is a part of the system, he will increase the detail on his mental map of it, and will periodically note any changes that occur in regard to it.

The aide is especially concerned with the part of the map containing his subsystem. As he identifies the objectives of the total system, the aide thinks of the objectives of his subsystem as fitting in with the overall system objectives. As he notes policy of the total system, he modifies his subsystem policies to reinforce it. Thus the aide provides for his area of responsibility to operate smoothly within the total system.

An aide in early childhood education usually has one or more of the following areas of responsibility:

1. An aide in a classroom: Teacher's Aide.
2. An aide on the playground: Playground Aide.
3. A tutorial aide in a child's home: Tutor or Sitter.

As a paraprofessional with professional personnel, an aide has a continuing responsibility for keeping the professional personnel informed about the progress and problems in his part of their system. An aide observes instances in which a child demonstrates competence he has not previously shown and makes a brief descriptive report about it. Furthermore, an aide observes exceptional behavior that may indicate that a child is having a problem in learning. By reporting such behavior immediately, the aide is able to reinforce the professional educator in guiding the learning of the child into more successful channels. Because of his important role as an observer and recorder of learning behavior, an aide begins his responsibility by finding out to whom and with what frequency he should report. "What kind of feedback do you need?" he may ask. "Shall we schedule a weekly conference?" he will inquire. By arranging for regular, periodic reporting, an aide sets up the basis for mutual confidence and smooth cooperation between his area of responsibility and that of the professionals with whom he works.

### Learning the Classroom System

When an aide enters a classroom, he is coming into a system that is guided by the classroom teacher. The teacher has in mind what the system is and what it is to accomplish. In welcoming an aide to set up and operate a subsystem within the larger classroom system, the teacher expects that what the aide does will fit into the classroom system, and at least will not interfere with smooth operation. The system of the aide must interlock with the system of the classroom teacher as an integral part of that system.

An aide begins setting up his subsystem by getting acquainted with each part of the teacher's system and figuring out how to have the corresponding part of his subsystem fit smoothly into it or parallel it. First the aide explores the physical situation and then he learns the routine procedures that provide the children with stability within their school day.

The first day at school an aide finds out what space he has for his things. Is there a locker to accommodate his coat, jacket, or sweater? Is there a high shelf on which to put his personal items?

And where is work space? Perhaps the teacher is sharing counter-top space that she uses for preparing and organizing craft materials for the use of each child. Maybe the aide can have a desk or share a drawer and desk top with another aide or with the teacher. An aide must be sure that he understands where he is to do his work. Each function he performs requires work space. Knowing what to do involves knowing where it is to be done.

Where is equipment stored? Usually equipment such as scissors and construction paper is stored adjacent to the work space on which it is to be used. It is easy to think about equipment, materials, and work space as a small system for preparing craft items for each child to use. It is also easy to think of tricycles, wagons, and playground equipment as part of the small system that enables children to develop themselves physically in playing roles of people driving to work, having fun, or serving as community helpers.

In discussions with the teacher, a classroom aide clearly gets in mind the usual succession of activities within a child's day. As he learns the various schedule patterns, an aide notes those times when a child may begin to show signs of being fatigued, thirsty, or hungry. "What reminders are the children accustomed to when they have to go to the bathroom?" an aide asks. "When I notice that a child is unusually wiggly, shall I ask him quietly about going to the bathroom?" an aide may ask in order to find out how to help an individual child improve his self-management.

As rapidly as possible, and within the first week, an aide learns the name of each child in the classroom group. By using the child's name the aide teaches the child to respond to him. At the same time, the aide uses the name of the child as a nucleus around which to build an increasingly detailed map of how the child learns, what is of special interest to him, how he reacts to what interests him and to what is not yet interesting, what kind of cues he is starting to use, and so on. The more an aide knows about a child the more easily and completely he can help him learn the beliefs, skills, and concepts that he needs to know.

### An Aide to Child Development

Both in and outside of preschool and primary school, an aide is concerned with child development. He leaves the guidance of curricular learning to fully qualified teachers, but he shares with teachers, parents, and others who work with young children the important responsibility of furthering their individual development. This means that an aide is responsible for helping a child:

1. Be self-confident.
2. Feel that he is an important person and an important member of his family and school group.
3. Move through learning experiences of a school day with his group.
4. Learn to look after his physical needs.
5. Explore safely.
6. Be interested in learning and creativity.
7. Accurately perceive and respond appropriately to the essential elements of his environment.
8. Develop and use an increasing number of significant concepts.
9. Be happy.

Essentially, an aide assists individual children in learning situations. Whether the aide is at home with one or two children or is with them in a school setting, he is encouraging them to perceive essential cues and respond to them appropriately. If he is serving as a Playground Aide, the individual children with whom he interacts most frequently include:

1. The stars of attraction for the children, the leaders of their own selection.
2. The child whose behavior is exceptional for him.
3. The child whose behavior is different from that of his group.
4. The child who asks for advice or other help.

With each individual, the aide provides material, encouragement, or information that the child needs to go ahead with what he is learning.

The aide will have advanced far toward becoming a teacher when he is also able to identify the withdrawing child and to help such a child advance toward involvement in learning activities and eventually to achieving satisfaction in them.

## Aide Beyond the Classroom

Outside of school, the parents, older siblings, grandparents, and sitters for a young child are important aids to his development. Such people of importance in his life nurture the child's development. It is desirable for these people to do this with warm affection and in harmony with the guidance that the child has from his teacher in his preschool or primary school group. Working together rather than at odds, teachers and parents and other aides help the child in building a pleasant and accurate map of reality that is readily useful to him.[7]

[7] Helen Heffernan and Vivian Edmiston Todd, *Elementary Teacher's Guide to Working with Parents* (West Nyack, N.Y.: Parker Publishing Co., 1969).

# HELPING CHILDREN LEARN DAILY ROUTINES

With the help of aides as well as their teacher, young children soon learn the basic patterns that give stability to their life at school. Learning these routines as soon as possible can make school more pleasurable for the child. Each day the child knows he can count on doing familiar activities as well as on having a new experience. Thus he is able to predict his school day with confidence, and to have a measure of control in his life at school. The confidence that the child gains through the routine aspects of school is a major factor in his enjoyment of school and his eagerness to continue going to school.

The teacher establishes the routines, introduces them to the children, and plans each school day in terms of them. But she depends on her aides to reinforce her guidance in keeping the children happily aware of the routines to follow—perhaps by saying clearly and firmly, "We have time to clean up before our group goes outside." The aides and the teacher make up the team that guides the children in learning how members of a group move through the day at school. "John," an aide may say to a preschool child, "let's put the blocks away," or he may say to a more experienced school child, "Tom, what do you think should be done with the blocks?" If Tom decides that the blocks should be arranged neatly and that he will arrange them, the aide commends his helping to place the room in order. If Tom chooses another activity at that time, the aide accepts his choice and says perhaps, "You may help put blocks away another time." In discussing such an incident with the teacher, the aide finds out how the teacher responds to a child in the situation and the reasons for the teacher's response. In this way an aide learns how to reinforce the teacher's guidance of child learning.

Before working with a new child or with a small group of children, an aide confers with the teacher about personal routines for the children. When will they need to go to the bathroom? Should the aide help them individually, or in small groups, or in accord with some usual procedure? Are there nutritional or rest patterns that the children are learning? What are the children learning about cleaning and putting things away?

The teacher and the aide also confer from time to time about the guidance of individual children. The immature child who is developing bladder control may need immediate help from the nearest adult. The preschool child who is learning to respond to others in a friendly rather than an aggressive fashion will also need consistent help from the nearest adult. The aide and the teacher work out a suitable adult response to a child who hits others. They also discuss how an adult interacts with the sensitive child who is exploring group activities from the security of solitary play in the sandbox. Through conferring with the teacher about guidance of such individual children in their problem situations, an aide learns an increasingly large repertoire of desirable ways for interacting with the children, and thereby becomes more effective as an aide.

At all times in dealing with the children and their teacher, an aide keeps in mind his role in assisting the teacher. The teacher is in charge of the class unless she has specifically requested an aide to temporarily take over the responsibility for it. When the teacher asks a question of the group, an aide observes how the children respond, but makes no response himself. If the teacher specifically addresses a question to the aide by name, or if the teacher makes a specific request of him, the aide responds at once. In responding to the teacher's request to help an individual child, an aide is careful not to wait on the child, but to set up a situation in which the child enjoys making the expected response.

From time to time the teacher points out a child or two who need the help of an aide in learning their daily routines. Sometimes the aide may recognize himself the child who is not quite sure of what to do or the child who is momentarily distracted from doing what the group is doing because of a great personal interest in something else. In either case the aide moves over by the child, watches for a transition point in what the child is doing, and then gives him whatever cues he needs to become part of the group in carrying out a daily routine.

In guiding children learning daily routines, the aide uses positive suggestions, for instance: "Here is room for yours," or "Walk quietly." If the aide does use a negative remark, it is only in contrast to the positive remark that he made first: "Walk; don't run," for instance. More often the aide simply makes a suggestion together with a simple explanation, for instance: "Walk. Don't run. The wet sidewalk is slippery." Usually the aide finds it sufficient to say, "Please close the cupboard door so that it is out of our way."

An aide who wanted the children on a study trip to look at exhibits rather than to touch them made the mistake of saying, "Don't touch the glass." Immediately each child was interested in touching the glass, and tried to do so. A more experienced aide says, "Remember to keep your hands down while we look at the. . . ." Thus the aide makes positive suggestions to guide the children in looking at what is exhibited rather than in touching the glass in front of it.

This chapter provides suggestions to help an aide to guide children in activities that are likely to occur each day in most preschool and primary school groups. The aide who has thought about each activity is ready to help children learn to participate in the activity in line with what their teacher suggests.

## BELONGING TO A GROUP

Learning to be a contributing member of a group is so important in a democracy that it is a major objective each year for a young child in school. Aides have a major responsibility in helping each child exercise his rights as a member of a group and to appreciate his consequent privileges and responsibilities. Aides, like teachers, use basic strategies such as the following as they guide the learning of the children:

1. They help the child be glad to be part of a happy school group. They may say, for instance, on the playground, "Aren't we glad to be here swinging high in the air?"
2. They leave the child room to explore not-being-a-part-of-the-group and gently help him observe that he misses pleasant experiences when he is out of the group activity. An aide may say, "Another time when we have games, you may play."
3. They give the child the opportunity to take his turn as leader of the group and to be visible to the group as a successful and helpful achiever. An aide may say, "Thank you, Jane, for putting the numeral 3 next to the three red disks."

An aide working with young children can do much to facilitate their learning and pleasure of daily routines.

Especially in neighborhoods that are economically impoverished, a child may be added on to a school or preschool group at any time of the year. If his family has to move back to where his grandparents or other relatives live when his father is out of work, a child has to shift to a new school group. An aide can be invaluable in giving this child the security that he needs in making such a transition. Although the teacher must maintain his relation to each child in the group, the aide is free to give an individual child continuing attention and companionship during transitions and other periods of time when he most needs them.

A child who is new to the group and just starting to learn its daily routines needs explanations and encouragement as he develops rapport with his teacher and with other children and learns to fit into the daily activities they have worked out together. An aide encourages and explains things to the new child whenever he needs encouragement and explanations.

In any preschool or primary school group, a slow child or two needs the help of an aide in learning the daily routines of the group. The child who has been ill with a contagious disease or a child who has been absent for some other reason may return to the group only to feel out of step with the daily routines that the group has learned in his absence. Such children need individual help beyond that which the teacher can easily provide them without detracting from her warm relationships with the other children in the group. An aide can serve as a supportive tutor for the child who was absent until he is able to move easily again with the group of children from activity to rest, refreshment, and more activity throughout the school day.

One way in which an aide can help one or two children to identify with the school group is to encourage their friendships in the group and at school. A child who looks forward to seeing his friend the next day at school is the child who attends school as regularly as his health permits.

With a child who distinguishes "real" from "pretend," an aide can develop the idea of an additional friend at school perhaps by calling attention to the fish in the fishbowl with the following poem:

MY FRIEND, THE GOLDFISH

My friend, the goldfish, has no feet.
He cannot walk like me.
He swims all day. He likes to eat
And dream about the sea.

He wants me to get in with him
And swim just like an otter.
But I'm so big. If I got in,
I'd splash out all the water.

With this poem, activities, and stories such as *My Goldfish* [1] to enhance it, an aide can create a personality for the little goldfish as a friend at school. The aide can encourage a child or two to make paper representations of the fish and fishbowl to have at home, as follows:

1. Use water-colored blue to finger paint.

[1] Herbert H. Wong and Matthew Vessel, *My Goldfish* (Reading, Mass.: Addison Wesley Publishing Co., Inc., 1969).

2. Cut a pattern for a fishbowl by folding a sheet of paper in half and cutting both sides of the bowl at once.
3. Place the pattern on the back of the dry finger painting and trace around it. Cut out the bowl.
4. Across the bottom of the bowl, spread paste. Then sprinkle sand on it.
5. Cut out a fish or two, and green plants to complete the fishbowl.

In this way a child not only has a live fish as a friend to welcome him to school each day, but he also has a representation of his friend, the fish, to keep the child reminded of his friend at school.

## CONCEPTS THAT UNDERLIE ROUTINES

An aide is constantly reinforcing the learning of the basic concepts that underlie daily routines. For instance, the aide helps children learn to take turns as a means for everyone to have his turn. If both John and Sue want the same truck at the same time, an aide reminds them to work out turns so that first one and then the other child has the truck to play with.

Using equipment carefully and taking care of school and playground facilities are part of group experience for the young child. An aide helps a child in forming useful lifelong habits when he helps him put his playthings away. With more mature children, he may point out that "If you put away the truck, it will work well the next time you use it. But if it is left outdoors, it may be rusty and unusable next time."

An aide can help more experienced children to think ahead and be prepared in advance. For instance, and aide can simplify the handling of outer clothing when the group of children comes indoors at the beginning of the school day. The aide asks each child to have his sweater or coat in his hand ready to put on a hook when his group has its turn. Often the area where outer clothing is hung is a small space that does not accommodate many people at one time. The idea of planning ahead also is a basis for the habit of putting left and right overshoes together, turning off a faucet that was turned on, and closing a door that was opened.

An aide is uniquely responsible for helping the children learn respect for their teacher. His own respect for the teacher is soon mirrored by the children. When the teacher, Miss Jones, rings a tiny bell or plays a signal for quiet attention on a musical instrument, the aide helps the children respond to the signal, perhaps by his example, or by putting his finger on his lips. Later the aide may explain to busy children not yet accustomed to responding to the signal, "Miss Jones wants us to stop, look, and listen when she rings her bell."

Respect for oneself and for others is a basic concept that underlies most rules and routines. With it in mind, an aide seeks opportunities to make the concept visible to each child. "Sand hurts our eyes," the aide may say when a child starts to throw it, or he may remind a child to use the happy voice he likes to hear others use with him.

### Identity

A young child first builds a concept of himself. "I am Tom," he says with dignity and importance, laying a foundation for saying at a later age, "I am the president." An aide helps a child build a good self-image when he appreciatively calls him by name, "Good morning, Tom," and "Good morning, Sue." At no time does an aide use the name of a child with derogation or derision.

With his self-image established, a child goes on to learn his identity as a helper. An aide guides such learning by making the helper roles visible, and by being appreciative of a child's help. An aide at school may say, for instance, "Mary hung up a blue sweater she noticed on the floor this morning. Thank you, Mary." Or, "Tom put his overshoes together with a clothespin and placed them under the hook where he hung his coat. Tom is a helper."

An aide helps to build only desirable roles for the children. At no point does he use derogatory labels such as, "stupid," or other deprecating descriptions.

One way in which an aide can help school-age children in building their self-esteem and their identity as group helpers is to have them take attendance and make a flannel board record of it. To prepare for such a responsibility an aide makes or obtains a flannel board, cut-outs of girls and boys, a set of numerals, and a strip marked off in ten boxes for a number line.

The conversation of the aide with the children may be as follows:

*Aide:* How can we find out how many children are here today?
*Kristin:* Count them.
*Aide:* That's a good way to find out. Kristin, will you please count the boys who are here?

The boys stand, and Kristin touches each of them as she counts. The aide and the other children count silently, making sure that the count is correct.

*Aide:* (to boys) When Kristin counts you, you may sit down. Then we shall all know that you have been counted.
*Aide:* (to Kristin) How many boys are here, Kristin?
*Kristin:* Fourteen. (Children nod assent.)
*Aide:* Kristin tells us that she counted fourteen boys here today. Our class has sixteen boys. Who are the boys that are not here?

Sue mentions David, and Bob mentions Larry.

*Aide:* Sue, you may put a boy on the flannel board for David. Bob, you may put a boy on the board for Larry. Now, can you find the numeral that shows us how many that is? (The child removes the numeral 2 from the number line and places it below the boy figures.)

The procedure for finding how many are absent is repeated for the girls. The flannel board shows four girls absent.

*Aide:* Look at the flannel board. What does it tell us?
*Jim:* Six children are not here.
*Aide:* Let's count the set of boys and the set of girls to see if six is correct. We're right. Jim you may find the numeral 6 and show us that a set of 2 joins a set of 4 to make a set of 6. Six children are absent today. (Jim completes the attendance record as shown.)

Depending on the experience of the children, the aide may have the children simply learn the one-to-one correspondence of a flannel board cut-out and an absent child. With more experienced children, the aide may use the number line to show the order of numbers one through ten. With children who are ready for additional mathematical thinking, the aide encourages computing the total number of absent children. Soon some children can tell quickly who is absent and put the correct set of figures and numerals on the flannel board, and some children will respond with such complete sentences as, "There are fourteen boys here today," and "Don and Bert are absent." Such accomplishment is praised by the aide.

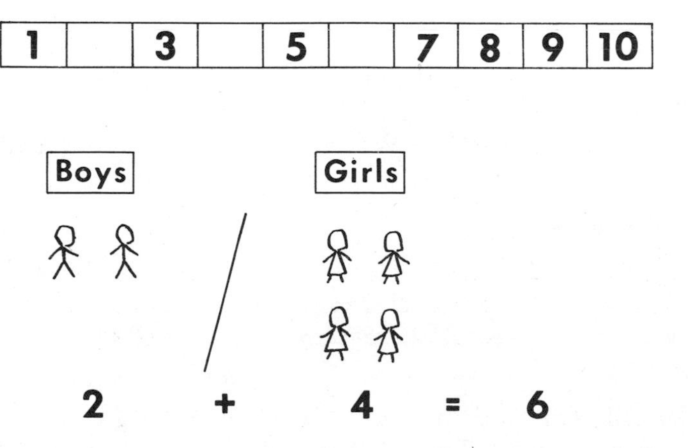


A SET OF TWO JOINS A SET OF FOUR TO SHOW ABSENCE OF A SET OF SIX.

## Equal Opportunity for All

Each day an aide has an opportunity to guide children away from selfishness and toward the fundamental democratic principle of equal opportunity for all. When John grabs a plaything from Steve, the aide firmly returns the plaything to Steve explaining to John that "He needs it," or "He had it first." Then the aide helps John and Steve work out plans for each child to take a turn with the plaything.

When Steve wants to continue his turn with the plaything past the time that John is to have it, the aide reminds Steve that it is John's turn now and helps Steve give the plaything directly to John, or to the aide to give to John.

When a more mature child is selfish, an aide helps his group in thinking about the effects of selfishness. The aide may dramatize the behavior of a hypothetical Mary and say as Mary would, "That's my buggy. You can't put your doll in it." Then the aide asks the group, "Would you like Mary for a friend?" A few minutes later she contrasts Mary's behavior with that of Bill who says to his friend, "Here. Ride my new bike. It's great," and then asks the group, "Would you like to be Bill's friend?"

At a Day Care Center, an aide is also prepared to be helpful when children begin to comment as Tom did, "You gave Jack a bigger sandwich than you gave me." The aide points out that the sandwiches are divided as evenly as possible. He may add: "Enjoy what you have. You may have a second serving if some sandwiches are left."

On the school playground when Ruth comes up to say, "The jump ropes are all gone and I want one," the aide is ready to suggest that Ruth work out turns with Sally who is using one of the ropes. Later with Ruth and Sally in a group, the aide dramatizes this kind of incident and discusses it.

*Ruth:* The watering cans are all gone. I want to water my garden.
*Sally:* Here. You can use mine.
*Ruth:* You take a turn first. Then I'll use it.
*Aide:* Was Ruth selfish? Was Sally selfish? Were Ruth and Sally able to work out a solution to the watering can problem?

## Please Follow Directions

In helping schoolchildren become increasingly skillful in listening to and following directions, an aide can play a game adapted from "Simon Says" with them. It is called, "Follow Directions, Please!" and is played as follows:

*Aide:* Listen carefully to each direction that I give you. If I give it politely, using, "Please," then follow the direction. But if I do not use, "Please," do not follow the direction, and just stay as you are.

An example of playing the game is as follows:

*Aide:* Please put your hands on your head. Please hop on one foot. Please touch your toes. Please touch your elbows. Put your hands on your knees.

Usually there is much laughter as the children either pride themselves on having listened carefully and followed the directions each time or are surprised that they followed a direction that others ignored—a direction given without "Please."

A few of the children may quickly come to understand how the game is played. They may act as leaders with two or three children not yet as knowledgeable as they.

Many games give children an opportunity to listen to and follow directions. One that is especially important for young children is entitled "Looby Loo" and gives them practice in distinguishing right from left. Following directions about putting a right foot toward the center of the circle can lead presently to following directions for bicycle or pedestrian traffic to turn right or left.

### A Rhythm of Activity and Rest and Activity

An aide is very helpful with young children as they develop daily rhythms of constructive activity, eating, constructive activity, resting, activity, and so on, alternating constructive activities with relaxing ones. The adult at hand, teacher or aide, must guide the child whenever he is choosing between constructive and destructive activity, or between responding or not responding to physical needs, or between other desirable and less desirable behavior. By interspersing activities with rest and nutrition, an adult helps children in choosing desirable behavior.

### Brief Relaxation

When children have been working with concentration such as is required in learning new concepts, they should have a change of pace for at least a few minutes. Weather permitting, if he has first arranged with the teacher, an aide can provide this change of pace by having the children go outside to skip or run. Indoors the aide can have the children stand up and stretch.

An aide should have at the tip of his tongue an ever enlarging repertoire of finger plays.[2] With these he can guide the children in moving their hands, arms, or bodies in a relaxing manner.

Playing a game or singing a short song also affords a change of pace for the children. At the request of the teacher, an aide is prepared to lead

[2] Louise Binder Scott and J. J. Thompson, *Rhymes for Fingers and Flannel Boards* (St. Louis: Webster Publishing Co., 1960).

either activity. The aide knows more active games such as "Did You Ever See a Lassie?" and his song repertoire is added to regularly with such quiet pantomime songs as: "My Hands,"[3] "I Wiggle,"[4] and "Two Little Hands."[5]

### Afternoon Rest

Many young children need toileting and an extended rest in the early afternoon, and an aide is prepared to provide the setting for rest and to guide children to relax. He knows where the mats, rugs, or cots are stored, when to take them out, and how the children can help in setting them up for use. He sees that each child has a place to rest, spaced away from nearby children and from doors and passageways. He can show the children how to relax through admiring a limp Raggedy Ann doll or by observing his own example of stretching, yawning, and replacing tensed muscles with relaxed ones. He may ask, "Have you seen animals asleep? Suppose we stretch the way the animals do. (He stretches and yawns.) And then show how they sleep." He has songs and poems to help the children to think about rest and sleep and relaxation.[6]

Sometimes at rest time an aide plays a soft lullaby on the record player, for instance, "This Is My Sleepy Time," or sings a quiet song perhaps accompanying himself with an autoharp.[7] The children like to hear their names said as the aide sings in a quiet voice that "Tommy is resting nicely; Kathy is resting nicely; Jane is resting nicely; Tony is resting too."

Sometimes as they lie resting the children like to think of themselves as being very quiet. An aide guides such thinking by saying softly, "Tom is as quiet as a mouse who steals a picee of cheese," or, "Sue is as quiet as snowflakes falling to the ground," or mentions whatever else he has observed as being very quiet. Then the aide asks, "How quiet can you be?" The aide writes down the creative expressions of the children and then says them the next time that he leads the children in thinking of how quiet they are. Here are some of the comparisons that one aide wrote down:

I'm as quiet as: peas inside a pod.
the clouds floating in the sky.
smoke as it curls up in the sky.
an ant as he crawls on the ground.
a fish swimming in the sea.

[3] Lucille F. Wood and Louise B. Scott, *Singing Fun* (St. Louis: Webster Publishing Co., 1954), p. 58.
[4] Ibid., p. 56.
[5] Ibid., p. 59.
[6] Louise Binder Scott and J. J. Thompson, *Talking Time* (New York: McGraw-Hill, Inc., 1966).
[7] "This Is My Sleepy Time" is in one of the recordings for *The Kindergarten Book*, by L. B. Pitts, Marbelle Glenn, and L. E. Watters. It is a 78 rpm record in Album K-A of *Our Singing World*.

Sometimes an aide tells a quiet story from the repertoire of teachers of young children, for instance, the story of "The Whispering Rabbit" by Margaret Wise Brown.[8] This story encourages rest and relaxation, especially when the aide who tells it yawns and stretches and becomes increasingly sleepy in appearance. By the end of the story each child should be resting quietly. If a boy has not succeeded in getting into the quiet mood of the story, a gentle reminder of that mood sometimes will help him relax. An aide may say softly, for instance, "Susan is like the sleepy little rabbit. Mary has closed her eyes and ears. Let's all close our eyes and ears and tuck our heads down too."

Besides pantomime, an aide can enhance the story by using a rabbit puppet made from a pattern or purchased from a toy store, and a bee such as can sometimes be found in a florist shop. Practicing with such properties and experimenting with quiet, rest-inspiring pantomime can help an aide learn to be an increasingly competent storyteller who can quickly get his group into the mood of whatever story he may tell.

## NUTRITION

Good nutrition, like good health, is important to young children both because it helps them to be ready for learning each day, and because it helps them lay a foundation of good health for subsequent years of their lives. What is important for children is of concern to aides as well as to teachers. Both should be aware of the children who are undernourished or who come from homes in which good nutrition is neither understood nor valued. Especially with these children, aides and teachers guide the development of such basic concepts as, "Milk tastes good and is good for us," and such beliefs as, "We like carrots."

Aides as well as teachers need to understand that a normal child who has good food available will select the food that his body needs. He does not have to be urged. He may eat only ice cream for one meal, but in the course of a week, he will have a balanced diet. An adult who offers food to a child accepts the refusal of it as readily as expressions of interest in the food.

Aides confer with teachers about the schedule of nutrition periods for the children. Since a child's stomach empties more quickly than that of an adult, the child needs more frequent nourishment. With the youngest children, snacks are probably served in the middle of the morning and in the afternoon. Snacks may consist only of fruit juice or milk, but are likely to include a cracker or cookie as well. If children are at school in both the morning and the afternoon, they should have a noon meal that provides

[8] Paul S. Anderson, *Storytelling with the Flannel Board* (Minneapolis: T. S. Dennison & Co., Inc., 1963), p. 177.

them with at least one-third of their daily requirement for food. If children come to school with a parent on his way to work, they may need to have breakfast served on their arrival at school, and if they are picked up late in the day by a parent returning from work, they may need to have supper. All of these scheduled periods of nutrition require preparation on the part of the aides and coordination by aides and teacher with the other activities of the children.

Each aide needs to know his responsibilities for preparing and serving food in relation to the learning and other needs of the children. If the children are learning to be part of a group eating together, they may be seated at a table and served with individual trays prepared and distributed by the aides. Usually each table has an aide or a teacher as its host or hostess. When the host starts to open his milk carton, the rest of the members at the table also start. When the children finish eating, they ask their host if they may be excused from the table. Then they put their scraps and their utensils in the designated places. In all of these small group activities, the aide acts as a guide to help the children learn to participate with pleasure. The aide provides an example of courteous consideration of others. He is a helper and a conversationalist, who makes nutrition time an especially pleasant part of the school day.

If the teacher thinks it important for the children to learn to serve themselves, the aide arranges food items as if they were in a cafeteria. Child-size napkins made by cutting paper towels in half are arranged handily, perhaps next to the milk cartons. An aide checks on the preparations that he has made by thinking how a child proceeds in serving himself: Will he have picked up each item that he needs? Will he be able to handle all of the items without much danger of spilling them? Will he walk only a short distance to the table?

If the teacher thinks it desirable for the children to learn the courteous custom of waiting until everyone is seated and served before starting to eat, she may ask the aide to use a poem as a signal for beginning the food rituals. One such poem that is popular is:

WE THANK YOU

For milk, for food,
For love and good,
We thank you.

## COURTEOUS SAFETY ROUTINES

"How does our group move quickly from one place to another?" is a question that a group of children has to answer early in the school term with the help of its teacher. As soon as the rules are established, an aide helps the children to develop habits in keeping with the rules. Usually three procedures are thought to be important:

1. Keeping hands at sides, rather than touching others and getting their attention away from what is to be done.
2. Forming a line to go quickly through a door.
3. Walking instead of running.

An aide often says: "Let's keep our hands to ourselves." "Form a line so we can each get into the lunchroom." "Walk. The wet sidewalk is slippery." In each case the aide is reminding children of a rule they helped to formulate, and is helping them to link the desirable action to a cue in their environment.

With a small group of children, an aide can ask questions that will lead the children to arrive at or learn the rules that the group has established. For instance, an aide may lead the children in discussing:

1. If you run instead of walk to get in line, what can happen to you? What can happen to someone near you?
2. What is a fair place for you to take in a line? Is it fair to step in front of someone in the line? Is it fair to go to the end of the line? Does each one have a turn?
3. When you have a place in a line, do you like to be pushed? Do you like to be stepped on by someone behind you? How much space do you need in front of you?

As rapidly as possible, an aide should learn to imitate the teacher in helping the children to move quickly from one place to another. In the event of an emergency such as a fire, it might be necessary for the aide to take the children through their procedure for moving from one place to another. If he has previously helped the children go quickly from a classroom to the auditorium, or from outdoors to indoors, or from playground to bus, the aide has their confidence and can calmly and quickly help them reach a place of safety. The wise aide anticipates what can happen and is prepared for an emergency because he has carefully observed the cues the teacher uses in guiding the children. He has also worked out with the teacher opportunities for practicing taking the teacher's place in moving a group of children from one location to another.

An aide can practice giving directions to a group on any day that the teacher asks him to guide the children outdoors for recess. An aide can make the departure an enjoyable learning activity with directions such as the following:

*Aide:* If you have on red socks, you may *walk* out for recess without touching anyone.

*Aide:* (while children with red socks leave) Why are we careful about that? (Children suggest reasons.)
*Aide:* If you have on blue socks, you may *walk* out without touching anyone.

The aide will continue through the range of colors until all children have walked out. In case a child forgets either to walk or to keep his hands to himself, he is called back to wait until the rest of the class is outside.

An aide can use variations in the leaving routine, perhaps having the children hop, skip, or go on tip-toe instead of walking. With the younger children in the group the aide gives more cues and may say, for instance: "Those whose names begin with the letter *B* may leave. That will be Barbara and Burnett." He watches for opportunities to encourage through realistic praise, and may say, for instance, "Charles and Linda skipped outside without getting in anyone's way."

An aide may talk for a minute or two with the children while they are waiting for some of the group to leave. He may ask, "Have you noticed how a group of birds flies from one place to another? How fast they fly without getting in each other's way! Let us try to leave without getting in each other's way."

Here are procedures that an aide is likely to observe and imitate. In using them, an aide guides the children with words. He does not move them physically as he would a two-year-old beginning to move with a group.

1. A group enters an auditorium: The leader of a line enters the row of seats assigned to his class, walks to the end of the row, and sits down in the last available seat. The rest of the class follows.
2. A group leaves an auditorium: The teacher or aide asks one row at a time to stand. Each child puts his seat back, faces the end of the row, and walks in single file along the aisle and out the door.
3. A group boards a bus for a study trip: While the children wait in line to board the bus the teacher or aide helps them think about how they conduct themselves on the bus. As they board the bus only one child is on the steps at any one time. The aide counts them. The aide or teacher asks the driver which seats are to be filled first and guides the children to them.
4. A group leaves a bus: An aide asks the children to leave the bus one row at a time as he designates. The aide counts the number of children, making sure that every child is present and reporting at once to the teacher the names of any children who are missing. Back in the classroom, the teacher or aide asks the children such questions as, "Did we stay together as a group?" "What did we do that helped us keep together?" Other questions will give the chil-

dren the opportunity to recall what they saw and learned on the study trip.

5. A group responds to the signal for a fire drill: A teacher or aide gives directions. For example, "Fire drill! Walk quickly outside. Remember to keep a safe distance away from the friend ahead of you." The group calmly forms a line outside of and away from the building. Then the children walk to the area designated for them.

### Air Raid Routine

An aide who has responsibility for helping a group of children respond to a signal for an air raid can help them calmly enjoy the safety routine if he has taught it to them as a way of playing "Jack-in-the-Box," or "Little Seeds Waiting to Sprout." The children learn to pantomime Jack-in-the-Box crouching down in his box, arms pulled down over his head from closing the lid to the box. Or they learn to pantomime seeds in the warm brown earth, with arms folded down like sprouts. The songs entitled "Jack-in-the-Box" [9] or "Little Seeds" [10] are fun for the children and are a way of guiding them in learning a protective position to assume on a cue.

With children who have played the Jack-in-the-Box (or Little Seed) game, an aide can calmly give simple directions when the air raid signal is sounded. She can say, "Air raid! Under chairs, desks, anything. Play you're a Jack-in-the-Box (or a Little Seed)!"

### Dismissal Routine

An aide has considerable responsibility at dismissal time. Often the teacher is completely occupied in taking care of emergencies and out of the ordinary happenings, leaving the aide to make sure that each child has his own outer wraps and his crayon picture or other completed material to take home. The aide expects each child to be responsible for putting on his own outer wraps as soon as he can, and to find what is to be taken home. If it is the first day of the school year, the aide also takes responsibility for helping a child leave his name tag and feel happy about returning the next day.

An aide should focus his attention on the most important part of the dismissal routine: he should try to have each child think of an enjoyable part of his day at school. He may say, for instance, "Let's say the words of the song we learned today," or "We had fun today. Now it is time to go home. Tomorrow is Thursday. See you tomorrow."

Another part of dismissal is to remind each child who walks home

[9] Lucille F. Wood and Louise B. Scott, *Singing Fun* (St. Louis: Webster Publishing Co., 1954), p. 57.
[10] Ibid., p. 33.

how to cross the street. A few minutes before dismissal is a good time for an aide to use a safety poem or a finger play such as the following one:

Stop, Look, Listen,
Before you cross the street!

Also at the end of the school day an aide can help the children evaluate their day. Together they may recall the highlights of the day. Sometimes the aide may ask, "What did we play today that you have never played before?" or "What did you like best about today?" or "If mother or daddy asks you what you learned today, what will you tell them?" Remembering something he enjoyed reinforces the eagerness of a child to come back to school the next day.

## LEARNING SAFETY IN TRAFFIC

An aide, like a parent, is especially concerned with helping children to be safe at school, at home, and on the streets. As rapidly as possible a child must expand his skill in keeping himself safe from bodily harm and in noticing and responding to all of the cues in his environment about what must be done to be safe.

An aide talks with the teacher to learn games, poems, stories, and other activities for guiding children to learn how to be safe. Aide and teacher consult together with the librarian to see if new safety materials have been prepared for young children.

Safety poems are made up and passed from teacher to teacher to delight the children and to help them be safe. Here is one poem an aide will find useful:

SAFETY IN CROSSING STREETS

Remember, when you cross the street,
That cars are swifter than your feet.
So if you see one coming fast,
Wait, please wait, until it's past.
—Anonymous

### A Traffic Signal [11]

To be safe, young children should become aware of traffic signals as early as possible. The flannel board and a simulated traffic signal can be helpful in guiding them to notice and respond safely to a traffic signal. This series of four lessons can be used by an aide with one or more children, as suggested by the teacher.

[11] Ruth Radlauer and Ed Radlauer, *Colors* (Glendale, Calif.: Bowmar Publishing Co., 1968). The book has an excellent photograph of a traffic light taken by Harvey Mandlin.

*Lesson 1*

1. Objectives
   a. The child reviews concepts of colors, a circle, and relative positions.
   b. The child learns the meaning of the three color cues in a traffic signal. The child enlarges his life-space safely.
2. Materials
   a. Flannel Board.
   b. Cut-outs: Red circle-edged disk, Yellow circle-edged disk, Green circle-edged disk.
   c. Traffic signal made from cardboard with three disks cut out and replaced by red, yellow, and green tissue paper; and with a handle at the bottom.

*Aide:* (places red disk at top of flannel board) What color is it? . . .

The aide interacts with each child encouragingly and uses the interests of the child to lead into a similar presentation of yellow and green disks. The aide arranges the disks one below the other as in a traffic signal. Then he presents the traffic signal.

*Aide:* Does this have the same shape? (points to red disk). . . . What color is the light? . . . What does the red light tell us? . . .
*Aide:* I know a poem about a traffic signal.

THE TRAFFIC SIGNAL

The yellow is a cue.
"Watch out," it says to you.
When red is at the top,
It's telling you to stop.
When green is down below,
It says, "Be safe. Let's go."

When the aide develops the idea of the green light in the same way, he puts the green disk on the flannel board below the red disk and at a distance from it. The aide repeats the poem emphasizing the green as well as the red and pointing to both the red and green disks.

The aide completes the lesson by developing the idea of the yellow light in the middle of the red and green lights in the same way.

*Lesson 2*

1. Objective: The child reinforces his learning of the meaning of the three colors in a traffic signal.
2. Materials: As in Lesson 1.

The aide reviews the previous lesson. The child or children enjoy saying the poem with him and place the red, yellow, and green disks on the flannel board one below the other as in the traffic signal.

*Lesson 3*

1. Objective: The child links the names of the colors to interpretations of the colored lights in a traffic signal.
2. Materials
   a. The hand traffic signal.
   b. A flashlight.

The aide repeats the poem as he illuminates a color of the traffic signal by shining the flashlight through the colored tissue paper in the hand signal.

The children take turns in making the traffic signal light up to tell people: Watch!—Stop!—Go! as each child repeats the poem.

*Lesson 4*

Objective: The child values the traffic signal as a safety aid.

The children create simple stories about what happens at the traffic signal. They tell the story using the hand traffic signal to show the cues for their hero or heroine.

When the children are eager to tell the story at home, an aide prepares materials from which a child can make a hand traffic signal, and mimeographs the poem for the child to take home stapled to the hand signal.

## PLAYGROUND AIDE

When children are on the playground for free play with their classmates, for recess from concentrating on new learning experiences, or for the noon hour, they have aides as well as teachers to guide them. Sometimes mothers volunteer to be aides for their own children and those of others and come to the school for an hour at noon or after school. Whatever the administrative arrangements, an aide has the opportunity to guide children in learning the following:

1. A child plays happily with his peers, sharing equipment with them, taking turns, and taking responsibility for his own and others' welfare.
2. A child becomes skillful in handling a ball, crossing an overhead ladder, and using other playground equipment.
3. A child enjoys group games as well as individual sports and recreation.

AN AIDE WHO LISTENS MAKES IT FUN TO PRACTICE SAFETY AND STORY TELLING.

4. A child keeps the playground clean, putting litter into trash containers.

**Courteous Safety Routines**

Courteous safety routines that the teacher and aides develop within the classroom setting carry over to the playground situation. An aide who has been with a group of children indoors is often helping the children to learn that interacting with classmates outdoors is like interacting with them indoors. The aide may remind children that everyone will have a turn walking the rail if they line up, let each person walk across, and then line up again for another turn.

When a child explores the limits of the rules, an aide has an opportunity to help the child perceive what the reasons are for the rules and what the precise limits of safety are. In general, the role of the aide is to help children expand their experience, and to be safely and consciously in control of it. Instead of keeping the children safe by preventing action, the aide encourages controlled action by helping the children make mental maps of how to act safely.

### Ball Handling

When children are on the playground, they are learning how to move themselves through space, and how to move balls and other game equipment in relation to their own movement. An aide observes their movements and is at hand to demonstrate good technique, to encourage additional trials, and to ask an occasional question that may help a child observe what he has not noticed or reinterpret what he is doing.

One of the skills to be learned early by young children is that of handling an object such as a ball. A skillful ball handler gets favorable attention and goes on to enjoy a great many sports and games that will further build his ball-handling ability. Even the youngest child in a group can have the fun of sitting down on the floor or sidewalk with his legs spread apart and his feet touching those of a friend while he and his friend roll a ball back and forth to each other in the enclosed space. Gaining control of the movement of the ball is a satisfying accomplishment for each child.

Here are suggestions that one school district makes for those who are demonstrating ball-handling skill or guiding children in developing such skill at their level of maturity.[12]

#### *Bouncing Ball*

*Starting position:* Stand with feet in easy stride position, one foot slightly ahead. Hold ball in both hands at waist height a comfortable distance from body. Look at ball.

*Action:* Swing weight to the forward foot and bend body forward slightly. Push the ball to the playing surface . . . continue bouncing by pushing it each time at the height of the bounce.

*Follow-through:* When catching the ball "give" with it, bringing the

[12] Oceanside Union School District at Oceanside, California, prepared for its personnel a booklet entitled, "Skills," and another entitled, "Games." Excerpts from the booklets printed in October 1967 are presented in this section with the permission of the district.

arms toward the body, and swing the weight to rear foot. When pushing the ball, extend arm in direction of ball each time.

*Catching Ball with Arms*

*Starting position:* Stand in a comfortable stride position, one foot slightly ahead, knees relaxed and easy. Extend the arms, slightly bent, waist high, palms toward the ball. Keep eyes on ball.

*Action:* As the ball approaches, close the arms around it, and bring it against body.

*Follow-through:* Bend the knees slightly and "give" with the ball, to help in absorbing its force.

As children develop proficiency in bouncing and catching a ball, they enjoy simple games that give them practice with their new skills. Here are games that an aide is prepared to suggest when young children are ready for them:

HEAR ME COUNT. A child bounces the ball and counts as he catches it. The aide encourages each child to keep track of the number of bounces he makes, and to increase the number of bounces each time that he plays the game.

BOUNCE BALL. A child bounces the ball a number of times while others watch. The aide asks, "How many times did he bounce the ball?" The child who replies correctly, "He bounced the ball __ times," has the next turn as ball bouncer.

BOUNCING BY NUMERALS. With more mature children, the aide prepares three circles, each with a numeral printed in it. A child chooses one of the circles and bounces his ball according to the number indicated in that circle. Then he chooses another child to continue the game.

BOUNCE-CATCH RELAY RACE. Eight to twelve players use two nine- or thirteen-inch balls. In each line, a leader bounces the ball to the player at the front of the line. One player catches the ball, bounces it back to leader, and goes to end of the line. If the player fails to catch the ball, he must recover it, return to the starting point, and bounce the ball back to the leader. The leader bounces the ball to the next player who bounces it back to him and goes to the end of the line. When each child has had a turn as player, the line that finished first wins. The game may be repeated with another player becoming the leader.

BOUNCE CATCH. Two, four, or six players use six-, nine-, or thirteen-inch balls. Two children each stand in one of two adjacent squares. A child bounces the ball into his opponent's square. The second child catches the ball and then bounces it back. If the second child fails to catch it on the first bounce, he is out, and a waiting child takes his place. After three bounces, both players are replaced by two waiting players.

To help preschool and kindergarten children with throwing and catching, a beanbag or a soft ball, nonrubber and of a size to fit the hands of the children, provides an opportunity for experimenting with vertical tossing and tossing into a container. It also helps a child learn to look at the target when he is throwing the beanbag, and to look at the beanbag when he is catching it. Here are two games for an aide to use:

BASKET THROW. Two to eight players form a circle around a basket or carton. The players face the center. The group leader stands inside the circle to return the beanbag to the players. A player in the circle tosses the beanbag toward the basket in the center. Whether the beanbag reaches the basket or not, the leader passes the beanbag to the next player. The game continues until each player has had several turns.

BEANBAG CATCH. Each player has a container with a handle made by cutting the bottom off a large plastic bottle. With two players, player one throws the beanbag. Player two catches it in his container and tosses it back to player one from his container. With four or more players, the children stand in line. The aide tosses the beanbag to one child at a time. The child catches it in his container and returns it to the aide. The aide then tosses it to the next player in line.

In whatever activity the children have on the playground, the aide learns to give the children pointers about how to move their bodies more efficiently. For instance, if the children are jumping, the aide notices whether each child starts with his weight evenly distributed on both feet, whether he bends his arms forward and springs up into the air, whether he lands on balls of both feet with knees bent, and whether he stretches his legs as he returns to standing position.

## Simple Playground Games

With the help of an aide, schoolchildren who want to observe or participate in an organized game can do so. What they are not yet able to plan and organize themselves, they are able to watch or take part in. Here are a few of the typical games that a Playground Aide is expected to make available to young children as they develop their game-playing skills. An aide first explains the game and then illustrates it by being "It." Subsequently the aide observes quietly while all parts are taken by the children.

### *What Can You Do?*

About twelve players form a circle. A child stands in the center of the circle as "It." Turning slowly, he moves his pointing finger around the circle saying, "One, two. What can you do?" On the word "do," the child to whom the finger points answers, "I can . . ." (i.e., hop, skip, jump, run, and so on). "It" then says, for instance, "Hop, hop, until I say 'stop.'" Whereupon all the players hop until "It" calls, "Stop." The player who chose the activity then becomes "It" and the game continues as before.

*Mother, May We Go Out to Play?*

Five to twelve players line up along a starting line. A child who plays the part of "Mother" stands on a goal line about three yards in front of the line. The players ask, "Mother, may we go out to play?" Mother answers "Yes, if you will . . . (i.e., skip, hop, jump, walk, run) all the way." The players go to the goal line and back to the starting line. Any player who does not follow the directions of the "Mother" returns to the starting line and starts over. The first player who completes the directed activity can be "Mother" for the next game, or can choose someone else for the part.

*Cat and Mice*

Six to fifteen players have the role of mice, and take their places in "rat holes." A child chosen to play the role of the cat hides behind a tree outdoors (or a desk indoors). The mice creep up to the cat. When all the mice are near the cat, one of them makes a scratching sound. The cat hears the mice and chases them back to their own places. The first player caught becomes the cat for the next game.

**Keeping the Playground Clean**

A Playground Aide has an excellent opportunity to help children learn fundamental concepts of antipollution such as:

1. A person puts in the trash container what he is discarding. (He does not throw it away for someone else to handle.)
2. A person puts in the trash container whatever he finds that might hurt him or someone else (e.g., nails, glass).
3. A person puts in the trash container whatever does not add to the beauty of the grounds (e.g., paper brought in by the wind or by people).

An aide is prepared to guide child learning in such ways as the following:

*Aide:* Please put the potato chip bag in the trash.
*Child:* I don't want to.
*Aide:* I'll help with the lid. . . .
*Aide:* Let's put our lunch papers in the trash before we start to play.
*Children:* You do it.
*Aide:* Part of eating lunch is putting the papers in the trash. (Starts helping them collect the papers and take them over to the container.)

An aide is willing to share a responsibility with a child as a means of helping the child get started in doing what should be done, but is always careful to have the child know that the responsibility is in his hands. The child learns to be responsible by assuming responsibility with the help of an aide.

An aide is careful to see that each child has the opportunity only for a constructive role of helper. At no point does an aide let a child build up a role of "objector" or "destroyer" in front of an audience of his peers. If a child momentarily gets into a destructive or competitive stance with an aide present, he is helped to think of better ways of solving his problems "next time." An aide may say, for example, "Next time let's put our lunch papers in the trash can as we finish, and before we start to play." The aide says this in much the same way as he says, "Next time let's make sure that no one is nearby when we swing a bat."

## PATRIOTIC RITUALS

In many schools all people present, including the young children, are expected to participate in patriotic rituals such as reciting the Pledge of Allegiance. The aide helps to dramatize the importance of the ritual by standing erect, looking proudly at the flag, and making each gesture that is part of the ritual. He repeats the words distinctly, enunciating each word clearly so that it can serve as a pattern of sound for the children.

If a child nearby remains seated when others are standing and the teacher has requested that everyone stand, an aide may whisper to him, for instance, as follows:

*Aide:* (whispering to Tom) Stand up.
*Tom:* I don't want to.
*Aide:* (taking Tom's hand and smiling) I'll stand beside you.

The aide discusses the incident with the teacher so that he will handle relationships with Tom confidently and with conscious competence.

As children become more experienced participants in a patriotic ritual, their teacher may give them the opportunity to have a leadership role in it. One way in which an aide can help the group and its teacher to be sure that each child has an opportunity to be leader is to prepare a container from which a child's name may be drawn each day.

To make such a container for name drawing, staple together two pieces of construction paper, putting staples down one side, across the bottom, and up the other side. Make the container into two pockets by adding a row of staples down the middle. Each child can write his name (or have it written) on a slip of paper and personally put it into the left-hand pocket, making sure that his name is there and that he will have a turn as leader. The day his name is drawn the child serves as leader and his name slip is put into the right-hand pocket with the names of others who have served.

Because a patriotic ritual is often scheduled as the opening activity that starts the school day, an aide may be asked to take responsibility for it while the teacher is out of the room for some exceptional situation such as welcoming a guest or helping a child who has become suddenly ill. The aide is careful to carry out the ritual with the children taking their accustomed parts. The aide is careful to give the children each cue that they need at their level of experience with the ritual, for example, a reminder that the flag is prevented from touching the ground, and a reminder as to which is the right hand (e.g., the hand on the side toward the window).

To enhance the patriotic ritual, an aide adds to his collection suitable songs and poems like the following:

FLAG SONG [13]

I stand up to salute the flag,
My hand is on my heart.
I know the love inside must be
The most important part.
—Virginia Pavelko

When an aide regularly takes responsibility for conducting the Flag Salute, he has an opportunity for guiding the children to take increasing responsibility. He may, for example, have more children participate in leadership roles in front of the group. If Dick has drawn the name of George to lead the group in saying the pledge, then he may invite one child to hold the flag and two or four other children to serve as color guards who stand proudly at attention on each side of the flag. The responsibility of the leader may be increased by having him wait until he sees that each child has put his right hand over his heart before starting to repeat the pledge. As children learn, they appreciate the opportunity to show what they can do.

## DEVELOPING THE CONCEPT OF A CALENDAR

By taking daily responsibility for a calendar, an aide can help preschool and primary schoolchildren to develop a concept of a calendar. Children who are just beginning to conceive time note the passing of days until the arrival of their own or someone else's birthday. Children who have more experience in noting time take an interest in the daily counting of days in each month. This counting procedure can be relatively simple—perhaps the daily covering of the date for that day. For children with increased experience with number concepts and numerals, the procedure may include the matching of the date numeral with that same numeral, or the daily

[13] From *Sing a Song* by Roberta McLaughlin and Lucille Wood. Copyright © 1969 by Bowmar Publishing Corp., Glendale, California. Used by permission.

placing of the date numeral on a calendar space. Later children will be able to write in numerals on the calendar from memory of their shape and sequence.

Conferring with the teacher, the aide works out a calendar procedure appropriate to the experience level of the children on the calendar committee. Together they may plan some of the following materials and procedures for maintaining the calendar.

### Making a Calendar

At the beginning of the school year, an aide makes a large calendar from tag board and hangs it at the eye level of the children. At the top of each of seven columns, the aide prints the succession of days of the week, printing each day without abbreviation. Horizontal lines divide the columns to form five or six rows. The names of each of the twelve months are printed on separate pieces of tag.

Using a symbol for each month (e.g., an apple for September), the aide makes a set of apples that shows the succession of numerals from the first to the last day of the month. These can then be used, one a day, to match the numerals on the calendar month, or to fill spaces on a calendar left blank. Here are monthly symbols that may be used by an aide for a group of young children:

1. September—red apple.
2. October—pumpkin.
3. November—turkey.

## Match the Numerals

| September | | | | | | |
|---|---|---|---|---|---|---|
| Sunday | Monday | Tuesday | Wednesday | Thursday | Friday | Saturday |
| | | | 1 | 2 | 3 | 4 |
| 5 | 6 | 7 | 8 | 9 | 10 | 11 |
| 12 | 13 | 14 | 15 | 16 | 17 | 18 |
| 19 | 20 | 21 | 22 | 23 | 24 | 25 |
| 26 | 27 | 28 | 29 | 30 | | |

4. December—Christmas tree.
5. January—snowman's hat.
6. February—red heart.
7. March—kite.
8. April—Easter egg.
9. May—May basket.
10. June—flower.
11. July—drum.
12. August—leaf.

In keeping with motion from left to right, an aide places the reservoir of numerals at the left of the calendar. With a group of experienced children as a calendar committee for the week, the aide may guide their thinking as seems appropriate to their level of experience. He may proceed as follows:

1. What month is this? (passing hand from left to right under the name of the month). Let's say the days of the week: Sunday, Monday, Tuesday, Wednesday, Thursday, Friday, Saturday (passing hand under the words on the calendar).
2. Yesterday was Monday. Who can tell us what day today is? (hand under Tuesday).
3. One, two, three, . . . (hand under each numeral in succession). Yesterday was the 18th (hand under 18). What number comes after 18? Who can tell us? Nineteen. Good. You may find the numeral 19 and match it with the 19 on our calendar.
4. Now can someone tell us what the day and date are? Good. You said a complete sentence. Let's all say the sentence together: "Today is Tuesday, September 19th."

The first day of a new month gives an aide the opportunity for the children to have additional experience with numbers as they take down the numerals of the preceding month, and get started with a new month. An aide may guide their thinking as follows:

*Who will take away the apple with the numeral 1?*

*Who will take away the apple with the numeral 2?*

As a variation, an aide may say, "Take an apple and tell us what numeral is on it." When the apple cut-outs are put away, the name of the new month is discussed and shown. The children talk about the capital letter with which the word begins and find that same letter in other places, for instance, in the alphabet chart.

The aide has the children enact the changing of the month by having one child take down the name of the past month while another child pins up the name of the new month. For Christmas and February and several other months, the children enjoy cutting out the symbol they choose for the dates on the calendar. They especially like to fold colored construction paper before cutting it so that the paper has a new shape when it is unfolded.

# CREATIVE ENRICHMENT MONTH BY MONTH

An aide can be an invaluable member of the team guiding the learning of young children if he reinforces, and does not interfere with, the guidance provided by the teacher. Many teachers of young children develop a new theme each month, and other teachers who prefer to work with larger units develop seasonal themes. These themes can be enriched by the involvement of an aide with individual children and small groups of children. Aides, like teachers, help young children to become pleasantly aware of the seasonal changes and the flow of events from one season to another.

## GUIDING EMOTIONAL EXPRESSION

An aide to a teacher encourages each child to participate fully and creatively in the activities of each day. A child should become so saturated with the current theme and should be so imbued with it that he wants to express ideas and his sad-to-happy range of feelings in words, in a variety of art-and-craft media, and in moving himself through space. Learning the joy of creative expression lays a foundation for active living and for a lifelong satisfaction in being alive.

Whenever a young child expresses himself, the aide encourages the child to find satisfaction in the process of expression and to continue that process as long as the child needs to work constructively with his expressions. In fact, by helping an individual child an aide can make it possible for a child to complete his project before joining the group in its next activity. The aide can, for instance, show the very young child how to hang his painting up to dry, encourage him to wash his hands, and then accompany him to make the transition to the next activity. With a mature child, an aide can say perhaps, "When you finish, rejoin your group." An aide can make the difference in whether or not flexible scheduling can be arranged to provide for individual differences in the children's learning rates.

### Encouraging Creativity

To encourage children to be creative, an aide allows each child to move in his own way toward what is to be learned. One child may temporarily seem to explore exactly the opposite of what is expected as a final outcome. Most children explore various alternatives to it, especially when they have learned one suggested procedure and are going on to determine the limits within which the given objective can be accomplished. The aide is an interested and tolerant observer of what the children do safely while keeping the objective and at least one way of accomplishing it in their view. In general, an aide continues to make visible the objective that the teacher developed with the children and to encourage each child to move toward it in his own way and at his own pace.

If the teacher emphasizes that a child should enjoy caring for a pet, the aide encourages the children to care for the pets that are an integral part of the environments of most young children. But if a child turns over a rock in the schoolyard and discovers a fascinating sow bug, the aide also encourages the child to care for this new found pet. "Will you put his house back in place for him?" the aide may say, or "Let's watch what the sow bug does."

If the teacher emphasizes the exploration of art media for the children in the group, the aide watches for opportunities to encourage a child in using whatever media are available. An aide may say to a preschool child watching others at the painting easels, "Would you like to paint next?" If the child is not ready for that experience, the aide accepts the shake of his head but encourages him to continue watching, perhaps by saying, "It's fun to watch painting," and possibly adding, "It's fun to paint, too." But if the child is eager to paint, the aide may ask, "Shall I call you as soon as it's your turn?"

The aide who has established good rapport with each child and has observed how each reacts to a new situation finds it easy to help a child move ahead into constructive and creative activities that extend his areas of interest. What a child says and does provide the aide with cues about the activities and materials the child will enjoy.

### Creative Art

When a child wishes to express his feelings and ideas in art media, he should be able to obtain the materials he needs quickly. In order to obviate problems and frustrations for the child, these materials should be at hand or at least in a convenient cupboard. An aide bridges whatever gap exists between the child and the materials the child needs. Anticipating what the aide will need to fit in with the teacher's plans for the day, he usually has gotten together just what he will want and is prepared to offer any explanation that may be needed in as few words as possible. For instance, anticipating that the children will want to paint at easels, an aide sees that the paints are ready for use and that a smock or old shirt is at hand to protect the child's clothing. The aide also has in mind several encouraging conversations he may have with the children, especially with a young child:

*Child:* I want to paint.
*Aide:* Good! What you need is right here (points out easel, paints, and smock).
*Child:* I don't want that (points to smock).
*Aide:* Painters wear smocks, just the way policemen wear uniforms.

Sometimes a child faced with a blank piece of paper suddenly thinks he does not want to draw or paint on it. An aide can help him recover his interest in expressing his feelings and ideas. He may say to a reluctant preschool child, "Look at this lovely color!" After appreciatively stirring that color of paint, the aide hands the child the brush so that he can use it. The aide may say to a reluctant but more mature child in school, "Shut your eyes for a minute and imagine what you are going to paint." The aide helps the child identify himself and the art materials with the experience he thoroughly enjoyed, perhaps like this:

*Child:* I can't draw it!
*Aide:* What is it you want to draw?
*Child:* Running.
*Aide:* Do you like to run?
*Child:* Yes.
*Aide:* How is your body when you're running?

The aide continues to guide the child in vividly remembering his experiences in running. The aide may ask, for instance: "When you run, how are your legs?" "How are your arms?" "How does it feel?" As the child thinks about such questions, his running experience is vivid in his thinking and it soon finds expression in some art medium.

As children paint, model, or otherwise use art materials, they sometimes express their pride in their own work with awkward words, perhaps attempting to build their own accomplishment by making derogatory remarks about the artwork of others. If Tom makes a negative remark about what Suzy has painted, an aide can reassuringly point out that:

"Suzy painted colors. Who can name a color that Suzy used?"
"Suzy paints the way she wants it."
"An artist has a right to choose his own colors."

"Tom paints what he wants to paint. Suzy does too. Each of us paints what he wants to paint."
"An artist paints for us to enjoy his painting."
"Does this picture make you happy or thoughtful?"
"Does it make you think about something you like to think about?
"Does it make you think of something you don't like to think about?" [1]

Whereas some children like to paint realistically what they see, others like to explore the media with which they are working and work with color, shape, or some other abstraction. An aide can guide the children to appreciate the individuality of painting, perhaps in this way:

*Tom:* Julie's painting is nothing.
*Aide:* Julie understands her picture. Maybe she will tell you about it.

Usually an aide does not distract children from their creative work. But occasionally when a child has reached a transition point or looks as if he is about to leave his work, the aide makes a remark to help the child appreciate what he has been doing. The aide may smile and say,

"I like the pretty color you used."
"I like your picture of color."
"It makes me happy to look at your picture."
"I can see that your arm really swung the color on."
"I like the way you used blue in your picture."
"I like where these two colors meet."

### Creative Stories, Poems, and Songs

With an aide to help individuals, children can have the satisfying experience of seeing written on paper what they have created in their thoughts. An aide can type or write out a story as a child tells it, and then read it back to the child later. An aide can memorize a poem or a song that a child has created, and repeat it for him and his friends later. When an aide writes out any of these creative expressions, he gives them to the teacher to keep in the child's file and to communicate to the child's parents. Every parent should have the thrill of having evidence on paper of his child's success in school activities.

## ENRICH THE THEME OF EACH MONTH

An aide often redoes with one, two, or a few children a theme activity that the teacher has introduced to the entire group. Thus an aide is often

[1] Maude Ellsworth and Michael F. Andrews, *Growing with Art, Book I, Fun to Begin* (Chicago: Benjamin H. Sanborn Publisher, 1950).

doing what the teacher does, but is doing it half-a-day or a day or two later. An aide also reinforces what a teacher does with a similar but not identical activity. In either case, the aide is helping the children understand the major theme concepts and generalizations that grow out of their pleasant experience at the time. Furthermore, an aide is helping the children to the point that they want to express their feelings and theme ideas. The aide who has well-tested plans at hand to guide the learning of the children month by month will find it easy to accomplish such guidance.

### September

What September is likely to mean to the children and to an aide as well as a teacher is "Getting Started." Day-care groups of young children who meet every working day often have new children joining them when public schools start in the fall. Furthermore, the informality and relaxation of summer vacations lead into new increased activity in the fall. Most children find themselves in a new room, with a new teacher, with a new aide, with children some of whom they did not know before, or with new sensitivities they have developed without being aware of them. All of these factors make it desirable for an aide to work with individuals and small groups of children to orient them to their life at school, and to help them feel worthy there.

In September an aide has an opportunity to help children feel more assured in being at school by leading a discussion about such questions as the following:

*What friends live near you and go to school when you do?*

*On your way to school today, what did you see? What streets did you cross?*

*On your way to school today, what did you pass by?*

Especially with young children who learn slowly, an aide can ask, for example,

*When you are thirsty, and are at the playground, where do you get a drink?*

*When it is cold enough to wear a sweater or a jacket, what do you do with it at school?*

*When you need to go to the toilet at school, where do you find one?*

The routines that will continue throughout the term, such as birthday recognition, begin in September. A teacher usually appreciates having an aide responsible for remembering the birthday of each child in the group. An aide can arrange the names of the children in order of their birthdays and keep a desk calendar that will remind the aide when each birthday occurs. Each child is thus assured of having his worth in the group noted on the day that is especially important to him—his very own birthday.

An aide may wish to reinforce the concepts of the succession of months in a year and the time lapses between different months, by making a Birthday Train to decorate the room. To do this, the aide cuts from construction paper an engine, a caboose, and a car, each of which is labeled for a month of the year. Under the aide's guidance a mature child makes a picture of himself to put in the window of the car of his birth month. The child writes or prints his name to put below the car if he has developed such skill.

As the children become familiar with the major parts of their new environment, an aide can direct their attention to the more detailed aspects of their world. Having the children close their eyes and think, the aide will ask such sensory questions as the following:

*On your way to school today, what colors did you see? (e.g., green grass, brown telephone pole)*

*What did you hear? (e.g., cars, airplane, birds)*

*What did you touch? How did it feel? (e.g., wet grass, rough bark of tree, cold metal)*

*What did you smell? (e.g., flowers, mowed grass, smog)*

With more mature children, the aide may ask such questions about other situations including those on the playground, going home from school, or being out-of-doors.

Children like to talk about what they know well. By doing so when they begin a new school year, the children are better able to link their home experience with their school experience and to carry their pleasure in one over to the other. An aide may want to have children talk together about such questions as the following:

*Who takes care of a pet? What is its name? What kind of an animal is it? What color is it?*

*What does your pet eat? How often?*

*Do you give your pet water to drink?*

*How do you hold your pet when you stroke it and talk to it?*

*Where does your pet sleep?*

*Do you brush your pet?*

An aide can also help the children get acquainted with people who are part of their new experience at school. He may help a small group of children think about:

*Who is our teacher? What does she do for us?*

*Who teaches the children in the room next to ours?*

*What is the name of our principal?*

*What is the name of our office secretary?*

*What is the name of the maintenance man who keeps our school clean and in repair?*

*Do you know the crossing guard? What does she do for us?*

Especially in September an aide can use "Too Big—Too Little" to help children build a sense of their own worth as pupils and as people. This is a story about a child who thought of himself as being too big to get attention as a baby but too little to take part in the activities of his big brother. The story enables the teller to guide the children in appreciating the activities of their own school group and lends itself to pointing out precisely the activities that their own group enjoys.

1. Formulate objectives
   a. The child will appreciate the privilege of going to school.
   b. The child will feel that school is just right for him.
   c. The child becomes aware of the succession of activities in his school day.
2. Tell the story.

TOO BIG—TOO LITTLE

A big, big tear rolled down Jodie's face, and then another, and another. Splash! Right down on his new book. Jodie did not care about the book. Somehow the book was not quite right for him. It did not have many pictures that he liked.

Jodie did so want to be just right for something. He was too big to be fed like Baby Rosa, but too little to go to the park and have hamburgers and fries like Big Brother Tim.

Too big to be pushed in the stroller like Baby Rosa, but too little to ride a bike down the street like Big Brother Tim.

Too big to be rocked to sleep like Baby Rosa, but too little to stay up and watch T.V. with Tim.

What size was the right size? Too big—too little. What could he do?

"Jodie, Jodie," called his mother.

Slowly Jodie stood up and went to see what his mother wanted. His mother did sound excited. He wiped his face so that she would not see his tears.

"Jodie, I have a surprise for you, something we've talked about many times. We'll meet a new friend, Mrs. Green."

"What about Baby Rosa? What about Tim?" asked Jodie.

"Tim will stay with Baby Rosa. She is sleeping now. So we can go by ourselves."

This did sound better. Mother had not taken him alone with her for a long time, not since the visit to the dentist.

Mother fastened his seat belt and started the car. She surely was being mysterious. She was taking just Jodie, and was not going to the doctor or dentist. And she seemed happy too.

"Where are we going?" asked Jodie.

"You'll see," said mother. "Here we are now. This is where everyone and everything is just the right size for you."

So mother did know what was bothering him. And now she had done something about it. Maybe, just maybe, things were not so bad after all.

"Hello," said a smiling voice. "My name is Mrs. Green. What is your name?"

Jodie gave his name and then looked around. He saw happy boys and girls about his size doing things he liked to do.

"Jodie," said Mrs. Green, "this is Billy. Billy, this is Jodie. Billy, will you be Jodie's special friend today? You can show him what we do, and where the bathroom and the drinking fountain are."

Mrs. Green went on talking, "Jodie, you may stay with us and your mother will come for you later."

Jodie's mother smiled at him. "There is lots to do here," she said. "You can stay and play, and I'll be back for you."

Jodie wanted to stay, although he had never stayed with people that he did not know before.

"Okay," said Jodie. "Be sure you come back."

"I'll be back," Mother said. "Have a good day."

Mother was gone. Jodie felt a little funny in his stomach. Before he had time to think about it Billy came up and said, "Hey, new boy, do you want to play rocket ship?"

Billy and Jodie played rocket ship. They played __ together. (Fill in major activities of the day in the sequence in which they often occur, e.g., they ate together; they sang together; and so on.)

Time passed quickly, and then Billy's mother and Jodie's mother came for them.

"Hey, mom," Jodie said. "This is my new friend, Billy. Can I come back tomorrow?"

Jodie was happy, and mother was happy too.

"See you tomorrow, Jodie," said Billy.

"Right," said Jodie. "I'll be here."

Jodie loved everybody now, even Baby Rosa and Big Tim, because in (fill in the name of the school group), Jodie was just the right size: not too big, and not too little.

—Marian Hager

## October

By October, if not earlier, young children should be aware of the fall season as the harvest time of the year. An aide can help the teacher to introduce the children to the locally available fall fruits and vegetables. The children should learn to know what they can see in the market, perhaps apples and pumpkins and pumpkin seeds.[2]

An aide can help children perceive elements in the world around them and build the concepts of *in, on,* and *middle,* by telling a folk tale entitled "Johnny Finds a Magic Apple." The aide should bring a shiny apple and a knife to cut it with so that the children can see for themselves the star in the middle of an apple—and then enjoy eating the apple slices.

### JOHNNY FINDS A STAR IN AN APPLE

Once upon a time, there was a little boy named Johnny. He was such a good observer that, when his Daddy lost his hammer, Johnny was always asked to look for it, and he always found it. Whenever his Mother lost an earring, she asked him to look for it, and Johnny always found it, because Johnny looked carefully and saw many things.

One day, when Johnny was visiting his Grandmother, he went out in the yard and saw a beautiful apple tree. It was full of apples. He asked his Grandmother if he could pick an apple. She said, "Yes," and added, "maybe you can find a star in an apple, since you are such a good observer!"

A star in an apple! Oh! Now Johnny was sure that he wanted to find a star in an apple! He went to the tree and looked and looked at its apples. He saw apples that were red and round. Some were big, and some were small. However, he couldn't see a star *on* any of the apples.

Then Johnny remembered his Grandmother had said, "a star *in* the apple," not "*on* the apple." Very carefully, he picked a lovely, red apple and ran into the house with it. He was eager to cut it open and find the star in it.

Very carefully, Johnny cut the apple in half. He cut the apple from the stem down through the middle. He looked, but saw no star. How disappointed he was! Then Johnny began to think. Grandmother had said there was a star in the apple. He'd try another apple!

Johnny went back to the tree. He looked and looked, then picked another apple. "This time," he thought, "I'll cut the apple in

[2] Stephen A. Yezback, *Pumpkinseeds* (Indianapolis: The Bobbs-Merrill Co., Inc., 1969). This is a story to go along with eating pumpkin seeds.

half around the middle." When he lifted off the stem end, he saw how the apple is put together. His eyes danced with surprise and joy! There it was. There was the star, just as Grandmother said it would be—a beautiful star—perfect in every way!

With his good observing Johnny found that an apple has a star in it!

—Adapted from a folk tale

The pumpkin at harvest time and the Jack-o'-Lantern at Halloween afford ample opportunity for an aide to provide vivid experiences that spill over into creative expressions. (See "The Life of a Pumpkin" in Chapter 8, page 183.)

A delightful story-activity experience that a teacher with an aide may provide for the group is that of "Toby's Surprise," a story that leads a child into freely cutting or tearing a Jack-o'-Lantern and often to the painting easel to create a Halloween picture. When the aide later tells the story of Toby's Surprise to an individual or to a small group of children, he will have for each child in his group a large sheet of orange newsprint or construction paper folded in half, and, if desired, a pair of scissors appropriate for the children. If the group includes children who are inexperienced in the use of scissors, the aide may suggest that they tear their paper instead of cutting it. Each child is encouraged to take home the Jack-o'-Lantern he has created and to tell his family the story.

### TOBY'S SURPRISE

Once there was a little elf named Toby who had no home at all. Daytimes he skipped from one mossy bank to another, napping under toadstools, feasting on seeds and wild berries, and sipping nectar from the wild flowers. Nighttimes he crawled into a milkweed pod to make his bed, or under a broad leaf he slept sheltered from the dew and the rain. He would have been a very lonely little elf had it not been for Peto, his wee pet mouse who went everywhere with him.

It was the time of year when real people begin to think of Hal-

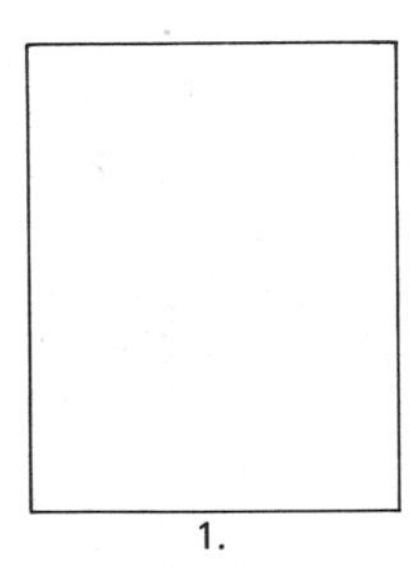

1.

loween and fairy folk begin to think of surprise. Toby thought what fun it would be to have a house of his very own and invite all his fairy friends for a celebration. So—he started out one morning in search of something with which to make a house. He found a sheet of paper, something like this one (Figure 1).

"Aah," said Toby, "the very thing!" Then he pulled and he tugged and he pushed and he sat on it 'til he managed to fold it like this (Figure 2). Taking his own little scissors from his vest pocket

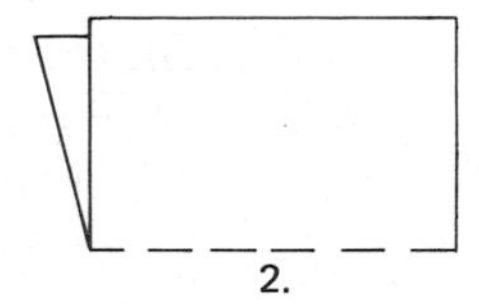

2.

and working very slowly and very carefully, he cut around the ends, like this (Figure 3). Toby was very proud of his work, and pulled it

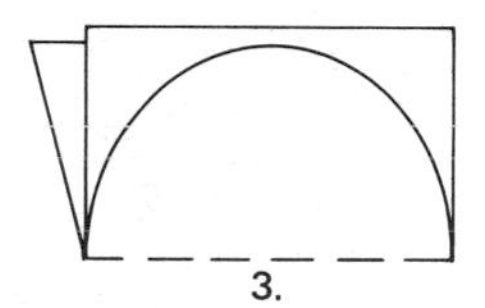

3.

up against a tall weed to have a better look at it. Of course it must have a tall door, and a window. So Toby cut a tall door right about here, and a window right about here (Figure 4).

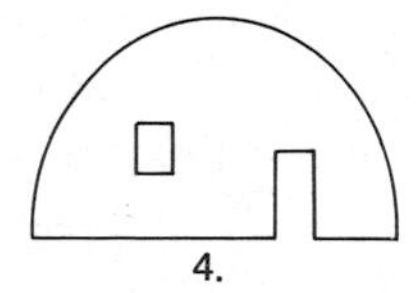

4.

By this time Peto who had not squeaked a single squeak was becoming very interested in Toby's work, and eager to know how he was to get in and out of the house. "Where do I come in?" he asked with a twitch of his wee mouse tail. Toby laughed and with a twinkle in his eye he cut another door, a very wee door right here (Figure 5).

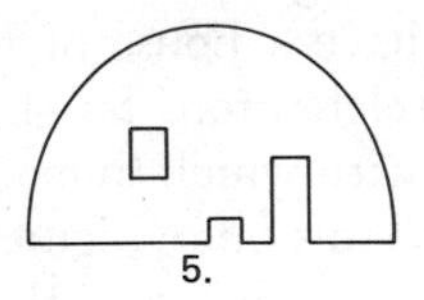

5.

He told Peto it would always be open so he could come in or go out whenever he wished.

And now it was Halloween! All the fairy folk were excited because Toby had invited them to his new house for a party. Toby and Peto were excited too, and when they opened up their house to their fairy friends it was all a-glow! There—sitting right in the middle of the living room floor was———WHAT DO YOU SUPPOSE????? Yes—the *very* thing to make it a real Halloween! A Jack-o'-Lantern like this! (unfold sheet) (Figure 6).

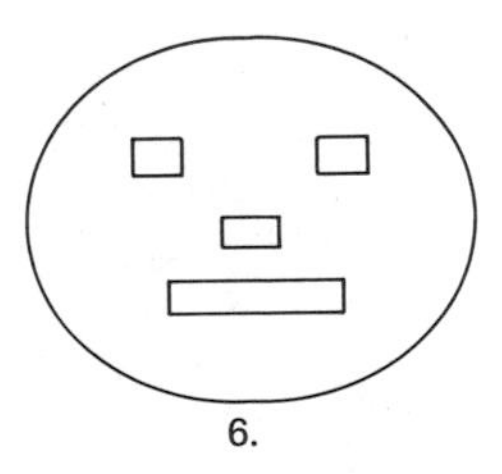

6.

**November**

The month of November rounds out the fall harvest theme with emphasis on Thanksgiving. An aide is prepared to help the teacher communicate the concept of giving thanks for what we have. He has at least one or two poems to use with whatever individuals or small groups the teacher thinks need more adult attention. One such poem that young children enjoy is by Maude Burnham and is entitled, "The Barnyard." [3] Here is another:

I'M THANKFUL

I'm thankful for my mother
And for my father too.
I'm thankful for my doggie Jim

[3] May Hill Arbuthnot (ed.), *Time for Poetry* (Chicago: Scott, Foresman and Company, 1961), p. 66.

And for my kitty Sue.
I'm thankful for my lovely home
And for my sister dear.
I'm thankful for the good God gives.
I'm thankful I can hear.
I'm thankful for my shiny jacks
And for my rubber ball.
But then there are so many things
I cannot name them all.
—Anonymous

While the children are drinking their milk each day an aide sits down at their table, notebook in hand, and asks, "What are you thankful for?" Then the aide writes down what each child says. When each child has had an opportunity to dictate his list, the aide duplicates the statements of all the children for the teacher to send home with each child. Here are three statements dictated by young children:

*Andrew:* I'm thank you for my table. I'm thank you for my clothes and windows and doors. I'm thank you for pianos and chairs. I'm thank you for trash cans.

*Gregory:* I'm thankful for flannel boards. I'm thankful for my house, apples, and pumpkins. I'm thankful for pianos that can play. I'm thankful for Mommy and Daddy, my doggie and my kitty.

*Kathy:* I'm thankful for my food, for birds. I'm thankful for Mama and Daddy. I'm thankful for rain. I'm thankful for teachers. I'm thankful for turkeys.

In addition to poems to enrich Thanksgiving time, an aide has stories to tell, including a simplified version of the adventure of the Pilgrims in coming to America. He tells this story as he shows the children pictures from the lovely book by Alice Dalgliesh entitled, *The Thanksgiving Story*.[4]

### December

Working with individual children, an aide is careful to have whatever is appropriate for the holidays that are recognized by the child. If greeting cards are taken home, "Merry Christmas" is what many children look for. But other children expect "Happy Chanukah" because they celebrate another holiday. Lights glow on Christmas trees to celebrate the birth of Christ, and candles are lighted for Chanukah, Feast of the Maccabees. Speaking of stars may mean the Star of Christmas just as it also means the Star of David.

Of course, for families of all faiths it is appropriate to extend greetings

[4] Alice Dalgliesh, *The Thanksgiving Story* (New York: Charles Scribner's Sons, 1954).

with "Best Wishes for Happy Holidays." Children are encouraged to share, especially with those they most love, their families and their friends. In all families, December is a special month for making and giving gifts, and for decorating rooms.

An aide follows the lead that the teacher takes in planning creative activities for the month of December. Perhaps he will help the youngest child to make collages from greeting cards collected the previous year; or he will help children to be creative with words by making up picture lists of toys all beginning with the same sound, or printing stories about what they have been doing; or the aide will help more sophisticated young children to plan original songs, rhythmic activities, and stories for a program for their parents to attend, perhaps about Christmas in other lands. In short, an aide uses the suggestions of the teacher in helping the children be creative as they use art media, music and dance, and both spoken and written words.

Working with the teacher, an aide can take responsibility for having a Christmas bulletin board display of a decoration that each child is making for his family. First the aide pins a gay Christmas alphabet along the length

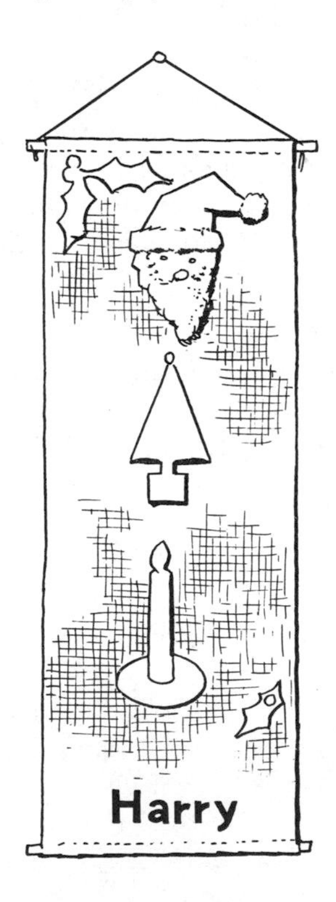


CHRISTMAS PRESENT: A DOOR PANEL.

of the bulletin board. Then he gives each child a burlap panel about six inches by thirty-six inches, hemmed at each end to accommodate a piece of dowel. A loop of yarn or heavy colored string for hanging the panel is tied to the ends of the top dowel, and a small bell is tied to the bottom dowel. At the bottom, a child or the aide writes the child's name with a red or green felt tip pen. "Whose panel will we hang under the letter A?" the aide asks the small group as each child finds a letter of the alphabet under which to hang his panel during the days he is decorating it. "What other word can we think of that begins with A?" the aide may ask to also help the children to link the letter symbol to the names of friends and familiar objects.

Each day during the weeks before Christmas, an aide can encourage the children to use their work period to make a different symbol of the season from construction paper and to paste it on their panel. The aide can bring an example and encourage the children to create symbols such as:

1. A miniature Christmas tree. (e.g., Fold over a rectangular piece of green paper and cut diagonally to the top corner at the fold. Sequins or glitter may be sprinkled on and additional ornaments added.)
2. A Christmas stocking.
3. A candle.
4. Round ornaments of different colors.
5. A candy cane.
6. Holly leaves and red berries.
7. Santa Claus. (e.g., A round face; cotton added for a beard, a red triangle bent over at the point to make a hat.)

Each day after he adds a decoration to his panel, the child returns it to its place under his letter.

Thinking about taking the panel home as a gift, the child will probably enjoy decorating a paper to wrap it in. He can use plain white paper with his name written on it in red or green crayon. The child prints on the paper with a sponge or potato that has a pattern of some Christmas symbol (e.g., Christmas tree or stocking) cut in it. After dipping the sponge or potato in red or green liquid tempera paint, the child then stamps the pattern on the plain paper.

The wrapped package is returned to its place on the alphabet bulletin board so that each child can easily find his gift and take it home on the day before vacation.

One of the ways in which an aide helps children develop skill with words is to say with them, clearly and distinctly, Christmas poems and stories they like to hear, such as "The Night Before Christmas," by Clement C. Moore, "Rudolph, the Red-Nosed Reindeer," and "Jingle Bells." Often the children like to say them in turn, too. If a child is hesitant about the next words of the poem or story, the aide casually joins in, and then phases out as soon as the child continues. The aide points out what each child does but does not call attention to what he does not do. Such well-deserved praise encourages the child to attempt more and facilitates his enjoyment and retention of it.

### January

During the winter months, the absence of many children may frequently keep an aide occupied with individuals and small groups of children who have been absent by repeating what the teacher did previously with the other children. He often uses much the same teaching techniques that the teacher used. For instance, the aide may show the calendar started at the beginning of the new year to a returning child. Thus an aide is invaluable in helping a group of children move ahead without some becoming laggards.

Since January is the heart of winter, an aide helps the children to perceive the essential elements of the season and to formulate concepts and generalizations about winter. The time for playing out-of-doors is an excellent time for an aide to help the very young children develop habits of getting in and out of winter clothing, and to help more experienced children use a hand lens for seeing the intricate beauty of a snowflake.

All young children enjoy working with snow to make a snowman, to roll a snowball, or to make a larger ball for part of the snowman. An aide reminds them to throw snowballs at a target other than people by suggesting that they see if they can hit a fence post. As the children become more skillful they step back to throw from a greater distance. "Look at the post," an aide may say to help them become habituated to aiming their throw.

When young children notice the cold, an aide has an opportunity to guide their learning of an important concept for survival, namely: "Keep moving to keep warm." If a child complains of cold hands, the aide may help him do part of the finger play they often do indoors. He says, "Open, shut them. Clap, clap, clap."

Indoors the children enjoy the help of an aide in doing some of the many science activities that can be part of any month of the year, but are especially enjoyable outdoors in winter. With Jack-o'-Lantern seeds kept dry since October, an aide can help the teacher develop the concept of the continuation of life through seeds from a plant that is gone. The aide prepares individual flowerpots from plastic cups (or bottoms of milk cartons) by filling them with good soil. After the teacher develops the concept of seeds as a means of continuing life, the aide helps her in seeing that each child plants and waters two seeds in his flowerpot. Each day the aide continues the development of the concept as he makes sure that the array of flowerpots on the window sill is kept moist by the children and that eventually a vine develops in each pot. From time to time the aide says with the children a verse entitled, "The Magic Vine."

THE MAGIC VINE

A fairy seed I planted,
So dry and white and old;
There sprang a vine enchanted
With magic flowers of gold.

I watched it, I tended it;
And truly, by and by,
It bore a great big pumpkin
That made a pumpkin pie.
—Anonymous

**February**

Working with the teacher, an aide plans how to further acquaint the children with the national heroes whose birthdays fall in February, especially George Washington and Abraham Lincoln, and to help the children to express love for and devotion to their native land by pledging allegiance to the flag. At the same time, an aide takes responsibility for helping individual and small groups of children to express their love for friends and family as Saint Valentine did. Thus, in February an aide encourages children to create imaginative valentines and to conform to patriotic rituals of the United States of America. Through experience with both patriotic conformity and loving creativity, an aide helps children to see that the occasion determines whether conformity or creativity is the more appropriate behavior.

Creating valentines can be a great deal of fun. In starting the activity an aide may point out that, "We give valentines to friends we like. A valentine is a thought put down on paper in pretty designs and colors. The best valentines are those we make ourselves."

Creating valentines is easy for those who know how to freely cut a heart. An aide encourages the children to cut hearts, first from newsprint as they experiment and then from red and other colored papers when they feel ready to cut hearts for valentines. The aide guides them in the following simple and exciting procedure:

1. Fold a square or rectangle.
2. Hold it in the left hand with the fold at the right.
3. Start cutting at the fold near but not at the top, and cut up and around to cut off the corner.

4. Cut on around to make a hump, cutting off the next corner.
5. Continue cutting down straight to the bottom of the fold.
6. Unfold the paper to find a heart.

While the children are cutting valentines the aide talks with them about valentines. He encourages the children to use the speech sound of "V" like the drone of a motor as they talk about giving valentines and having them to give. With older children who print their own names or want to learn how, the aide encourages them to sign their names on each valentine. With children who can print more extensively, the aide encourages them to address their valentines to their eventual receivers. By giving valentines, many children have learned or improved their speaking, reading, and writing skills.

An aide may ask the teacher about helping each child to make his own mailbox for receiving valentines. A twelve inch by eighteen inch piece of white, pink, or red construction paper is folded like an open envelope and stapled together at the sides. Each child creates his own decoration with the hearts he has learned to cut out, and labels his mailbox with his own name. When these mailboxes are pinned on the bulletin board in alphabetical order, the children can mail a friend's valentine by putting it into his individual mailbox. This creative learning activity for the children saves a great deal of time in the delivery of valentines on Saint Valentine's Day.

### March

An aide can make the windy month of March a very meaningful and happy time for preschool and primary schoolchildren by sharing with them a variety of experiences and reinforcing the guidance of the teacher in having the children develop basic concepts about air in motion.[5]

Besides reinforcing the learning of concepts about the wind, an aide can use the activities with the wind to reinforce the learning of other concepts. For instance, an aide helped a small group of children to practice counting as they enjoyed their pinwheels. The aide introduced the following verse, which the children pantomimed while the aide counted.

My Pinwheel

I've made a paper pinwheel.
I blow it like the wind.
I blow and blow;
The wheel goes 'round.
I blow my paper windmill
Until you count to ten.

—Anonymous

[5] Mae Freeman, *When Air Moves* (New York: McGraw-Hill Book Co., 1968). Photographs and text show activities that an aide can do with children.

| CONCEPT ABOUT AIR IN MOTION | LEARNING ACTIVITY WITH AN AIDE |
| --- | --- |
| Wind is fast moving air. | Watch how small pieces of paper move in the breeze. |
| Wind has force to move things.<br>Blowing makes a small wind. | Each child makes a pinwheel from a square of colored construction paper by cutting in a straight line from each corner toward but not into the center of the square; and then putting a pin or thumbtack through every other point, the center of the square, and the eraser of a pencil used as a handle. Blow on the vanes to make the pinwheel turn. |
| Blow hard for more wind and faster turning of a pinwheel. | |
| A soft blow makes the "wh" speech sound in when, what, why, white, wheel, etc. | Make the pinwheel turn by saying "wheel." |
| Wind makes sounds. | Listen to the air as it escapes from a balloon. Blow up a paper bag. Hold it tightly closed and hit it on a table. Explain the noise. |
| A person can play with the wind. | With a silk scarf, dance in the wind. |
| Wind can move things usefully. | Watch a pinwheel turn in the wind. Move a toy sailboat across water by fanning. |
| Wind blows in one direction at a time. | Observe a wind sock and record its changes. |
| An airplane rides on air. | Fold a sheet of paper to make a glider. Throw it and watch it ride on air. |
| Wind makes a person feel cool. | Blow on the back of a hand. Notice how cool it feels on a windy day. Notice the change in feeling when a fan turns on. |

Then the aide encouraged the children to use one breath to spin their pinwheels while first one child and then another took a turn in counting. Thus through a fun activity, the aide helped the children with breath control and with counting.

An aide can also use the song entitled, "Five Kites," to help children to learn counting and communication skills.[6] With his flannel board and cut-out figures for key words, the aide goes over the song with a small group of children.

[6] "Five Kites" reprinted by permission from *More Singing Fun* by Lucille F. Wood and Louise Binder Scott. Copyright © 1961 by McGraw-Hill, Inc.

### Five Kites

One, two, three, four, five.
Five little kites flying up in the sky,
Said "Hi" to the clouds as they passed by.
Said "Hi" to the birds.
Said "Hi" to the sun.
Said "Hi" to an airplane.
"Oh, what fun!" Then——
Whissh! went the wind, and they all took a dive.
One, two, three, four, five!

—Louise Binder Scott

*Cut-out Placement*

1. Place five kite cut-outs from left to right across the top of the board.
2. Down one side, place: cloud, bird, sun, airplane.
3. Across the bottom of the board: 1, 2, 3, 4, 5.

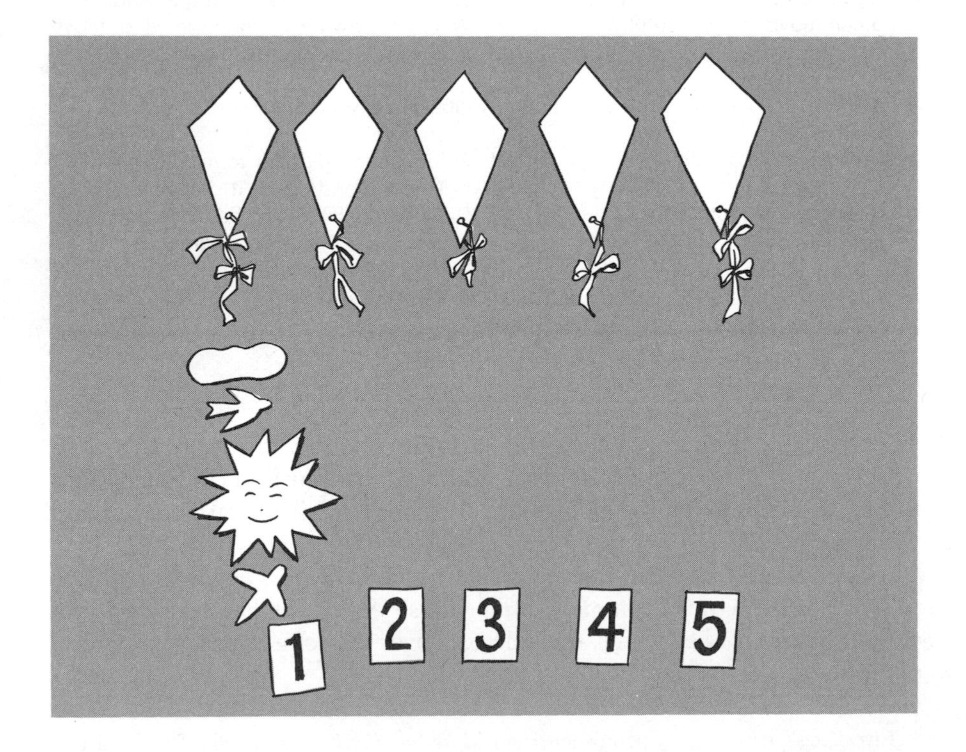


A CHILD'S CUT-OUTS ARE HIS CUES.

The aide can help the children create their own set of flannel board cut-outs, and think about sharing the kite song with their family at home. The aide helps the children prepare an envelope with the kite song stapled on it. Each child puts his cut-outs in it ready to take home. When a child feels ready to sing the song by himself, the aide helps him find a try-out audience. Using the cut-outs as cues, the child has the confidence-building satisfaction he needs to encourage him to sing the song at home. The next day the child is eager to discuss his experience with his friend, the aide.

**April**

With the advent of Easter, the aide reinforces the teaching of delightful, creative anticipation of the spring holiday as well as an imaginative enjoyment of the legendary character, the Easter Bunny (which has evolved probably from the hare, an early symbol of the moon that determines the date of Easter). With small groups of absentees and slow learners, the aide retells stories and poems that the teacher has introduced to the children. With small groups of children needing an enriched program, the aide uses additional stories, songs, poems, and activities, such as "I Am Bunny Pink Ears." [7]

*Related Craft Activity*

"Would you like to make Bunny Pink Ears?" Fold a sheet of white construction paper lengthwise. Free-cut a pattern of a rabbit ear and use it as a pattern to trace on the white paper. Cut around the pattern, making two ears alike. From flesh-colored construction paper, cut pieces to paste in the center of each ear. Staple ears to white headbands.

*Dramatizing the Song*

When the group of children sings: "I Am Bunny Pink Ears" and wears the ears they have made, two children can dramatize it. An Easter basket with plastic Easter eggs is needed for Bunny Pink Ears to give to the child who thanks him for it.

As he guides the learning of an individual child or a small group of children, an aide endeavors to make them consciously aware of reality in contrast to imagination. The aide may say, "Let's make believe for a little while," and then guide the children into imaginative thinking, perhaps using Aileen Fisher's verse entitled "Thinking." [8] "What would you like to turn into?" the aide asks. After the children talk about their preferences

[7] Lorrain E. Watters, et al., *The Magic of Music-Kindergarten* (Boston: Ginn & Co., 1970), p. 87.

[8] Aileen Fisher, *Runny Days, Sunny Days* (New York: Abelard-Schuman Limited, 1933), p. 29.

for a few minutes, the aide suggests, "Show us what you would like to be. Here is paper, and here are crayons (or paints, or some other medium)."

As he guides children in imagining Easter bunnies and Easter eggs, the aide, like the teacher, also guides the children in learning about real rabbits, which are mammals who bear naked young, and about the fascinating facts of egg-laying chickens. These facts include:

1. In the spring, a hen lays an egg every day for about two weeks.
2. The hen sits on the eggs to keep them warm.
3. Inside each egg warmed by the mother hen, a little part starts growing into a chicken.
4. Three weeks after the hen starts sitting on the eggs, the baby chicken takes up all the room inside the shell.
5. The baby chicken pecks a hole in the shell and pushes its way out of the shell.
6. The baby chicken is covered with down, which will be replaced by feathers when it is older.

If the aide takes the responsibility of having children care for the pets each day, the children can observe for themselves that rabbits have young, and

IN THE SPRING, CHILDREN OBSERVE GROWTH AND DEVELOPMENT.

that chickens lay eggs from which baby chickens develop. The aide can easily do this if he is familiar with some of the many written materials that have been prepared by experts.[9]

The teacher will suggest to an aide that he guide the children in some of the many delightful craft activities based on the egg theme.

1. Dipping a hard-cooked egg into food-coloring solution contained in a discarded shallow tin can with smooth edges.
2. With dainty cotton-tipped toothpicks as brushes, painting delicate egg shells.
3. Free-cutting oval shaped eggs by rounding off the corners of rectangular pieces of colored construction paper.
4. Making egg flannel board cut-outs: a set of one egg, a set of two eggs, and so on, each set in a different color.

An aide can easily extend these craft activities into flannel-board practice by linking together color sets and numerals. The aide can use the following verse in setting up the flannel board:

SETS OF EASTER EGGS

I have some colored Easter eggs,
Some sets of many colors.
A set of one is ___ (e.g., red).
A set of two is ___ (e.g., yellow).
. . . . . . . . . . . . .
A set of nine is green.
Don't you think them pretty?
As nice as you have seen?

The aide helps the children take turns in selecting from a set of numerals the one that accurately describes the set. "We need to find the numeral that tells us how many ___ (e.g., red) eggs there are," the aide says to the child having a turn placing a numeral on the flannel board opposite the set of eggs of that color.

### May

In the month of May, an aide helps children to understand and enjoy spring. On the playground or during a study trip, an aide helps each child to be a better observer of the world he lives in. An aide as well as a teacher can have the joy that comes from helping a child see for the first time such things as buds swelling, leaflets spreading into the sunlight, the birth of a

[9] Martha Shapp, Charles Shapp, and Sylvia Shepard, *Let's Find Out About Babies* (New York: Franklin Watts, Inc., 1969); Ruth Jaynes, *Three Baby Chicks* (Glendale, Calif.: Bowmar Publishing Co., 1967). Millicent E. Selsam, *Egg to Chick* (New York: Harper & Row, Publishers, 1946, 1970).

kitten, the first butterfly of the spring season, a sow bug curling up protectively, and the infinite details of spring. Helping a child to perceive sounds he has not distinguished before, or to feel a surface that is lovely to the sense of touch, or to know the pleasure of meaningful communication and response through movement or through words—such are the rewards of being an aide to young children in any month, but especially in the month of May.

In May an aide also has opportunity to help children forge more securely the link between home and school by preparing at school to enrich Mother's Day for the family at home. Here are some of the ideas that aides have used:

*A Song to Sing*

The children learn a song to sing on Mother's Day, the second Sunday in May, for instance: "On Mother's Day." [10]

*Greeting Cards*

Parents and grandparents appreciate a card the child creates expressly for them, using perhaps pieces of colored yarn, roving, colored tissues, construction paper, and other materials of different textures to create flower and leaf designs. The child uses his writing skills in keeping with his level of maturity, perhaps signing his name, perhaps printing a simple greeting, or perhaps composing his own verse. Here is a greeting he may want to use:

> Can you guess who it is
> Who loves you best?
> I'll give you three guesses:
> One, two, three.
> There, I knew you'd think of me!
>
> —Anonymous

**June**

To continue the dialogue between home and school into June, an aide encourages the individuals or small groups of children with whom he works to take home the evidence of new skills they have learned during the school year. For much of his time, an aide is working with absentees who have returned to school and who need help in bridging the span between where they were when they became ill and where the group has progressed in the meantime. But an aide also helps small groups as they work on craft projects or other time-consuming activities. An aide guides them in working at their own pace on a project of interest to them. In June the aide may have a series of small groups make a necktie-shaped card from construction paper. Each child folds the long sheet of paper, matching top to bottom.

[10] *Birchard Music Series—Kindergarten* (Sacramento, Calif.: California State Department of Education, 1960), p. 79.

Then if the child is sufficiently mature in his cutting skills, he cuts a double necktie to look like what he sees between the points of the collar on his father's shirt. With paints or crayons, the child makes a suitable design on the top of his paper necktie. Then inside his necktie greeting card he writes his name, a copy of a favorite verse, or his own greeting to his father. The completed card is then ready for the child to take home for Father's Day.

In another take-home craft activity in which an aide is prepared to help, each child is provided with a copy of a poem entitled: "My Handprint," together with a piece of construction paper on which are labeled prints of his "Left Hand" and his "Right Hand." These prints are made by the child by dipping first his left hand and then his right hand in colored finger paint of his choice and then pressing it on the paper he has selected. The poem is adapted for use on Father's Day.

My Hand Print

Sometimes you get discouraged
  Because I am so small,
And always leave my finger prints
  On furniture and wall.

But everyday I'm growing up
  And soon I'll be so tall,
That all those little hand prints
  Will be difficult to recall.

So here's a current hand print
  That you can put away.
You'll know just how my fingers looked
  This year for Father's Day!
—Anonymous

**July**

For Independence Day in the month of July, an aide works with the teacher to help the children learn about their country and be proud of it. Patriotic rituals of saluting the flag and pledging allegiance to it can take on added significance if the aide leads the children in learning such patriotic poems as "The Flag Goes By," or the poem that follows.[11]

Our Flag

Red means be brave.
White means be good.
Blue means be true.
—Anonymous

[11] May Hill Arbuthnot (ed.), *Time for Poetry* (Chicago: Scott, Foresman and Company, 1961), p. 195.

An aide can help more experienced children to think about the expanse of the United States if he prepares a large outline map on which they can print the names of cities where their relatives and friends live. This can be done on paper in the classroom or on sand outdoors. Children who are less experienced with words can place preprinted words at the appropriate places on the map, and more experienced children can print the words themselves. The aide guides their thinking about how they get from where they live to where their grandmother and grandfather live. If they go by car, it may take an hour. Can they get there in an hour if they walk? By such questioning, an aide can help the children understand that by going faster, a person can cover a distance in less time. The children who are working with printed words will enjoy making a list such as the following:

I can go on foot,
on my bicycle,
in a car or bus,
in a train,
in an airplane.

### August

In August an aide makes sure that the individuals and the small groups with which he works have ample opportunity to understand and appreciate the season of summer. Out-of-doors with the children the aide helps them perceive the growing things around them and formulate basic concepts about their relationship to plants and animals. As the aide and the children watch a long line of ants, an aide may say, "Let's watch what these ants are doing." Sometimes the aide may say the poem entitled, "Ants Live Here." [12]

If a child says, "I step on ants," an aide has an opportunity to help that child and other children nearby as he says, for instance, "Sit here by me and let's see what they are doing." In this way before many days are past, the children take on the role of observer, adding to the roles they learn at home and at play.

Similarly an aide can guide children in learning to be admirers of wild flowers as well as pickers of cultivated flowers. "Let's leave the pretty flower right where it is so that we can come to see it again," and aide may say on a study trip. The aide, of course, makes sure that the children do return to that spot either to admire again the beautiful blossom or to observe how it has progressed in its life changes. In some instances, the children return to learn that someone else has selfishly taken the lovely flower away and robbed everyone of the joy of seeing it in its wilderness home.

More experienced young children can learn to collect fallen leaves or

[12] Lilian Moore, *I Feel the Same Way* (New York: Atheneum Publishers, 1967).

pick an occasional leaf from among a treeful of leaves in order to bring a leaf to school for use by the class. An aide can take a group of children around the playground to collect leaves of all sizes and shapes. Holding up first one kind of leaf and then another, the children see the variety of leaf shapes and sizes. More experienced children can also perceive the differences in the way that the leaves are arranged on a stem. Such perceptions help children to form concepts about each individual being unique. "No two individuals are exactly alike."

Back indoors with their leaf collections, the children can use them to create new shapes. An aide may guide them into such activity as follows:

*Aide:* Does this leaf remind anyone of anything?
*Child:* It looks like a clown without a head.
*Aide:* Let's put some paste on the leaf and press it down on a piece of paper. (Pastes and presses.) Now what shall we look for?
*Child:* A head!

If no child finds a leaf for a head, the aide suggests finding a leaf for a hat and drawing a face under it. Then the project is continued to create the whole clown.

*Aide:* What will we look for next?
*Child:* Arms! Here's one!
*Aide:* Good! Can you find another small, narrow leaf for the other arm?

A few minutes later two other slender leaves are pasted and pressed onto the paper to make long, floppy feet for the clown. The final result is a leaf clown. By using a "fix-set" kind of spray, the aide can make the leaf clown sufficiently durable to be displayed and serve as a spur to other creations. Next to the leaf clown are other stimuli for creativity, including pie tins containing leaves that were collected, paper and paste for working with them, colored toothpicks, pipe cleaners, yarn, and other colorful bits. A great variety of leaf pictures are the result: leaf people, leaf planes, leaf houses, leaf fish, and so on.[13]

When an aide leads children to evaluate what they have created, he encourages each child to tell about his leaf picture. The aide records what the child says and places a typed copy of it on the back of the picture, or next to the picture when it is displayed. In such ways an aide encourages individual children to be creative with things around them and with words.

[13] Josef Guggenmos and Irmgard Lucht, *Wonder Fish from the Sea* (New York: Parents' Magazine Press, 1971). The author and her children gather leaves and transform them into fish and birds.

# GUIDING PERCEPTION

Working with a teacher, an aide can help preschool and early elementary schoolchildren to lay the cornerstone for their continued learning and richer experiences throughout their lives. An aide helps the children to perceive the essential elements of the social and physical environment in which they live. Through sharing their experience with a person older than they, the children become consciously aware of important aspects of the world around them. This awareness linked with the ability to create first oral and later written symbols of communication enables the children to develop control of their environment.

As an aide works with one or more children, he guides them in observing the routine of their day, the succession of activity and rest, the succession of activity and nourishment, and, in general, the patterning that people build into their lives. He also guides the children in observing the seasonal patterning within a year: the succession of fall, winter, spring, and summer; the sequential development of plant and animal life within the year; the national holidays and community celebrations associated with each of the seasons. Furthermore, the aide guides the children in observing what is new and different because this novelty usually involves an opportunity for learning.

It is important for a child to enjoy making use of his ability to discriminate. He must trust his own perceptions. When an adult with a less sensitive sense of taste asks a child to eat what is no longer fresh and delicious to him, the adult respects the child's refusal of the food and thus encourages him to learn to discriminate between what is and what is not desirable to do. A child who is so trusted becomes a trustworthy person of good judgment.

An aide, like a teacher, respects and trusts the observations of each child. If a child makes an erroneous report, an aide accepts it and acts on it as if it were valid until it is evident to the child that he should correct his report. Thus the child sees the importance of observing and reporting accurately, so that he can accomplish what he wants.

*Aide:* Do you want milk?
*Child:* No.
The aide goes on to other children without leaving a milk carton.
*Child:* Gimme one.
*Aide:* Oh, do you want milk? (Serves a carton.)

Realizing that most learning situations are multisensory in nature, an aide encourages each child in multisensory perception, observing what is sensible to feeling as well as to touch, to smell, to taste, to hearing, to kinesthesis, as well as to sight. Thus the child is encouraged to observe widely in each situation and to enjoy learning not only through a single sensory channel but through all of the channels. This concomitance is important if a child is to learn in his subsequent years of schooling and apply what he learns and transfer it easily from one situation to another.

Furthermore, multisensory perception is a learner's best guarantee of validity in his learning. For instance, if what the child sees is in accord with what he "feels in his joints," he knows that his observations are valid and he thus has confidence in what he sees. His confidence enables him to proceed to action.

## INCREASING PERCEPTION

Whether he is working with an individual child, with a few children, or with a larger group of children, an aide helps the children to focus their attention sometimes on one sensory aspect of a situation and sometimes on another. Within a single day, an aide endeavors to help children become aware of what each of their senses can show them. Whether he is a parent, a Playground Aide, a Classroom Aide, or one who is guiding child learning in some other role, an aide always endeavors to increase the child's perception.

### Perception Through Tactile Sensations

An aide uses primarily three questions to help a child increase his tactile perception. He asks:

*How does it feel?*
*Do these feel alike, or different?*
*How can you tell that these two objects feel different?*

*My Bunny Feels Soft* [1] and *What Is Your Favorite Thing to Touch?* [2] are excellent books for helping children link the vocabulary of descriptive words to how an object feels to the sense of touch. Passing around different objects and talking about how they feel is also an effective way of getting children into conversation that motivates better observations. "The stem of a rose is prickly," "Soap feels slippery," "First metal feels cold, and then it feels warm," are descriptive kinds of response that an aide encourages, rather than only the evaluative response, "I like it," or "I don't like it." If a child responds with an evaluative remark, an aide continues the conversation to get it into descriptive observations that can lead into useful activity.

An aide helps children to see similarities and differences in tactile sensations, and to make the children aware of such contrasts as:

1. Soft—hard.
2. Cold—warm.
3. Rough—smooth.
4. Wet—dry.
5. Warm—hot.
6. Sharp—not sharp.

The aide occasionally uses a few minutes in the course of a school day to guide children in thinking about such a question as: "How can you tell the difference between a cat and a kitten?" As the child responds to the question he uses words such as "big," "little," and "size," and helps himself and the other children to use the words both more extensively and more exactly. Other key comparisons for tactile perception include:

1. A sheet of sandpaper and a piece of tile (rough and smooth).
2. A rubber ball and an apple (bouncing and not bouncing; elastic and nonelastic).
3. A cube of ice and a cube of cheese (cold and warm).
4. A handshake and a touch (pressure and nonpressure).
5. The end of a wire and the side of a wire (sharp and not sharp).

An aide uses the "Touch and Tell" game with an individual child or a small group of children to increase their sensitivity to the feel of objects. The aide prepares a box or bag that contains objects that a child can identify by feel:

| | |
|---|---|
| a ring | a sponge |
| a pencil | a crayon |
| a nut | a marble |

[1] Charlotte Steiner, *My Bunny Feels Soft* (New York: Alfred A. Knopf, Inc., 1958).
[2] Myra Tomback Gibson, *What Is Your Favorite Thing to Touch?* (New York: Grosset & Dunlap, Inc., 1965).

| | |
|---|---|
| soap | a feather |
| an earring | a piece of: |
| a bracelet | leather |
| a pine cone | velvet |
| a paintbrush | fur |

The game is played with a child putting his hand inside the container, selecting something he thinks that he recognizes by feel, telling how it feels, and then identifying it. The child removes the object from the container to see if he identified it correctly.

### Perception Through Olfactory Sensations

To guide children in developing their sense of smell, an aide frequently asks three major questions:

*Does it have an odor? Does it have a fragrance?*

*Do these smell alike, or different?*

*When does it have this smell?*

In asking such questions, an aide encourages children to make observations beyond the usual evaluative remark, "It smells good." The aide guides children in accurately observing the world around them.

An aide helps children to note similarities and differences in smell. He may say, "This flower has a stronger smell than this one. I can smell it better." An aide also guides children in noticing smells when they come into a room, perhaps the appetizing aroma of the noon meal, or the fragrance of a gardenia. He may remark on what he smells, helping the children to link names to smells, for instance, "I smell bacon frying."

Sometimes more discerning observations made by an aide are caught by children who are ready to link them to their experience. A child who has accustomed himself to using his sense of smell with discrimination can notice that the smell of gasoline or tobacco interferes with smelling more subtle odors such as that of perfume. Usually just by responding to the observations that a child makes and encouraging him to use his sense of smell is the principal way that an aide helps a child develop his olfactory perception.

"Smell and Tell" is a game that an aide can use to increase the child's sensitivity to odors. In advance of playing the game, the aide prepares small containers each having a familiar item with a distinctive smell, such as:

| | | |
|---|---|---|
| onion flakes | cantaloupe | lemonade |
| soap | mint | leather |
| cinnamon | rose petals | peppermint |
| cloves | orange peel | eucalyptus |

A child closes his eyes so that he will perceive with his sense of smell. He selects one of the containers, smells its contents, and completes his turn by attempting to identify what it is.

### Perception Through Taste Sensations

Since the sense of taste combines with the olfactory sense in helping people appreciate foods, the aide who is with a group of children at mealtime has an excellent opportunity to help them enjoy each of the foods they eat. Knowing that a pleasant experience with a new food leads to further experience with it, and aide attempts to make each meal or snack delightful. Enjoying each food with the children is one way of doing this. "My, this is delicious," says a child echoing what he has heard an aide say.

Usually a new food is served at meal or snack time after its introduction by the teacher. Then the aide guides the children in remembering their initial pleasant experience and in again enjoying the taste as well as the color and texture of the food. "Do you remember Miss Smith making a Jack-o'-Lantern from a pumpkin yesterday?" the aide may ask the children. "When our cook made this delicious bread today, she used a pumpkin just like the Jack-o'-Lantern." Making such linkages with the children is an important function of an aide.

### Perception Through Auditory Sensations

An aide can do a great deal to help children become perceptive about sounds, and interpret them realistically. The older person who is at hand when the thunder rolls can say calmly and pleasantly, "That's thunder. It comes after a flash of lightning." The child observes not only the thunder but also the calmness and pleasantness of the aide and thus links lightning and thunder together, and also links each of them with calmness and pleasantness.

An aide can help a child identify and interpret the loud noises of his environment—the siren on the helpful ambulance or fire truck, the muted rumble of a passing truck carrying construction materials, the whirring motor of the lawn mower, and so on.

Sometimes an aide also helps a child reinterpret sounds that have been misinterpreted. Here is a story that an aide can use with a child who is learning about thunder.

#### THE PUPPY WHO LEARNED ABOUT THUNDER

Once there was a little puppy who had not learned to like thunder. When he saw thick, dark clouds in the sky, he ran and hid. His puppy playmates knew this and teased him about it. "Bow, wow! Thunder! Thunder! Run!" they would cry. Then they would run after the little puppy until he ran away and hid.

One day the little puppy went for a long walk. The day was hot and soon he said, "I'm thirsty. I want a drink. I am so very, very thirsty!"

Just then it began to thunder. The little puppy was so thirsty that, for a moment, he did not hear the thunder. Then another great thunderous roar rolled out of the sky. The little puppy began to run.

As he ran, the little puppy passed a frog. "Chugurumph! Thunder!" shouted the frog to the little puppy. "Am I glad to hear it thunder! Now my pool won't dry up." The frog was happy about the thunder.

The little puppy ran on. He passed a duck. "Quack! Quack! Thunder! Hurrah! Thunder!" he shouted to the little puppy. "I like mud. I like thunder. Quack! Quack!"

As the little puppy ran on, he thought to himself, "They are glad to hear thunder. Why are they glad?" He thought and thought about their gladness.

"I know!" he said out loud. "When it thunders, we have rain. And rain is good. If it rains now, I can have some water, and I am so thirsty!"

The little puppy was right. Soon raindrops fell on his face. It rained some more, and the little puppy got a drink of water.

The little puppy walked along while the thunder rumbled and rumbled. He did not run. He walked. Then he looked up at the sky and said, "You don't scare me any more, you thunder."

And do you know, the thunder did not frighten the little puppy ever again.

—Adapted from a folk tale

An aide can also help a child in perceiving and appreciating the soft sounds in his environment—the quiet sounds of leaves and needles moving in the breeze, insect noises such as those of a cricket or a Sphinx caterpillar, or the tones of the scale played softly on a musical instrument. Hearing the sounds and reproducing them is fun for everyone, child and aide alike.

Children who are perceptive about the sounds in their environment often are ready to link remembered sounds to present sounds, to note similarities and differences in sounds, to recall a short melody from a television program or commercial, or to create a new melody. Note the typical responses that an aide can make to encourage such activities and auditory perception.

When an aide has responsibility for a small group of children, he can use simple games and then gradually more complex games that give the children experience in noting the likenesses and differences in sounds. Several games of this type follow on page 90.

| CHILD ACTIVITY | AIDE ACTIVITY |
|---|---|
| Listens attentively to a familiar melody. | Asks, "Have you heard that before?" |
| Taps a rhythm. | Taps the same rhythm, or a different one of the same length, and asks, "Is this it?" |
| Hums a note or a familiar melody. | Asks, "Isn't that. . . ?" |
| Sings a new melody. | Says, "I like that. Let me write it down." Writes it out on staff paper. Gives a copy to the teacher. Uses a copy the next day with the composer. |

AN AIDE GUIDES AUDITORY PERCEPTION; THE CHILDREN LEARN NEW SKILLS.

*Listening Game*

*Aide:* Close your eyes. Just listen to sounds. (Children close eyes briefly.)

*Aide:* What did you hear? (Children mention: a dog, a plane, a truck, etc.)

Aide repeats and embellishes what the child says (e.g., a dog barking, a truck rumbling by).

*Aide:* How did you know it was? . . . (Child mentions shrill, low, fast, etc.)

*Find the Object*

"It" is chosen from volunteers. Aide hides an object. (Later a child can do this.) "It" hunts for the hidden object guided by the loudness of clapping by other children. The children clap more loudly when "It" approaches the object, and more softly as he goes away from it.

*Guessing High or Low*

The aide uses the piano, autoharp, bells, pitchpipe, or other instrument to make a single tone. He begins with notes that are far apart and gradually reduces the distance between them as the children become increasingly able to discriminate between tones.

*Aide:* Which tone is higher? Is the first tone higher (or lower)?

If the group understands the terms *first* and *second,* the aide may ask, "Which is higher, the first or the second tone?" The aide may instruct the children as follows: "If the first note is higher, raise your hand up high. If the first note is lower, lower your hand." Doing the first example together enables the children to observe the demonstration of the aide at the same time that they do it themselves.

*It Is I*

With his eyes closed, one child (e.g., Tommy) sits on a chair (representing his house) with other players in a circle around him. A second child (the visitor) quietly takes his place behind the chair while players and aide recite:

Little Tommy Tiddlemouse
Lives in a little house.
Someone's knocking, me-oh-my,
Someone's calling. . . .

*Visitor:* It is I

The first child, playing the part of Tommy, tries to guess the identity of the visitor from hearing his voice. If he is not successful, a player gives him a clue by asking the visitor a question and Tommy again tries to identify the visitor by his response. Clues include:

*Player:* (to Visitor) Are you a girl or a boy?
*Player:* (to Visitor) What color . . . do you have on?

The game concludes when Tommy successfully identifies the visitor.

Like a teacher, an aide guides children to be good listeners and thus reinforces the teacher's guidance. An aide listens attentively to what a child says and notices children who do likewise. He praises evidence of good listening. He may remind a talkative child to explore the listener role by singing, "I'll Listen." [3]

An aide is also prepared to tell the story entitled, "The Little Elf Who Listened," and any other story or poem that the teacher recommends as an aid to encourage good listening.[4]

When a child shows that he has listened to what the teacher said, an aide lets the child know that he noticed it. Thus he helps the child appreciate what he has done. For example, if a child brings to school something that was mentioned the day before or related to it, the aide praises his alertness and good "ears for listening." The aide helps him display what he brought by adding to it a sign such as:

| Bob's Book |
|---|

Thus the aide helps the child develop self-confidence and encourages others to likewise earn recognition.

### Kinesthetic Perception

An aide also encourages a child to be aware and proud of the ways in which he uses his kinesthetic perception. An aide is alert to notice when a child first pumps his swing, balances for a step or two first on the walking board and then on a more narrow curbing, goes from rung to rung on the overhead ladder or from ring to ring on the playground apparatus, or completes a pleasing sequence of other movements. Then the aide helps the child to be aware of what he can do, perhaps by exclaiming, for instance, "You can swing by yourself!" Such encouragement leads a child on to greater physical achievements of coordination and movement.

It is important to help a child build both large muscle movements and small muscle movements. Outdoor play in space is essential and so is the opportunity to develop the finger control necessary for handling a tool such as a paintbrush, a pencil, or a hammer; or material such as finger paint or a book; or a small toy such as a truck or a magnet. An aide is invaluable

[3] Louise Binder Scott and Lucille F. Wood, *Singing Fun* (St. Louis, Mo.: Webster Publishing Co., 1954), p. 55.
[4] See Chapter 8, page 175.

when a child is physically exploring the feel and the mobility of an object. If a child's awkward gesture results in his making a mess, an aide is quick to procure cleaning materials for both the child and himself. If the experimentation is rough to the point of breaking the object, the aide is at hand to provide a similar object for further experimentation.

An aide is careful at all times to encourage and not to derogate either the child or his attempts to learn.

### Visual Perception

As early as possible a child benefits from guidance in visual perception. An aide is invaluable in helping him find pleasure, use, and satisfaction in what he observes. The poems, stories, and letters that children write to magazines come out of an environment that encourages them to make observations, provides them with exact words for what they observe, and guides them into a satisfying experience in arranging words meaningfully and well.

The older people around a child growing up in a primeval forest guide the child into being able to survive in a primitive environment. But an aide to a child growing up today in the United States guides the child toward survival in a social order that emphasizes quite different perceptions. The primitive child learns to observe and respond to one set of cues—for instance, a bit of fur on a broken twig two feet above the ground is a cue for proceeding with great alertness. But the child from surburban United States learns to observe and respond to other cues—for instance, English words that sound alike are a cue for putting them with other words into a meaningful poem.

An aide is eager to have each child be a good observer of both his natural setting and his social setting. On one day an aide may read "Johnny Finds a Star in an Apple" (see Chapter 3, page 63). On another day the aide may work with a young child or a small group of children to help them think about clouds in the sky. The aide may read with them *It Looked Like Spilt Milk* and let them illustrate the story by placing cloud shapes cut from white pellon from left to right on a sky-blue flannelboard.[5] Then the cloud shapes can be memory cues that enable a child to tell the story.

Another day the aide may encourage the children to create their own set of flannel board cut-outs of their own observations of clouds. The children use construction paper and small pieces of adhesive material in making cut-outs to help them tell the story at home. In these ways an aide enriches a primitive experience of cloud-watching into a more extensive learning experience on which subsequent school experiences can be built.

[5] Charles G. Shaw, *It Looked Like Spilt Milk* (New York: Harper & Row, Publishers, 1947).

An aide can extend perception for survival into perception for living in the world of today. How an aide helps a teacher guide children in perceiving color will illustrate ways in which an aide can reinforce teacher guidance of a child's perception.

## COLOR PERCEPTION

Working with children individually or in small groups, an aide has the opportunity to observe what colors a child perceives and names, and what other colors he needs to have further experience with. An aide can help a child lay a foundation for learning easily by means of color-coded materials, and for enjoying both natural and man-made worlds with their infinite array of tints and shades of all the colors.

An aide has a simple strategy for guiding a child to learn a color that he does not yet know, namely:

1. Provide a succession of experiences with the color, first by itself and then in contrast to other colors, first one at a time and then with several colors.
2. Use the name of the color in many, many situations in which it is noticeable, thus helping the child link the spoken name to the color, and to familiar objects (e.g., brown potato, brown nut).
3. Make use of the flannel board in letting the child use representations of what he has linked the color name to.
4. Presently help the child in linking the printed name of the color to the visual representations he has worked with before, perhaps by putting both on the flannel board, or by using such picture books as *Colors*.[6]

### Experience with Each Color

An aide can help a child notice the color that is new to him. The aide comments on the color whenever it is in the immediate environment of the child. Here are some of the gestures and comments that an aide can make to the child about each of the primary and secondary colors:

*Red*

1. Point out a picture of a big red apple posted on the bulletin board.
2. Ask the child to bring something that is red and post it on the board.
3. Prepare a "frame" from red construction paper for a picture that the child draws.

[6] John J. Reiss, *Colors* (Englewood Cliffs, N.J.: Bradbury Press, 1969). "Things to eat, to wear, to chase, to pet come in all colors."

4. Read books such as *What Is Red?* [7] and *An Apple Is Red.*[8]
5. Comment when a child wears a red shirt or sweater.

*Yellow* [9]

1. Let a child use on his flannel board such yellow cut-outs as: a yellow daffodil or daisy, a yellow leaf, a yellow sun or star, or a yellow duck.
2. Talk with a child about pictures cut from magazines and backed with a length of adhesive material for use on a flannel board, for instance: a slice of lemon, yellow flowers, a glass of lemonade, an ear of corn, pineapple rings, a cube of butter, half a grapefruit.
3. Share a poem about a "Yellow Duckling."

YELLOW DUCKLING

Yellow sunshine
  Out of blue sky.
Yellow flowers
  Standing waist high.
Yellow leaves
  Falling from trees.
Yellow duckling,
  Tell me, oh please:
In the white snow
  You will not freeze!

*Blue* [10]

1. Have the children, on several days and at different times of the day, look at the sky.
2. Look at colored pictures of the sea and sky, and talk about their blues.
3. Use the broad side of a broken crayon to color the sky in a picture.
4. Use a blue flannel board as a background for *It Looked Like Spilt Milk.*[11]

*Green*

1. On a walk, notice the green grass.
2. At the easels provide yellow and blue paint for mixing.[12]

[7] Suzanne Gottlieb, *What Is Red?* (New York: Lothrop, Lee and Shepard Co., Inc., 1961).
[8] Nancy Curry, *An Apple Is Red* (Glendale, Calif.: Bowmar Series, Bowmar Publishing Corp., 1967).
[9] Robert Jay Wolff, *Hello Yellow!* (New York: Charles Scribner's Sons, 1968).
[10] Robert Jay Wolff, *Feeling Blue* (New York: Charles Scribner's Sons, 1968).
[11] Shaw, *It Looked Like Spilt Milk.*
[12] Leo Lionni, *Little Blue and Little Yellow* (New York: Astor-Honor, Inc., 1959).

3. Help children make a collection of magazine pictures with green objects. Help children cut or tear them out and talk about objects and colors in the pictures while putting the cut-outs on the bulletin board under the word, *green.*

*Orange*

1. Display a large picture of an orange on the bulletin board. Discuss it.
2. Score an orange and strip off its peel in pieces.
3. Section the orange and let the children each enjoy a section.
4. Tie in orange color with pumpkin activities at Halloween.

*Purple*

1. Use a real bunch of purple grapes, or a large picture of a bunch, as a lead into talking about purple and into choosing purple crayons for drawing such a bunch.
2. Procure samples of cloth to make a display of purples that differ in how they feel.
3. Help children look through old magazines to find purple objects in pictures. They can cut or tear them out, and pin them on a bulletin board, to show to other children.

*Brown* [13]

After the teacher had introduced the color brown, one aide helped children to become aware of the color by telling them the flannel-board story entitled, "The First Teddy Bear" (see Chapter 8, page 191). The next day after telling the story to the children who were not yet certain in recognizing the color brown, the aide worked with them using a flannel board and the cut-outs to make the brown teddy bear.

"Let's put the brown teddy bear together the way the Great Toy Maker did," the aide said. "Who can tell us what the Great Toy Maker started with?"

Jeff volunteered and the aide said, "Jeff, you may find the first piece, and tell us about it."

As a different child volunteered and put a part on the flannel board, the aide stressed the color brown whenever possible. "Are all teddy bears brown?" the aide asked, for instance, and elicited the answer that not all are brown, but the first one was.

"If you would like to make your own flannel board story of 'The First Brown Teddy Bear,' you may cut or tear pieces of brown paper. Let's get

[13] Jean Carey Bond, *Brown Is a Beautiful Color* (New York: Franklin Watts, Inc., 1969).

it from the supply shelf," the aide said to get the children started to prepare to tell the story at home.

### Color Discrimination

An aide can help children enjoy learning to identify each of several colors. He may want to tell them about "A Gay Little Clown" (see Chapter 8, page 173), and encourage each child to create a picture of the clown and his balloons. An aide asks, "Have you a balloon of *each* color?" and obtains visual evidence of the colors that each child has learned to perceive.

Here are several games that an aide can use with a small group of children:

*Which Color Is Missing?*

Squares made from different colored paper are arranged on a flannel board either in a circle or in a straight line. The players hide their eyes while the aide removes one colored square. (A child is chosen to do this the next time.) Then one child is asked to tell which colored square is missing. An aide gives a less mature child a cue such as, "It is the same color as the sun," helping the child feel successful in playing the game by linking object and color.

The game may be played with triangles, disks, rectangles, or other

VISUAL EVIDENCE OF A CHILD'S PERCEPTION OF COLOR.

shapes, each of a different color. It can also be played with children who have been naming colors a great deal by removing two colors at a time.

*Musical Color-Chairs*

The aide places a different colored paper under each chair. As many children are players as there are chairs. Another child is "Caller" and calls out a color. The player sitting on the chair with the called color under it stands and skips to music. When the music stops (or the aide claps), each player and the "Caller" try to find a chair to sit on. The child who is not seated chooses another child to become the "Caller" for the next game.

*Rainbow Color Game*

Arrange colored papers on the floor as they are arranged in a rainbow.

While "It" hides his eyes, a child changes the position of one color (or two colors are interchanged if children have become familiar with the colors).

The child who is "It" must say what color changes have been made and then rearrange the rainbow as it was.

*Stepping Stones*

Using the rug as a "brook," the aide places across it a series of "stepping stones" each made from large construction paper of a different color. The players are seated on one side of the brook while one child takes a turn by naming the color of the first stepping stone and then stepping on it, and proceeding in this way across the brook. When the child gets across the brook, he sits down and watches his friends come across in the same way one at a time. Players clap as each new player gets across.

When an aide is to work with children who are linking written color words to their respective colors, he may use gray paper stepping stones on which color words are written. In advance of the game, the aide prepares a color-word chart showing the written color word opposite a square of that color. A player can use the color-word chart to make certain that he is calling each stepping stone correctly before he steps on it. Thus he feels successful in playing the game.

**Evidence of Color Perception**

Working with individuals or small groups of children, an aide has the opportunity to observe what colors each child has yet to learn and what colors he identifies readily. He can thus provide feedback to the teacher to help the teacher to plan further experiences for the children. One way to do this is for the aide to make up a set of name plates that can be kept in a pocket chart and can show each child, his parents, the teacher, or the aide exactly what color perception is already developed. As soon as a child has demonstrated his command of colors, perhaps by successfully providing the clown with a range of colored balloons that he can name (see page 96), then the aide lets him make a rainbow on the back of his name plate. Then perhaps the aide will read to a small group of the children Don Freeman's delightful book entitled *A Rainbow of My Own.*[14]

## MULTISENSORY PERCEPTION

Individual sensory perceptions reinforce each other to help a child learn more rapidly and more completely from an experience. An aide, like a teacher, chooses activities that are multisensory, in preference to those that are primarily visual, auditory, or monosensory. Furthermore, an aide encourages children to learn through multisensory experience whenever possible. He asks in general about their experiences and he asks specifically, "How does it feel?" "How does it smell?" "How does it taste?" "Does it make a sound?" "What do you use it for?" He appreciates the replies that the children give, and from time to time he reminds them of a poem such as "A World to Know" [15] or reads to them the book entitled *Open Your Eyes.*[16]

### Perceiving Similarity and Difference

In everyday activities, an aide often sees opportunities for guiding children to observe ways in which two objects are alike and ways in which they are different. Two children may bring to school the same toy. The aide can help their owners and other children nearby to observe the toys. The remarks of the aide in the course of the discussion will probably include the following:

*How are we going to tell these toys apart?*

*The toys should have the name of the owner on them. If they don't, how can the owners be sure they each have their own toy?*

*Are the toys* exactly *alike?*

*Can we find something that is just a little different about them?*

Questions of this type guide the children in making observations of likeness and difference.

Sooner or later an aide usually has an opportunity to help children observe the similarity and differences between two sweaters, shirts, or other articles of clothing. If a child takes home the wrong red sweater and returns it the next day, an aide can help him compare his own sweater with the one he has returned. The discussion will undoubtedly include new words

[14] Don Freeman, *A Rainbow of My Own* (New York: The Viking Press, Inc., 1966).
[15] James S. Tippett, *A World to Know* (New York: Harper & Row, Publishers, Inc., 1933). Out of print.
[16] Roz Abisch, *Open Your Eyes* (New York: Parents' Magazine Press, 1964).

and phrases: "a wide red band," "a design of light and dark blue," "a narrow black band down the front," "a plain sleeve," and so on. One such discussion can easily lead into others both at that time and later. An aide can thus provide the children with opportunity to perceive differences in weight, texture, the feel of material, and so on.

In addition to the similarities and differences observable in the course of a day, others are observable on study trips, a walk around the block, and play times out of doors. An aide is quick to engage children in observing similarities and differences in buildings, trees, telephone poles, and other objects that differ in size and shape. He listens carefully to the comments and questions of the children and extends their observations through his few comments and thought-provoking and perception-stimulating, questions.

*Which is bigger? Smaller?*
*Which is larger? The same size?*
*Which is shorter? Taller?*
*Which ones are almost alike?*
*Which one is different?*

To help children who are just becoming sensitive to similarity and difference, an aide can work with a small group of four children. He can have three out of four children face the windows in the room, and have the fourth child face in the opposite direction. Then the aide says, "Here are four children. Three are doing something alike, and one is doing something different. In what way is he different?"

After arranging the children in the same and different activities, an aide can similarly arrange objects. He can place four pairs of scissors on the floor, three pointing toward the window, and the fourth pointing in the opposite direction. The aide can also guide the children to see similarities and differences by having part of the group stand up while others are seated, by having some of the group read books while others are working with crayons, and so on.

Another way in which an aide can help children to become sensitive to similarities and differences is to prepare sets of pictures on eight-inch by ten-inch cards for use in a pocket chart or on the chalk rail. Sets in graduated difficulty are as follows:

1. Set 1. Four or five pairs of identical pictures cards. For example:
   a. Two red apples
   b. Two bananas
   c. Two balls
   d. Two tops
   e. Two boys

   Aide uses two pictures alike and one different, perhaps two apples and one banana.
   Aide asks, "Which one is different?"

2. Set 2. Picture cards for matching on the basis of kind and size. For example, add to Set 1 the following:
   - a. Two smaller apples
   - b. Two smaller bananas
   - c. Two larger balls
   - d. Two larger tops
   - e. Two larger boys

   Aide uses two pictures alike and one different, perhaps two large apples and one small apple.
   Aide asks, "Which one is different?" "How is it different?"
3. Set 3. Picture cards for matching on the basis of kind, size, and color. For example, add to Set 2:
   - a. Two tops different in colors
   - b. Four trees, two the same shape and size
   - c. Four Jack-o'-Lanterns, two with identical facial expressions

   Aide uses a set of four pictures, perhaps four tops of which two are colored alike.
   Aide asks, "Which are alike?" "How is this other one different?" "And how is this one different?"
4. Set 4. Picture cards for matching on the basis of small as well as gross details. For example, have the cards include:
   - a. Two red balls
   - b. Two red balls with a white stripe
   - c. Two red balls with two white stripes
   - d. Two red balls with a white star

   Aide uses a set of four pictures, perhaps two red balls, one red ball with one stripe, one red ball with a star.
   Aide asks, "Which are alike?" "How is this other one different?" "And how is this one different?"

An aide can also use the flannel board to guide children to see likenesses and differences. For instance, four identical yellow ducks cut from felt can be arranged on the flannel board with three facing in one direction and one facing in the opposite direction. "Which one is different?" the aide asks. "How is it different?" "How many are facing toward the window?" the aide asks children interested in counting.

To help children link together objects that are commonly associated, an aide develops a kit of pictures of items such as the following:

1. A baby—a cradle.
2. A knife—a fork.
3. A hand—a glove or mitten.
4. A shoe—a sock.

Another useful set for helping children build common linkages is a set of mother and baby animals, such as:

1. A hen—a chick.
2. A deer—a fawn.

3. A horse—a colt.
4. A cow—a calf.
5. A sheep—a lamb.

An aide can also make use of a set of animal pictures with each animal shown at rest and in action, including:

1. A kitten running—a kitten curled up asleep.
2. A rabbit hopping—a rabbit sitting ready to run.
3. A bird in the air flying—a bird on a twig.
4. A dog walking—a dog sitting down.

"Which animal is hopping?" the aide asks a child or a group using, say, four of the pictures, perhaps the rabbit hopping, the rabbit resting, a dog walking, and a dog sitting. "Is any other animal hopping?" "A rabbit hops. A dog walks or runs."

An aide is also prepared to guide more mature children to observe accurately in classroom activities, and to remember what they have perceived. Here are examples of such games:

*Remember*

An aide shows a picture to a child or a group of children. Then he puts it away and asks, "What did you see in the picture?" The children see how many things they can remember. The aide selects a picture that:

1. Is large.
2. Has only a few objects in it.
3. Has a plain background, uncluttered.
4. Has a familiar subject.
5. Is colorful.
6. Is interesting to the children.

*What Is Missing?*

Players are seated in a circle with a number of objects in the center. One child volunteers to leave the room as "It." Another child removes one of the objects. "It" is called in, by name, to answer the question, "What is missing?"

The aide determines the number of objects according to the maturity of the children and their experience in playing the game. With more mature children, the aide helps the children to make complete sentences. He may say, for example, "Did you notice that Diane used a complete sentence? She said, 'The square block is gone.' "

*Other Games*

Picture puzzles help children become increasingly sensitive to form and shape. An aide at school probably will have several puzzles to use with the children. An aide at home can find simple puzzles in inexpensive stores and can select ones with as many pieces as the child can enjoy at his level of experience and maturity.

With a small group of children, an aide can use Picture Bingo to help children gain speed in the recognition of objects on the basis of their shape and color, and in associating a picture of an object with its name. With children who are experienced at playing the game, an aide can have players take turns as callers of the cards.

## APPRAISING ABILITY TO PERCEIVE

Can aides help in the appraisal of a child's progress in perception? The question is an important one because a child needs to see that he is making progress and needs to see what others consider evidence of his progress. At the same time, parents like to see that their child is accomplishing what both they and the school consider important. Furthermore, a teacher should have visible evidence of the progress her pupils are making to show to other educators.

An aide indirectly helps in the appraisal of a child's progress by helping to make it visible. The teacher has the responsibility of deciding on appraisal methods, but her decision is likely to take into account the time required for it. With the help of an aide, a teacher can spend more time and attention on such things as making a child's progress more visible to him and to others interested in his progress.

One teacher who had the help of an aide was impressed with the drawing of a person as an indication of a child's ability, according to *Measurement of Intelligence* by Dr. Florence Goodenough.[17] At the beginning of the year, the teacher said to the children, "Today let us each draw our own picture. We shall keep our pictures of ourselves in a special place. We shall draw other pictures of ourselves. Then later on when we have been in school a long time, we shall each make a book of our pictures to take home. Mother and Daddy will like that!" The aide helped with the project by duplicating a caption to be pasted on each picture.

| A Picture of Me in September |
|---|

In the early part of December, the children again drew pictures of themselves. The aide prepared for them the caption.

| A Picture of Me After Thanksgiving Dinner |
|---|

[17] Florence Goodenough, *Measurement of Intelligence* (Yonkers, N.Y.: World Book Co., 1926). Out of print.

In January the children each drew a picture entitled

A Picture of Me in the New Year

and again the aide prepared captions.

When the teacher and the children talked about families, the children made other drawings.

A Picture of My Family and Me in March

The aide helped by preparing the captions and by adding the picture to the personal ones prepared previously and collected in a folder for each child.

In May the children were able to prepare final drawings.

A Picture of Me in May

As a group the children decided to prepare a Mother's Day gift booklet made up of their series of drawings. With the help of their teacher and their aide, the children prepared a table of contents. Each child created a cover and printed his own name on it. He did as much else as he could in assembling it, and he numbered its pages. The child checked with the aide to be sure that he had the pictures in the same order as in his Table of Contents and had the aide staple the booklet together. Just before taking their booklets home for Mother's Day, the children talked with the aide in small groups about what to say to their mothers and how to present their gifts.

Working with the children gave the aide the opportunity to help them see the improvement in their drawings, especially the greater detail that accompanies better perception. It also afforded many situations in which the aide could guide their learning, for instance, in seeing how a booklet is made and in writing the numerals from one to five. Whenever the aide noticed that a numeral was not accurate, he was careful to point out how people always write it, but he avoided making discouraging evaluative remarks such as, "That's wrong." In many ways, the aide did much to make the appraisal project both enjoyable and valid.

# REINFORCING BASIC CONCEPTS

When a child has had a series of related experiences, he is up to the point of conceptualizing what is common to those experiences. For instance, if the child has perceived a black cat, a tawny cat, a Persian cat, and his own cat sufficiently, he combines his perceptions into the concept of *cat*. Perhaps a teacher is guiding his perception of $cat_a$ and $cat_b$. "These are both cats. When you see another animal like them, you call it a cat," the teacher may say. After the child has grasped the concept of *cat*, an aide reinforces his concept by pointing out a flannel-board story using cutouts of cats, and by providing many other opportunities for the child to bring to mind the concept of cat. Through such experience a child moves from the perception of individual cats to a conceptualization about *cat* in general.

The ability to conceptualize is so useful to a person that teachers, aides, and others who work with young children look for every opportunity to guide children in developing and reinforcing concepts. A child can add the tonal patterns of many words to his vocabulary but behind the pronouncing of each word must be a concept built from real life experience. Meaningless words are useless in a world that depends on genuine communication. A child needs to develop concepts from vivid perceptions.

A teacher plans environments and experiences in which a child's perceptions are pyramided into useful concepts. Aides contribute to this conceptualization process by enabling each child to have additional experiences in suitable environments to the point of meaningful concepts and to have further experience in which concepts are reinforced through use. A wealth of guided experience helps a child to develop a wealth of concepts.

## FROM SPECIFIC TO ABSTRACT CONCEPTS

An aide at home or at school working with a young child strives particularly to build generalized concepts out of concrete experience. Helping a young child develop a concept of *dog* will illustrate the ways in which an aide can guide the child's learning process. These include the following:

1. Call attention to a dog passing by, perhaps by saying, "There is a little black dog," "See the police dog," or "That little dog has a little bark."
2. When helping a child get acquainted with a dog, recall other dogs that the child has seen, perhaps by saying, "This dog is bigger than the one we saw yesterday," or, "Yesterday we saw a little black dog, and today we see a big brown dog. Dogs are of different colors."
3. Read a story about a dog, and talk about it afterward.[1]
4. Provide experience with many dogs within a short space of time, perhaps a study trip to a dog show, a dog grooming shop, or a dog pound; or with a book or chart showing different breeds of dogs.
5. In the classroom, with models of dogs, pictures of them, and flannel board cut-outs, reinforce and enlarge the child's concept of *dog*, perhaps by talking about what a dog needs each day: food, water, and people with whom to play.

As a child develops a meaningful vocabulary, he is really formulating a reservoir of names developed from a series of specific experiences. The teacher and aide facilitate this process by providing many experiences in which words are an integral part of the experience. Helping a child attach names to objects is a very important part of the work of a teacher or an aide.

A child who recognizes and uses the names of many objects goes on to concepts of relationship. A child who understands and uses the concept of *dog* relates it to eating, running, barking, and other actions of a dog as well as to playground, home, and other locations. Presently the child will go on to relate it to more abstract concepts such as time, for example, *yesterday* and *today*, and later to other concepts such as *quickly* and *slowly*. An aide as well as a teacher can do much to guide the conceptualization of a child toward mastery of his world. An aide, like a teacher, takes advantage of each opportunity to help a child understand and talk about the *what*, *where*, *when*, and *how* of his world.

The child who has many word-linked experiences has a good foundation for abstracting a concept based on their interrelationships. For instance, out of the many experiences of measuring his height and that of others in his group, a child develops a concept of *height* that is new, or a further development of a rudimentary concept formed from having his own height measured periodically.

[1] For instance: Lisl Weil, *Alphabet of Puppy Care* (New York: Abelard-Schuman Ltd., 1968); Norman Bridwell, *Clifford the Big Red Dog* (New York: Four Winds Press, 1969).

The child who has the word *democracy* linked to many experiences will develop the concept of democracy as readily as he has developed the generalized concept of *parent*. His concept of the word *happy* will emerge from its linkage to many happy experiences. From these and many other examples of word-linked experiences that lead to abstract concepts, it is clear that a very important function of teachers, aides, and others who work with young children is that of "word-linker" as well as "experience-provider."

This chapter focuses on various experiences that a young child can have in his environment and can link to basic science concepts. The illustrative experiences discussed are a very small sample of the innumerable experiences that an ingenious teacher or aide can use as an environmental base for the children's basic vocabulary and other concepts. These

AN AIDE HELPS CHILDREN LEARN THE CONCEPT *I LIKE FRUIT.*

in turn provide a base to which a child can link more concepts as well as more abstract ones.

## CONCEPT: LEAF

In the fall of the year it is easy to help a child link the word *leaf* to many happy experiences. A walk through a residential area includes shuffling through fallen leaves; perceiving a leaf falling from a tree to the sidewalk; picking up leaves that are yellow, leaves that are still green, leaves that have become brown, and leaves that have delightful combinations of the green, red, brown, and yellow colors. The aide who accompanies a child or a small group of children makes a point of guiding the child's perception of the leaves and at the same time of helping him link words to his perceptions—color words, size words, simple but botanically correct words such as *leaf* and *stem*.

Back in the classroom with the collections of leaves, the children are further guided in developing concepts. Working with a variety of leaves, each with a unique coloring, enables the children to develop the concept of *individuality*. The aide points out that each leaf is individual in its coloring.

The aide also watches for opportunities to guide the children to recognize that each leaf is also individual in its shape and that at the same time it has a shape similar to the shape of other leaves from the same kind of tree. To help each child in thinking about the shapes of the leaves, the aide works with a small group of children at a table on which are scissors, paste, construction paper of different colors, and an eight inch by eleven and one-half inch sheet for each child to use as a base for creating a leaf picture. The conversation may proceed in this way:

*Aide:* (holding up first one leaf and then another) Does this leaf remind you of anything?
*Mark:* A dog without a head.
*Aide:* Would you like to paste it on your paper?
*Mark:* I'll find a leaf for his head. (Rummages through the pile of leaves that the aide brought to the table.) Here's a good one.
*June:* Here's a long one for his tail.
*Phyllis:* Here's another one.
*Mark:* Find some for his floppy ears.
*Aide:* See what you can find to finish your leaf dog, Mark. The other children might each like to think of something else that they could make.
*Aide:* (placing on the table a pie tin containing yarn, pipe cleaners, small pieces of colored paper) You may need something else to go with the leaves.

WHAT CAN A CHILD DO WITH LEAVES?

A few minutes later Cynthia shares her problem with the other children at the table:

> *Cynthia:* I can't find a leaf for my little girl's head.
> *Aide:* What else can you use?
> *Cynthia:* Paper?
> *Aide:* That's an idea. Try it.

Cynthia uses crayons to make a face and then finishes her leaf girl with a strand of black yarn for hair.

Kelly, who likes cars, creates an interesting picture of a car made only of leaves. Each child works to his own satisfaction. As the children work, the aide adds to their observation of leaves by making such comments as: "Keep looking. Each leaf is a little different you know." or "That little elm leaf has just the right shape." With children more experienced in observing shapes, an aide encourages more precise discrimination perhaps by saying, "If you think you need a maple leaf, look through these to find just what you want."

Through the creative activity of making pictures from leaves, the aide guides the children to build the concept the uniqueness of each leaf, or to reinforce their understanding that people, like leaves, are individuals, each a little different from anyone else, and each useful in his own way.

## CONCEPT: BUG

The young child notices small as well as large animals. Any day he may bring his teacher a bug and an aide will have the opportunity to help him develop his concept of *bug*.

The aide who has anticipated the arrival of a child with a bug is prepared to help him link his perceptions of the bug to concepts he has already formed, to new concepts in science and in literature, and to new activities to be enjoyed both at home and at school. Here are ways in which an aide can help the child with a bug enlarge his understanding of it:

> *Aide:* Do you know that your bug is really an insect? If it has six legs, it is an insect. How many legs does your bug have?

The aide guides the child in counting the legs of his bug.

> *Aide:* We can see your insect better if we look at it with a hand lens. A hand lens makes it seem larger. (Aide provides magnifying glass.)

Depending on the experience and interest of the child, the aide can guide the child to notice the mouth of the insect, its eyes, and other parts; or to notice that the legs have the ability to bend as do human legs.

> *Aide:* We need a home for your insect. (Aide gets a suitable container.)

The aide helps the child to provide the same kind of environment that the bug is used to, perhaps leaves for it to eat or to give it shade, and a drop or two of water.

> *Aide:* I have a picture of an insect like yours. (Aide goes to picture file for enlarged pictures to show the child and his friends.)
>
> *Aide:* Would you like to hear a story about bugs? [2]

When other children bring bugs, the aide receives them enthusiastically and guides their learning into activities that reinforce existing concepts and help to build additional ones. Providing the visiting bug with suitable living conditions is always in order, and an aide is prepared to produce a cricket cage or a wide-mouthed glass jar with a lid that has holes punched through it to provide air without letting the insect or spider escape. The aide also helps the child to see that the small pet has both food and water in amounts appropriate to his size and taste. With children who are becoming interested or are already interested in words, an aide makes a point of adding an identifying sign as well as a magnifying glass to the bug display on the science table, for example,

| Bill's Bug |
|---|

[2] Gladys Conklin, *We Like Bugs* (New York: Holiday House, 1962).

With more experienced children, an aide can guide the children to learn more about the bug that Bill brought. The aide asks such questions as:

*What kind of bug is it?*

*Where does it live? Did you find it there?*

Children who read and write enjoy working out a written story or account of what they know about bugs. Children who are less experienced with writing will enjoy dictating their account to the aide so that he can type it for them and read it to them. When the aide puts what he has typed on the bulletin board at the eye level of the children, they often reread it themselves.

With a small group of interested children, the aide is also prepared to guide them in thinking appreciatively about bugs. Perhaps the aide leads them into a discussion with a question such as, "What kind of bugs do you like?" and then listens attentively while each child responds.

The aide has a delightful poem to contribute to the thinking of the group, as follows:

BUGS

I like bugs:
Black bugs
Bad bugs, mean bugs,
Any kind of bug.

A bug on a rug.
A bug in the grass.
A bug on the sidewalk.
A bug in a glass.
I like bugs.

Round bugs, shiny bugs.
Fat bugs, buggy bugs.
Big bugs, lady bugs.
I like bugs!

—Anonymous

A small group discussion leads easily into creative activities at the painting easel or pasting table, as an aide guides the children in enlarging their concepts of *bug*.

Before the children go on to other conceptualization, the teacher with the help of the aide makes sure that the children know the necessary limits of liking bugs, namely:

1. How to recognize the kind of spider, which, in that locality, might hurt a person.

2. How to remove a bug to the out-of-doors or how to arrange so that there will be no bugs indoors.

## CONCEPT: THE SPEECH SOUND OF *S*

When the teacher has guided the children to conscious awareness of the speech sound of the letter S, the aide can help them formulate and apply their concepts of the sound, until they are each habituated to proper usage of it.

To help the children to be continuously aware of the speech sound of S, the aide can arrange a bulletin board or chalk board display such as the following and talk with a few of them at a time about the display:

| | |
|---|---|
| S s | This letter looks |
| | and sounds like me. |
| S,s,s,s,s,s,s. | I'm a s,s,snake! |

Hear the sound of the letter S in these words:

| | | |
|---|---|---|
| sun | Santa | soap |
| sock | sail | sea |

Working with an individual child or with a small group, an aide can use a flannel board cut-out of a snake, or a toy snake, as he guides the children in learning a verse that gives them practice with the speech sound of S, for instance:

SAMMY SNAKE

Sammy Snake is a good little snake.
He lies on a rock all day.
He sleeps, and sleeps, and sleeps in the sun.
And when he awakes, he will say,
"S-s-s-s-s!"

—Anonymous

The aide is also prepared to tell and retell an imaginative story in which each child can participate, making the speech sound of S. The flannel board can be used together with a grass background and cut-outs of each of the animals mentioned:

1. Cow.
2. Dog.
3. Frog.
4. Rooster.
5. Owl.
6. Sammy the Snake.

### THE STORY OF SAMMY THE SNAKE

Once upon a time there was a little snake named Sammy. He wanted very much to have spots, but he was all one color. One day he decided to take a walk and ask everyone he saw about how he could get some spots.

First he met Mrs. *Cow.* (Place the cow cut-out on the flannel board.)

Sammy said, "Mrs. Cow, how can I get some spots?"

Mrs. Cow said, "If you will say 'Moo' like a cow, then maybe you will have some spots."

So Sammy said, "Moo, moo."

But did he get some spots? No.

Next he met Mrs. *Dog.* (Place the dog cut-out.)

Sammy said, "Mrs. Dog, how can I get some spots?"

Mrs. Dog said, "If you will say 'Bow-wow' like a dog, then maybe you will have some spots."

So Sammy said, "Bow-wow, bow-wow."

But did he get some spots? No.

Then he met Mr. *Frog.* (Place the frog cut-out.)

Sammy said, "Mr. Frog, how can I get some spots?"

Mr. Frog said, "If you will say, 'Ugh, ugh, like a frog, then maybe you will have some spots."

So Sammy said, "Ugh, ugh."

But did he get some spots? No.

Then he met Mr. *Rooster.* (Place the rooster cut-out.)

Sammy said, "Mr. Rooster, how can I get some spots?"

Mr. Rooster said, "If you will say, 'Rrr, rrr, rrr,' like a rooster, then maybe you will have some spots."

So Sammy said, "Rrr, rrr, rrr."

But did he get some spots? No.

Next he met Mr. *Owl* sitting in a tree. (Place the owl cut-out.)

Sammy said, "Mr. Owl, you are so wise. Can you tell me how I can get some spots?"

Mr. Owl said, "Sammy, you will not have spots until you can make the snake sound."

Sammy tried very hard, but his tongue always came out like this, "S-th, S-th."

Mr. Owl said, "Your tongue keeps coming out. Keep it in your mouth behind your teeth and try again."

So Sammy did and it sounded like this, "S-, S-, S-, S-."

All of a sudden Sammy had a spot. He was so proud and happy about that spot!

But Sammy was also so tired from trying to have spots that he decided to ask his friends to make the snake sound for him so he could get more spots.

First he asked Mr. Rooster, but Mr. Rooster could only say, "Rrr, rrr, rrr."

He asked Mr. Frog, but Mr. Frog could only say, "Ugh, ugh."

He asked Mrs. Dog, but Mrs. Dog could only say, "Bow-wow, bow-wow."

He asked Mrs. Cow, but Mrs. Cow could only say, "Moo, moo."

Do you suppose that we can help Sammy Snake get more spots?

—Anonymous

"Polly, can you make the snake sound? You try it, and you may put a spot on Sammy!" (Each child in turn has an opportunity to attempt making the sound. Any effort is rewarded with placing a spot of felt on Sammy.)

With more experienced children, an aide can use a simplified version of the story, as follows:

Here is our friend, Sammy Snake. He is interested in having spots the way his older sister Sally does. The wise old owl has told him he will get some spots when he can say the snake sound.

Who would like to help Sammy?

### CONCEPT: ANIMAL FAMILIES

Concepts can be linked to other concepts to provide the background for more concepts. For instance, a young child forms concepts of various animals by linking each specific animal to the concept of animal, and thus builds that concept into one that is increasingly useful in more and more situations. The child should be guided into linking the concept of snake to the concept of animal; and the concepts of cow, dog, cat, pig, and so on, to the general concept of animal. An aide, like the teacher, helps each child to make such linkages, and then helps them further to make additional linkages among concepts of family relationship and animals.

When the teacher has introduced the concept of animal families, the aide can reinforce it and help the children to extend their application of it in many situations. Here are some of the situations in which an aide helps the teacher guide the children to link concepts of family and animals.

An animal family at the school provides the opportunity to see that the animals have the food and water that they need, but it also offers the opportunity to talk about "the mother hen," "the daddy rooster," and "the baby chick."

Pictures of animal families afford a similar opportunity for children and aide to think together about the daily lives of the members of an animal family. They talk about such events as the tomcat resting after his trips out hunting for food, the mother cat licking her kittens clean and carrying them in her mouth to safe places, and the baby kitten just opening its eyes and learning to take food as it needs to.

On a study trip to the zoo, the aide is careful to see that each of the children in the group for which he has responsibility stays at a safe distance from the animals but has the opportunity to observe their behavior. The aide talks with the children and encourages them in using the correct terms for the animals, for instance, a pride of lions, a lion, a lioness, and a lion cub.

Back at the school, the aide can help a child or a small group of children to enjoy one of the several books available in most libraries about zoo animals and their families, for example, *Mr. Stripes, The Gopher.*[3]

In much the same way, the aide on a study trip to a barnyard helps the children think about young animals growing up to be daddies and mothers. Later, back in the school, the aide makes use of appropriate books[4] and pictures as he reinforces the children's conceptualizations about animal families. Especially useful is a book entitled *Everybody Has a House and Everybody Eats.*[5]

In preparing to guide children to develop concepts about animal families, an aide arranges a collection of appropriate books, colorful pictures, and models, and makes copies of pertinent fugitive material such as the following poem from a book no longer in print:

> Connie Calf can say "Moo, moo,"
> She likes a lot of grass to chew.
> Although she doesn't know it now,
> When Connie grows up—she'll be a cow.[6]
>
> —Doris G. Tobias

In short, the aide is prepared to help the children have vivid, multisensory experience that will lead them to conceptualization and to creative activities such as making pictures of animal families, dictating or writing a story, or talking about what they have heard or observed outside of school about animal families.

[3] Charles Philip Fox, *Mr. Stripes, The Gopher* (Chicago: Reilly & Lee Books, 1961).

[4] Ann Weil, *Animal Families* (Chicago: Children's Press, 1956). This book gives correct terms for describing families. For instance, ram, ewe, and lamb are members of a family of sheep. Jerry Seibert, *Animals on a Farm* (Chicago: Encyclopaedia Britannica, Inc., 1964). Excellent photographs in color. Gladys Conklin, *When Insects Are Babies* (New York: Holiday House, 1969).

[5] Mary McBurney Green, *Everybody Has a House and Everybody Eats* (New York: Young Scott Books, 1944, 1961).

[6] Doris G. Tobias, *Zoo's Who* (New York: Vanguard Press, Inc., 1948). Reprinted by permission.

With more experienced children, an aide can help expand their concepts of families into realistic ones about variations in family composition. An aide can point out, for instance, that "All babies have a mother and a father. They make a family. Sometimes later on, the family may have just a mother or a father that lives with the children."

With a small group of children, the aide can encourage the children to talk about the people who make up their family. Such discussions lead into concepts about grandparents and aunts and uncles, and into concepts of the world having boys and girls and grown-ups who group themselves into families. An experienced aide with a group of experienced children wrote out their concept of a family as follows:

> Little girls who grow up are mothers, aunts, and grandmothers.
> Little boys who grow up are fathers, uncles, and grandfathers.
> All of these make families and friends.

An aide is also prepared to guide children in enriching their concepts about their own families and their place in their family, after their teacher has introduced the class to such concepts. An aide can read to a small group of children a book such as Muriel Stanek's *My Family and I* [7] or Jo Ann Stover's book entitled, *I'm in a Family*,[8] and can guide them in talking about such things as "What responsibility do you take in your family?"

The concept of animal families can readily be linked with concepts of family responsibility. Observations of animal families lead to such concepts as:

1. Mother has an important role in looking after the babies.
2. Father has an important role in food getting and in protection of the family.
3. Each child has an important role in becoming self-sufficient as soon as he can.

Additional concepts about human families can be linked to these concepts, for instance:

> Each one in a family has his own special work to do each day, his share of family living.

In leading discussion about family responsibilities, an aide sees that points such as the following are clear:

1. Each member of the family wants to do his part.
2. Taking care of one's own belongings helps the family.

[7] Muriel Stanek, *My Family and I* (Westchester, Ill.: Benefic Press, 1967).
[8] Jo Ann Stover, *I'm in a Family* (New York: David McKay Co., Inc., 1966).

3. Jobs in the household may change.
4. Children take turns on each job.
5. After finishing your work, you help others in the family with their family work.
6. You see what needs to be done and do it without being asked to.
7. You try to do "special" things for other members of your family, especially on birthdays, and such days as Mother's Day in May and Father's Day in June.

An aide can help a group of children to make a list of family jobs they can help with:

1. Emptying wastebaskets.
2. Bringing milk in.
3. Bringing the newspaper in.
4. Setting the table.
5. Clearing the table.
6. Running an errand.

An aide can also encourage children in creative activities using art media. Talking about families leads children to draw a picture of "My Family," and to tell others about it. The aide shows these pictures to the teacher because the teacher may think it appropriate for the child to take home his picture of his family and provide another link between home and school.

## CONCEPT: I OBSERVE THE WEATHER

In learning about the world around him, a child readily learns concepts that are directly related to him. He learns concepts that are at a distance less readily. He will have much experience before he handles with ease concepts that are abstracted from impersonal concepts. An aide as well as a teacher can help children link concepts to experience, and then concepts to previously formed concepts. Such linkages are so important for a child to build that he should have as much opportunity as possible to formulate the basic linkages between firsthand observation and simple concepts. It is important for an aide to assist the children in formulating a concept that "I am an observer of the weather."

After the teacher has developed with the class the practice of observing and charting the weather each day, an aide can guide the children in this daily activity and in formulating the concept of being a personal observer of the weather. The aide can use a flannel board and felt cut-outs to have the children show a variety of weather conditions.

| WEATHER | CUT-OUTS |
|---|---|
| a sunny day | a yellow sun |
| a rainy day | a red umbrella, light blue raindrops |
| a cloudy day | white, light gray, dark gray clouds |
| a windy day | a tree bent by the wind |
| a foggy day | a light gray, open-weave piece of material |
| a snowy day | a snowman |

"What kind of weather do we have today?" is a question that starts a group thinking about the kind of day it is. A child may be asked to step out-of-doors to observe and then report back to the group. The aide encourages and expands his report with such questions as:

*Is it a warm day? Is it a cold day?*

*Is it a rainy day? A foggy day? A windy day?*

The weather observer makes his analysis, and the group verifies it. Individual members of the group place the appropriate cut-outs on the flannel board to show an accurate description of the weather. If the weather changes in the course of the day, an alert child can record his observation of it by changing the weather symbols on the flannel board.

On the playground, an aide can guide young children in the scientific method of forming concepts about the weather. On a rainy day an aide can ask, "How do you know that it is raining?" and help the children to answer such simple questions as:

*What do I see?* (*e.g., drops of water coming down, dark clouds, puddles*)

*What do I hear?* (*e.g., patter of the drops*)

*What do I smell?* (*e.g., damp leaves, dust-free air*)

*What do I feel?* (*e.g., wet leaves, dampness*)

*What can I taste?* (*e.g., raindrops without taste*)

Each child makes his own observations and then compares them with observations that others make. In this manner he experiences a method of forming valid concepts.

Each day on the playground an aide can encourage individual or small groups of children to notice what the weather is. Here are a few of the simple concepts that an aide can help the children develop:

1. On a bright day, looking directly at the sun can hurt eyes.
2. The sun looks different in color from time to time because we look through different air pollutions.
3. At sunset, the sun may seem orange colored.

4. On a cloudy, or a foggy day, the sun may seem almost white.
5. We do not see the wind but we do see what it does.
6. Fog, rain, or snow gives a day a pleasant feel.

Each kind of weather condition provides the children with different things to do. With more experienced children, an aide can ask questions that lead into more precise observations and into new concepts of relationship. Questions that relate observations to a person—for instance, "Can you see the wind?"—are then followed by questions that begin, "Have you noticed that. . . ?"—and lead into formation of scientific concepts.

Indoors, an aide can help children relate their firsthand experience out-of-doors to concepts that their teacher has emphasized. Such discussions can be enriched by reading delightful picture books and engaging in creative activities with different art media.[9] To guide the discussions, an aide should have in mind basic concepts such as the following ones that should become clear in the thinking of the children:

1. The sun provides heat and light that any living plant or animal must have to live.
2. Our sun is one of the many stars, each of which is far, far away in outer space.
3. Our earth receives only a small part of the light and intense heat from the sun.
4. The earth is small compared with the sun, and our moon is smaller than the earth.
5. A cloud is made up of tiny drops of water that come out of the air.
6. Fog is a cloud touching the ground.
7. When droplets form and add on other tiny drops of water, they become heavy enough to fall as rain.
8. On very cold days rain can freeze into sleet before it reaches the ground.
9. On very cold days droplets come out of the air in the form of snow.
10. Wind is air moving.
11. The rush of air after lightning is like the rush of air from a balloon that is pricked, and is called thunder.[10]

[9] Vivian Edmiston Todd and Helen Heffernan, *The Years Before School* (New York: The Macmillan Co., 1964, 1970). Selected lists of children's books follow each chapter that discusses a phase of the school curriculum; for instance, science books are on pages 351–352 in the second edition.

[10] John Lewellen, *The True Book of Moon, Sun, and Stars* (Chicago: Children's Press, 1954); Franklyn Branley, *A Book of Planets for You* (New York: Thomas Y. Crowell Publishing Co., 1966). Such books as these have illustrations and simple basic information that are useful with young children.

## CONCEPT: WE ALL KEEP WELL

The importance of being well should be developed in young children through everyone who works with them. It is important for a child to come to the school group but it is even more important for him to see the doctor to be immunized, or to see the dentist for a filling for a tooth cavity. Realizing the priority of health, an aide is ready to take a child to see the school nurse at any time that a teacher thinks the child may have an elevation in body temperature or any other symptom of illness. An aide who drives a car may need to use that skill to get immediate medical help. In leaving the group, the aide explains to the children he has been with the reason for his departure and the fact that he will return as soon as the child receives the help that he needs to be well.

The concept that "We all keep well" implies that keeping well is important. It also implies that keeping well is important not only for each individual but also for the group as a whole. As soon as young children are sufficiently mature to link the concept of *me* to the concept of *you*, the *I* concept can be shaped by aides as well as by the teacher into the *we* concept. Teachers and aides encourage children to look after their personal health at the same time that they contribute to the good health of the group.

After the teacher has introduced children to such concepts as that of using only clean and individual eating utensils, an aide can tell a small group of children a story such as the following:

### A HEALTH STORY ABOUT THE PLAYHOUSE

> In the playhouse, a Mother set the table for lunch. Mary sat down to eat it. Pretending that she was eating the food on her plate, Mary put the fork into her mouth. Pretending that she was drinking her milk, Mary put the glass to her lips. Then she left the playhouse.
>
> Soon in the playhouse Father came home late for lunch, and Mother fixed a plate for him. He used the same fork that Mary had used, but he only pretended he was eating with it. He drank milk from the same glass that Mary had used, but he only pretended to drink.
>
> Another day Mary did not come to school. She had the flu.

In talking with the children about the story, an aide can help them build concepts about what to do to stay well. He can ask, for instance, "What should Mary do next time?" The aide can also help the children with their pantomime of pretending to eat so that they do not run risks of infection for others as well as for themselves. In such ways the aide as well as the teacher guides children in forming health concepts about themselves as individuals and as members of a group that stays well.

# ENCOURAGING COMMAND OF SPACE AND QUANTITY

A child lives in space and learns to think in terms of it. In his first year of life the child explores two-dimensional space as he crawls around and relates spatially the various objects with which he shares the floor. But very early in his second year the child goes on to explore the three-dimensional world, standing upright and then moving out into his enlarged life space by walking.

Parents and subsequently aides and teachers help the child extend his understanding of space and his relation to it. They also help him realize the limits of his safety within space, and help him gain command of himself within wide limits. They help him link words to his experience, and to rethink verbally what he had learned through sensation, saying, for instance:

I can be:
As *tall* as a tree. (Hands and arms stretch up tall.)
And as *short* as a bush. (Stoop down.)
As *wide* as a building. (Arms stretch out.)
As *narrow* as a crack. (Hands show a vertical line.)
As *round* as a ball. (Arms make a circle.)
And as *flat* as a pancake. (Hands show it horizontally.)
As *big* as a giant. (Stand big and reach tall.)
And as *tiny* as a mouse. (Stoop and crouch.)
And I'll grow. (From stooped position slowly grow up.)
And I'll grow, and I'll grow! (Up, up, up, and up!)

A classroom aide helps the children to link words to large-and-small-muscle experience in space and to describe it. A playground aide helps the children to link words to large-muscle experience in space, and to describe

it. An aide is constantly helping each child link concepts with his spatial experience.

In general, an aide reinforces what the teacher does in guiding children to perceive shapes and positions in space, and to work with numbers in harmony with the ways of the adult world. The aide helps children feel successful with and enjoy experiences that soon will be labeled "mathematics."

## SPACE PERCEPTION

### Fundamental Shapes

Basic to a command of space is the ability to perceive the fundamental elements from which Americans build elaborate and effective mechanical tools. These include:

1. Point, or dot.
2. Line, curved or straight.
3. Circle.
4. Square.
5. Triangle.
6. Rectangle.

A child has a good feeling of being in command when he realizes that his pencil, his crayon, or his paintbrush can make a picture of a dot whenever he wants it to do so. A mark may be accidentally made, but a dot or point is made purposefully.

A child who makes a dot can go on to further command of space because he can picture a series of dots, purposefully creating a segment of a line. He can arrange the series of dots to picture a curved line, and at other times to picture a straight line. Thus the child can offer himself, or someone else, a choice. "Shall I do a curved line, or a straight line, or a dot?" Asking and answering such questions is evidence to a child that he is powerful. An aide, like a teacher, helps the child to realize his power.

A child who can make a picture of a dot or a line can go on to recognize those that have been made by other people. In fact he can go on to recognize shapes that others have constructed and named, especially the circle, the triangle, the square, the rectangle, and the diamond. The child enjoys imitating patterns of blocks, patterns of diamonds, patterns of triangles, and patterns of circles that others have made. He admires the patterns in quilts that his grandmother made, but he also enjoys creating patterns as he uses and talks about these basic shapes.

An aide guides the experience of the child on the playground, helping him recognize that the ball he bounces looks like a *circle,* and that the snowman made from round snowballs looks like a small *circle* on top of a larger one. Older children like to form a *circle* to play an organized game or use the *ring sets* to help them move through the air.

Indoors an aide guides the children more intensively into using and recognizing the basic shapes. With a set of one red square, one blue square, one yellow square, and one green square, the aide is equipped to use his flannel board in guiding children who perceive colors accurately but have had only an initial introduction to the basic shapes. The aide can use a square of each of the four colors and ask each of the children to select a square of a given color. He may say, "Please put a red square on the flannel board," or "Please *remove* the red square."

With felt cut-outs in one color but of different shapes, an aide can guide a small group of children to recognize and name each shape. "Please put a green square on the flannel board," he may say, or "Please *remove* the green triangle." As the child places or removes the cut-out from the board he tells what it is. The child may say, for example, "A green square."

An aide can use the set of different shapes to play the game of "What Shape Is Missing?" The child who is learning the game plays it with three shapes, and the more experienced child plays it with additional shapes.

The aide also uses books about shapes to stimulate interest in them, and guides children to recognize them in everyday situations. The children enjoy such books as *The Little Circle* by Ann Atwood.[1]

Children who are sufficiently mature like to follow directions given to them in terms of shapes. With such children an aide can say, for example, "On this sheet of paper are three different shapes. Please use your orange crayon to put a mark on the oval." In this way an aide reinforces the learning of a color and guides a child in recognizing a named shape.

An aide working with children individually or in a group may suggest their using shapes to create a picture. Perhaps the teacher or the aide has read to them books that suggested the idea.[2] Perhaps it is Halloween time, and the teacher has encouraged the children to create a Halloween witch out of black triangles. The aide can see that the children have:

1. A sheet of nine-inch by twelve-inch manila paper.
2. Paste.
3. Many different sizes of black equilateral and other triangles.
4. Length of orange yarn and black yarn for witches' hair.

[1] Ann Atwood, *The Little Circle* (New York: Charles Scribner's Sons, 1967); Ed Emberley, *The Wing on a Flea* (Boston: Little, Brown Co., 1961); Karla Kuskin, *Square as a House* (New York: Harper & Row, Publishers, 1960); Cliff Roberts, *The Dot* (New York: Franklin Watts, Inc., 1960).

[2] Ethel Kessler and Leonard Kessler, *Are You Square?* (Garden City, N.Y.: Doubleday & Co., Inc., 1966); Fredun Shapur, *Round and Round and Square* (New York: Abelard-Schuman Limited, 1965).

AN AIDE ENCOURAGES CREATIVE EXPERIENCE WITH SHAPES.

The aide can introduce the activity by reciting the following poem:

A WITCH IN A TRIANGLE-SHAPED HAT

I saw a witch in a tall, triangle-shaped hat,
Riding a broom with a coal black cat!
I saw a witch, but she didn't see me,
For I was hiding behind a tree!

And when she went by,
I jumped out and called, "Boo!"
Oh my, she was frightened and shaking
As away in the sky she flew!

She left her broom, her tall, triangle-shaped hat,
And her painted mask, and her coal black cat.
I don't know when I've had such fun,
As on Halloween when I made a witch run!

—Anonymous

The aide places a tall black triangle in the upper central part of the flannel board. "Does this tall, thin triangle make you think of anything special?" the aide may ask. "Let's place a taller and wider triangle below it. What do you think now?" With talk about witches in the air, the aide can continue with comments about the many black triangles in the box—tall and thin triangles, short and fat triangles, and so on. Soon the children are busy creating Halloween pictures. As each child completes his picture to his satisfaction, the aide can arrange the pictures on the bulletin board —perhaps a display on a large black triangle.

The creative use of basic shapes is appropriate at holiday times throughout the year. At Halloween the children can cut black triangles from the corners of a sheet of black paper, and at Christmas time, they can cut Christmas trees from a folded sheet of colored paper. At Valentine's Day, an aide encourages the children in free cutting of hearts, and at Easter time, the children may cut oval-shaped eggs.

At any time of the year an aide can encourage the children to paste basic shapes of different sizes onto a sheet of paper to make a picture of a house, a truck, or some other familiar part of their community. Less experienced children may merely enjoy the activity of pasting, but others will create pictures of buildings. By using these activities, the teacher can guide the children into creating a map of their community. The aide helps guide the children to see that their house has its own house number and is located on its own street. He encourages the children to add trees, shrubs, flowers, fences, other houses, and even their school with its flag flying in front of the building. At all times, the aide is careful to be a questioner rather than a director, and to be a person who encourages the children to learn through their own doing.

From time to time as he works with children involved in activities with basic shapes, the aide brings out by comment or question the fundamental concepts about each basic shape, especially its boundary.

1. A circle is round.
2. A rectangle has four straight sides and four right-angle corners.
3. A square is a rectangle that has four sides of the same length.
4. A triangle has three straight sides.

When the children have worked with basic shapes for some time, the teacher may ask the aide to test them individually to make sure that each child can identify and name each of the shapes. With a small group of the children, the aide then uses a one-color set of different shapes on the flannel board. Holding up one of the cut-out shapes, the aide asks, "Who can tell us the name of this shape?" The child who names it places it on the flannel board. In this way the aide guides the children in reviewing the names of the shapes. Then the aide asks, "Who thinks he can name all of the shapes as he removes them from the flannel board?" After one child has removed all of the shapes, another child may name them as he puts them back onto the flannel board. In this way, each child has an opportunity to demonstrate that he has mastered the identification and naming of the basic shapes.

### Comparing Size

As the aide works with children learning to perceive different shapes, he soon makes a point of using descriptive words with the shapes. "Mark the large triangle with blue. Mark the small triangle with red." Thus the aide guides the children to enlarge their vocabulary meaningfully. Especially useful to the children are such contrasting words as:

1. Large—small.
2. Tall—short.
3. Long—short.
4. Wide—narrow.

The aide extends such simple linkages with others that children need to know from their daily experience as a basis for perceiving areas and three-dimensional shapes and later measuring them:

1. Heavy—light.
2. Dark—light.
3. Old—new.
4. Old—young.
5. Thick—thin.

An aide collects visual materials with which children can talk about differences in size, perhaps a picture of a stair-step arrangement of a family, or a picture of a gymnastic or dancing group in which the members are arranged in order of their height. If each picture is covered with clear plastic, the aide can suggest, "Put your finger on the shortest girl," or, "Put your finger on the girl that is most thin," and so on. As each child points, he describes what he is pointing out: "This is the shortest girl," thus linking appropriate words to his concept.

The aide at school works closely with the teacher to help the children perceive and identify similarities and differences in shape. The teacher diagnoses a difficulty that a child has and with the aide plans learning activities to help the child learn quickly what the other children in his group have already learned. For example, a teacher may ask the aide to work with three children who are not yet accurate in identifying and describing differences in shape. The teacher may suggest certain activities for the aide to use, and may point out in a "Teacher's Guide" paragraphs and illustrations that show the aide how he can proceed.[3]

[3] One such guide is: *Greater Cleveland Mathematics Program* (GCMP), *Teacher's Guide for Kindergarten* (Chicago: Science Research Associates, Inc., 1961).

### Position in Space

An aide also helps children to be aware of their positions in space. If a child is talking loudly, the aide may say, "Let's use an inside voice," or, "That is the kind of voice people use outdoors."

As the occasion arises, the aide helps children to understand such contrasting positions as:

1. Over—under.
2. On top of—underneath.
3. Up—down.
4. In—out.
5. Here—there.
6. This—that.

By using the flannel board and a set of disks or other cut-outs in a variety of colors, an aide can guide a small group of children in a review of colors and a practice with relative positions. For instance, simulating a traffic signal with a column of green, red, and yellow disks, the aide can ask, "Which color is *at the bottom*?" "Which color is *at the top*?" "What color is *underneath* the red?" "Is the green *above* or *below* the red?" Or, after making a row of disks of different colors, the aide can ask, "Is the blue disk *on the right* or *on the left* of the green disk?"

An aide can use the flannel board and two sets of disks, each set having disks that correspond in color but differ in size, Then the aide can guide the children not only in thinking about which of two disks is larger and which of two is smaller, but also about which of the four disks is *nearer* to the top of the flannel board and which is *farther* from it, and so on.

An aide notices each occasion during the school day when he can point out qualitative relationships in space. On a walk in the neighborhood, for instance, an aide can probably mention walking *on* the sidewalk, *between* the marked lines, and *through* the trees. He can probably point out an airplane flying *above* the houses, a man walking *along* the street, or a pair of dogs playing *in front of* a house.

To help children learn to identify and talk about placement in rows, an aide can prepare a set of five-by-eight-inch cards for use in a pocket chart, perhaps by drawing shapes with a black felt-tip pen. He places three cards having a circle in the first row of the pocket chart, three cards having a square in the second row, and three cards having a rectangle in the third row. The aide can say, "Tom, please remove a card from the first row and tell me the name of the shape," or, "Larry, please remove a square and tell me in which row you find it. Is it in the first row? Second row? Or third row?" On other days, an aide can use a set of cards with different shapes or with shapes in different colors, or with a larger set of cards.

## Matching Shapes and Sizes

An aide can use a pocket chart and a set of cards together with Key Cards to guide children to see similarity in shapes and sizes. In making such sets of cards, the aide prepares two sets of the cards that the children are learning. The second set of cards constitutes Key Cards. Selecting one of the Key Cards, the aide places a card that is just like it and two other cards in a row of the pocket chart. Then the aide displays the Key Card and says to the small group of children, "Look at this Key Card. Now who will remove a card that is exactly like the Key Card?"

By using a small triangle, a large triangle, a small square, and a large square, the aide can guide the children in distinguishing a small triangle from a small or large square and also from a large triangle. Showing a small triangle as a Key Card, the aide helps the children focus their attention on the size as well as the shape of a small triangle. Then using a large triangle as a Key Card, he helps them focus their attention on a different size. The aide continues in this way to guide the children to perceive first difference in size and then in shape, and then in both size and shape.

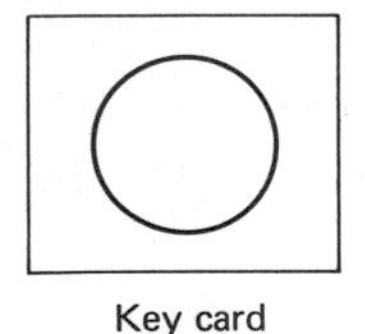

Key card

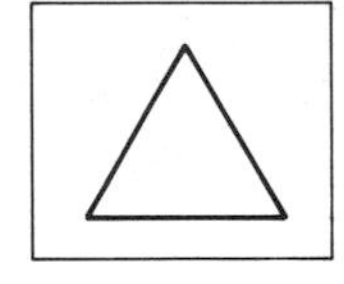

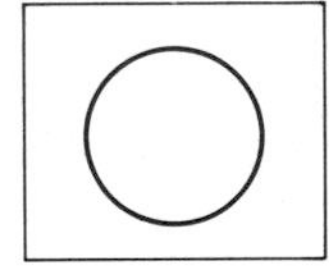

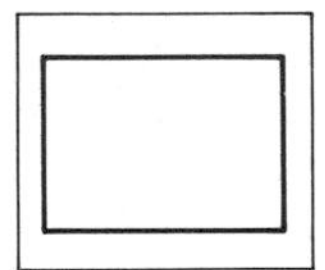

FIND A CARD LIKE THE KEY CARD.

The Key Card matching experience gives the children early confidence in the kind of perception that they will use at later ages in a variety of activities, for instance, in taking tests of their ability to handle spatial and related concepts.

## Making and Seeing Patterns

When children have become proficient in matching two identical shapes selected from an increasing number of shapes, the aide working with them helps them to develop the concept of *pattern*. Perhaps the aide will suggest:

1. Each child holding the same kind of card stands in a row to make a "line pattern," or in a circle to make a "circle pattern."
2. When children free cut a shape, they place several of them in regular formation and create a pattern.
3. The children talk about patterns as they create them from a collection of shells, leaves, or other similar items. (The aide guides them in seeing patterns that match.)

### Sequence

An aide can help more mature children develop the concept of *sequence* at the same time that they have a variety of enjoyable experiences. For example, on a walk around the school grounds an aide can help the children see that each tree has a trunk from which limbs grow, and that limbs have branches with twigs, and leaves are on the twigs.

Back in the classroom with a flannel board after the teacher has introduced the song, "Tree in the Woods," the aide can help some of the children further enjoy the song.[4] From a column of the cut-outs in sequence, the children make a tree by selecting the cut-outs in the same sequence as that in the song:

1. The tree trunk in the ground.
2. A limb on the tree.
3. A branch on the limb.
4. Some twigs on the branch.

When the song is finished and the tree is made, the aide guides the children to put away the flannel board cut-outs in the same sequence as in the song. The children will have had a great deal of experience with the sequence before they will explore the same sequence in reverse, putting away first the twigs and then the branch, the limb, and finally the tree trunk.

When the children have the opportunity to sing the "Tree in the Woods" and then draw a picture of it, the aide notices which children make their drawing in the same sequence as in the song, which ones are able to complete the entire sequence, and which ones need further experience with certain parts of the sequence. As soon as possible, the aide guides each child to have the additional experience he needs.

## BASIC EXPERIENCE WITH NUMBERS

A child who has a concept of himself as an important entity can go on to formulate the concept of *unity*. When he has the additional concept of another person, he can formulate the concept of *two*, as well as the concept of *both of us*. However, an aide should not leave such conceptualization to chance. A competent aide soon comes to see the presence of two people as an opportunity to have the children think of counting "one, two." If the children are to use materials, the aide also has the opportunity to guide them in developing the concept of one-to-one correspondence as

[4] *Music for Early Childhood*, California State Series (Morristown, New Jersey: Silver Burdett Company, 1952), p. 92. Hilde Hoffmann, *The Green Grass Grows All Around* (New York: The Macmillan Co., 1968). This poem edition is especially appropriate for the urban child.

COSTUMING PAINTERS CAN BE A NUMERICAL EXPERIENCE.

he sees that each child has a set of the materials. He may say, "Here are two sets of materials, one set for you, Tom, and one set for you, Kathy."

Many times a day an aide can guide children in meaningful enumeration. He asks, "How many girls are here today?" and leads the children to count both those present and those who are absent (see Chapter 2, page 32). When a group of children is working together, the aide finds time to have them realize their number, perhaps by asking, "How many pieces of green paper do we need?" or, "How many glasses of juice will Jane need to serve all of us?" On the playground an aide encourages the child who is bouncing a ball, as well as the children waiting for their turn, to count the number of bounces. At snacks or mealtime an aide has the children practice setting the table with as many spoons, forks, glasses, or napkins as there are children.

As the children become experienced with counting and enumeration, an aide goes on to guide them in identifying and reproducing a given amount. The aide may ask, "Can you find a headband with a set of four dots?" "Please make a set of four dots." "Can you bring four napkins please?" Such identification and reproduction should be a meaningful, even though contrived, activity time and time again. An aide sees that no day passes without guiding the children into situation after situation that involves the identification or reproduction of numbers that the teacher is teaching the children—or smaller numbers.

When children have experience with enumeration, identification, and reproduction, an aide guides them to make quantitative comparisons and to join and separate sets. All of these activities should be in keeping with and paced by what the teacher is doing with the children.

### Working with Numbers and Measurement

Working with space leads to working with defined segments of it or with defined shapes within it. Working with distance leads to working with definite intervals within it, and to measuring such intervals in terms of an agreed upon unit of measure. The length of a royal thumb as far as the first knuckle has been decreed to be a basic unit of length. This unit of length with its multiples now enables people to measure inches, feet, and yards of material, and to determine areas of land that are owned, bought, and sold.

Working with time leads to defining units of it such as minutes, seconds, and hours. Working with lengths of musical sounds leads to using units of it for the purposes of playing or singing a song or other musical composition. The aide helps the children experience activity with basic units of length, area, and time.

Whenever a teacher helps her group of children with such concepts of units or with other number concepts, the aide goes on to help individual and small groups of children do further work with such concepts. The aide provides the children with firsthand experiences from which the concepts are developed. Especially with children who have had little experience with numbers and with quantitative relationships, the aide must provide as much opportunity as he can for children to link abstract mathematical concepts to firsthand everyday kinds of experience.

### Counting and One-to-One Correspondence

A child is a visible unit. A second child is another unit of the same kind. An aide who has two children in a group can help them in counting, "One, two children." If each child has a set of three crayons, the aide can guide each of them to count, "One, two, three crayons." By putting the two sets of crayons together, the children can count to six. The aide carefully guides such everyday activities of counting and/or working with units so that each child understands and talks about:

1. Units.
2. Sets.
3. One, two, three, and so on.
4. Patterns made from various units.

Whenever an aide helps pass out materials, he has an opportunity to help the children with one-to-one matching. The set of children and the set of juice glasses for them must correspond. A child can see that the set of napkins also matches. As the children become experienced with matching they can go on to conceptualize about it. They think of a set of children being equivalent to a set of cookies having the same number, and they determine whether or not the two sets are equivalent by counting each of them, unit by unit.

The flannel board is an important help for an aide to use to guide children to understand one-to-one correspondence. The aide can use flannel-board cut-outs to tell the story of "The Three Pigs," and then talk with the children about the one-to-one correspondence of the set of pigs and the set of houses. The story of "The Three Bears" also lends itself to a flannel-board display of a column for the set of bears and a corresponding column for the set of bowls of porridge, or a column for the set of chairs, or a column for the set of beds.

"How many?" is a frequent question for an aide to ask. A typical day will include such questions as:

*How many are in our group?*
*How many pieces of paper do we need?*
*Can you find the numeral that tells us how old you are?*
*How many of us can find places at the painting easels?*

On the playground, an aide also finds opportunities to ask "How many?" He may ask:

*How many swings are there?*
*How many children can have a swing?*
*Jane wants a swing. How many more can have swings now?*
*How many can play on the jungle gym?*

### Numerals

An aide is invaluable in reinforcing the teaching of numerals representing each of the numbers. When the teacher is introducing the children to the numeral *1*, the aide can work with two or three children who are primarily motoric in their learning at that time and can encourage them to cut out of magazines illustrations having the number one—one boy, one car, one house, and so on. Collecting each of these unitary sets in a box conspicuously labeled with the numeral *1* makes a set of materials that a child can use in mastering the concept of the number *one*. In the same way, as each of the numerals is introduced by the teacher, an aide can work with small groups of children who learn the number concept by cutting out appropriate sets, and link it to the numeral that names the set and is written on the storage box for the set.

An aide can also use a game of matching pieces to reinforce the linking of a set of objects to the numeral that represents the number of objects in the set. For instance, an aide can use commercially prepared rectangular pieces of wood or plastic each two inches by four inches. One piece may have a large black dot and the corresponding interlocking piece, the numeral *1*. Similarly, other pieces may have a sequence of sets of dots and interlocking pieces with the corresponding sequence of numerals *1*, *2*, *3*, and so on as far as the children are ready to go. When the set of pieces with dots are arranged in a column at the left, the children can select from the numeral pieces the numeral that shows the number of dots in the set. The child can check to see that his work is correct by noting whether or not the two pieces can fit together. By having a child or a small group of children work with the matching pieces, an aide can guide them in linking together a set and the numeral representing it, and, at the same time, a linking together a mathematical process and a means of checking its accuracy.

When the teacher has presented each of the numbers and the children are familiar with them, the children enjoy representing the numbers by the appropriate numeral. A set of one object can be represented by the numeral *1*; a set of two objects, by the numeral *2*; and so on. Children like to put on the flannel board the numerals that show the number of children who are absent, are in the small group using the flannel board, have parts in a dramatic play, are in the playhouse, and so on.

To make sure that each child is linking the correct numeral with the number he has in mind, an aide can make up a series of cards, each having a numeral on it. The aide places these cards in rows on a pocket chart. At the same time the aide has a box containing a series of sets, each having as many items as can be represented by a numeral on a card. Then the aide shows one of the sets to the children with whom he is working. "How many pencils are in this set?" the aide may ask. Then he asks, "Can you find the numeral that represents that number?" If the child seems to be unsure of the answer, the aide gives him a further clue, perhaps by asking, "Is the numeral in the first row?"

When the child can identify the numerals from 1 to 5 corresponding to the number of items in the sets, the aide makes a record of the child's accomplishment, perhaps by proudly writing the numeral 5 on his name card. Similar accomplishments of understanding the number concepts six through ten and linking them with the corresponding numeral can likewise be noted on the child's name card. This notation device enables the aide to give the teacher the feedback that she needs to plan the next number experiences for the children, and enables the aide to work with the children to learn exactly what is most needed for them to work well with the rest of their group.

Working with a small group of children or with children who have been absent, an aide leads the game of "How Many?" and encourages the children to make further use of the numbers and numerals they have been learning. The aide asks, for instance, "How many doors are there in this room?" When a child responds with the correct number, the child selects the corresponding numeral from the sorting box and places it on the flannel board. In this way, the aide guides the learning of the children through such additional questions as:

*How many windows are there in this room?*
*How many wheels are on a bicycle?*
*How many fingers are on your hand?*
*How many thumbs have you on one hand?*
*How many toes have you on one foot?*
*How many are in your family?*

Using a flannel-board set of numerals from 1 to 10, an aide can help the children to link numerals with each other in the game, "What Numeral Is Missing?" As the group of children says the numbers in sequence, they place them on the small flannel board in a straight line reading from left to right. After the numerals are arranged, the aide turns the board away from the group and removes a numeral. "What numeral is missing?" he asks as he shows the board. Depending upon the experience of the children in the group, the aide may provide a clue such as, "It comes before five," or "It comes after three."

When the teacher introduces the children to the numbers on the clock, the aide arranges the numerals as on the face of a clock. When he works with more experienced children, the aide arranges the numerals at random for the game.

On the playground, an aide can encourage the counting and recording of counting. A young child can count the number of times be bounces a ball, or jumps a rope, and his friend can find in a model digit sequence the numerals to copy on the chalk board scorecard. A mature child who can write numerals as well as count the bounces of a ball or other scores can act as scorekeeper. The other children can check his score keeping.

When the teacher is guiding children to learn the use of numerals to represent sets with which they are working at school, she may suggest to the aide that he have the children help him make appropriate bulletin board displays; that he check out books from the library that will help the children think with sets of numbers; and that he be prepared to play educational games with children who need further experience in working with sets of numbers. The aide is prepared to do each of these activities.

An effective bulletin-board display that an aide can make with the help of the children is a display of colorful disks with each set linked to a numeral of the same color:

| | | | |
|---|---|---|---|
| 0 | 0 | 0 | 0 |
| 1 | 0 | 0 | 0 |
| | 2 | 0 | 0 |
| | | 3 | 0 |
| | | | 4 |

Such a display helps the children to work from left to right with a sequence of numerals, and at the same time to work from the top to the bottom of a column. The display can be made from construction paper using whatever shapes the children need practice in free cutting, perhaps triangles of different sizes and angles, or ovals, or whatever shape is of current interest to them.

A verse that an aide can use with flannel-board cut-outs to give children practice in counting and linking numbers and objects is entitled "Ten Chicks." It requires ten eggs, one hen, and ten chicks as cut-outs.

TEN CHICKS

Five eggs here and five eggs there—
That makes ten, you see.
Here on top sits Mother Hen
As happy as can be.

"Cackle, cackle," clucks the hen.
The eggs begin to hatch.
Five chicks now and five chicks then.
Ten makes quite a batch.

Crack and crackle. Peek-a-boo.
Five chicks come tumbling out.
The other five are hatching too.
Ten chicks now run about.

The aide first places the eggs on the flannel board and then makes two rows, one directly below the other, counting each egg in turn:

1, 2, 3, 4, 5
1, 2, 3, 4, 5

Then the aide can ask, "How many eggs does that make all together? Let us count them, 1, 2, 3, 4, 5, 6, 7, 8, 9, 10."

When the aide asks, "Who sits on top of the eggs so they will hatch?" he places the Mother Hen cut-out on the flannel board.

With the children who are interested in one-to-one matching, the aide uses ten chick cut-outs, and emphasizes that the set of eggs and the set of chicks have the same number and are equivalent. With children to whom the teacher has introduced numerals, the aide makes use of the numerals *5*, *5*, and *10*, placing them at the end of the rows to describe the set in each row. In these ways, the aide uses the poem to reinforce concepts of quantity that the children are practicing.

### Reteaching a Number Concept

When the teacher or an aide notices that a child is hesitant in the use of one of the numbers between one and five, or between six and ten, the aide can work with him individually or in a small group, to give the child the additional experience that he needs to develop confidence with the number. The following activities are described for the number three, but have their counterparts with any other number:

1. The child selects a set of three flannel-board felt cut-outs. The child counts them in sequence as he places them in a row from left to right on the flannel board: one, two, three. Then he selects from his sorting box the numeral 3 that shows how many there are in the row. He concludes the activity by putting the cut-outs and the numerals away, naming and counting them.
2. From old magazines the child selects pictures that have three similar objects, or three objects that seem related. He cuts or tears out each picture and pastes it on a sheet having a large numeral 3 written on it.
3. The child reads, tells, hears, or dramatizes such stories as "The Three Pigs," "The Three Bears," or "The Three Little Kittens."

### Building Confidence with Number Concepts

As children build habits of correctly linking numerals to numbers and both numbers and numerals to sets of objects or events, an aide is invaluable in providing the additional satisfying and successful experience that each child needs to make him confident in using numbers and numerals. Here is a repertoire of simple games that an aide is ready to use at the suggestion of the teacher.

"Beanbags in the Box" can be used to help children read the number symbols. The game is played by the same number of children on each of two teams, perhaps Mary and her team, and John and his team. Mary stands with her toes on the line and has two chances to throw the beanbag into a box. The aide records Mary's score. John tries next, and has his score recorded. After the children on each team have had their turn, the scores are added and the results tallied. The game can be played indoors with the aide writing the scores on the chalk board, or it can be played outdoors with the aide writing the scores on newsprint with a broad, felt-tipped pen. Wherever it is played, the game is followed by a discussion, during which the aide may ask, for example, "What did Mary's team score?" "Which team had the larger score?" "Which team won?" Sometimes the aide may have the children work with larger numbers by having each child have a larger number of chances to throw the beanbag into the box.

"A Fishing Game" is useful in helping children read numerals at the same time they review color recognition. The aide provides a small group of children with:

1. A fishing pole with a magnet tied on the end of its string.
2. A fish cut from construction paper in different colors, with numerals from one to ten printed on each, and with a paper clip at its mouth.
3. A pond outlined by heavy blue roving on the rug in the classroom.
4. A number chart that can be used by players to make sure they read a numeral correctly.

Each child takes a turn fishing. A child may say, "I caught a *blue* fish with a numeral 3 on it." He keeps the fish and gives the pole to the next player, who says, "Thank you," and takes his turn fishing. As the game continues, the aide suggests that the children check to be sure that the numeral is read correctly. Then a child goes to the number chart, counts the set of objects that the numeral represents, and reports back to the group.

When the children understand the number concepts of eleven through twenty and the teacher has introduced the children to the corresponding numerals, the aide reinforces the recognition of those numerals by playing the Fishing Game with a set of large fish having the numerals 11 through 20 printed on them.

"Bouncing the Ball" is a Follow-the-Leader game that an aide can use to guide children in counting accurately. One child from a small group of children bounces the ball counting *to himself* the number of bounces that he makes. Other children raise their hand if they know how many times the ball was bounced. One of them then bounces the ball the same number of times as the first child did.

"Hear Me Count" is used to help children link numbers to movements they make in bouncing a ball. The children count the bounces aloud and then select the numeral that shows the score made.

"Flash Cards with Numerals" are used to tell a child how many times he is to bounce a ball or clap his hands.

"Thinking of a Number" is a game in which a child thinks of the number on a card he chooses. Then he answers questions that the aide and other children ask him until someone guesses the number. Those questions include: "Does it come after __?" and "Does it come before __?"

To provide further experience with linking sets, numbers, and numerals, the aide uses a song such as "Ten Little Indians" and makes up ten Indian headbands, each with a set of dots to show the number to be represented by the wearer of the headband. The aide also prepares a set of cards with the numerals 1 through 10 printed on them. After each child has selected a headband and a corresponding numeral card to hold in front of him, he finds his place in line. The children squat to sing the first part of the song, and each child stands as his number is sung. With the additional properties made by the aide, the children who sing "Ten Little Indians" learn to link appropriate numbers with sets of dots and with numerals.

### Linking Counting to Experience

Each school subject moves from qualitative relationships into quantitative ones. Knowing this, an aide who is working with a small group of children can extend their experience at the same time that he provides practice in counting. For instance, an aide can have the children listening to a song make a downbeat at the beginning of a measure of music and an upbeat in between. Soon each child is not only hearing the beat of the music but is also counting, "One, two. One, two." When the aide plays a waltz, the children count, "*One*, two, three," and show with a strong downbeat what they hear in the music. A great deal of listening to music in this way lays a foundation for understanding and appreciating music with complicated rhythms in later years.

In general, an aide guides children to be sensitive to some new phenomenon by pointing out a countable aspect of it, and having the children use the simple numbers from one to ten, especially one, two, and three.

Probably the experience that best enables a child to build an abstract concept of a particular number is his birthday. A three-year-old child can count to three. After spending a year thinking about "three," he goes on to think of himself as having a fourth birthday and becoming four years old. He happily holds up four fingers to show how old he is.

An aide is invaluable in helping each child feel important on his birthday and in helping him count. With a flannel board, and cut-outs of a birthday cake, a set of candles and a set of yellow-colored flames, the aide simulates the traditional putting-on-birthday-candles-by-the-child. With a six-year-old birthday child, the birthday ritual may be like this:

*Aide*: Today is your birthday! Do you know the date?

*Child:* (Answers and learns the date.)
*Aide:* How old are you today?
*Child:* Six.
*Aide:* (Place cake cut-out) Here's a big pink birthday cake—For your very special day. Choose the number of candles—Place them on your cake.
*Aide:* Now light each candle with a flame.

The child places a yellow felt flame over each candle and all sing the traditional "Happy Birthday" song to the birthday child. Then the aide says the poem, "Six Birthday Candles."

SIX BIRTHDAY CANDLES

Six birthday candles on your cake!
What is the wish that you will make?
Blow out each candle with no tricks.
Let's count: one, two, three, four, five, six.

One year ago your cake had five
To say five years you've been alive.
What do these candles say today?
It's fun to have a sixth birthday!

The aide or the birthday child removes each flame as the child "blows" and the other children count.

The birthday cake is left on the flannel board with the caption:

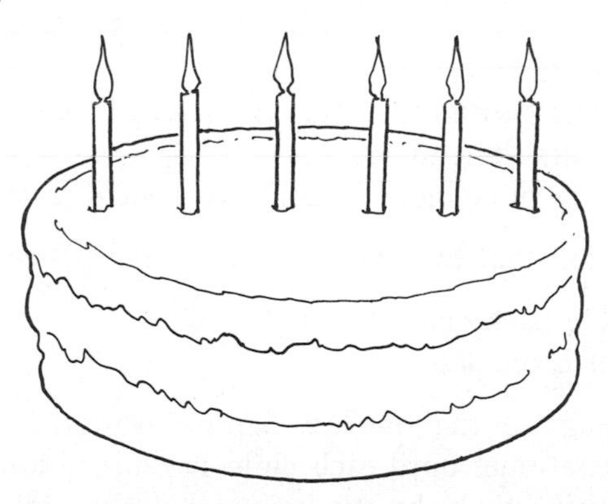

**Joan's Birthday**
**October 6, 19--**

### The Concept of Zero and of Unity

When the teacher introduces the concept of *zero*, an aide can help each child to understand both that concept and the concept of *one* by marking off units on a straight line. The units should be step size, perhaps one foot in length. The aide and a small group of children select a point on the line segment and label it zero. With this as a starting point they go to the right counting in sequence—One, two, and so on—and labeling each end point of a unit with the corresponding numeral.

Next the aide helps the children realize that they could do the same thing by starting with zero and going in the opposite direction. To distinguish the two directions, the set of numerals going to the right is each labeled with a positive sign (+) to indicate the positive direction and the set of numerals going to the left is each labeled with a negative sign (−) to indicate the other direction. At that time the aide points out the zero (0), the point lying between the two sets of lengths but having no length itself. Thus the aide helps the children to understand the fundamental distinction between something and nothing, and the basic concept of *zero*.

### Linking Addition to Subtraction to Experience in Space

The teacher who is fortunate to have an aide can plan to have each child experience the addition and subtraction processes in two-dimensional space with the guidance of the aide. A line segment is drawn and marked off in one-foot units. A small group of children and their aide pick out a point on the line segment and label it zero (0). The one child stands there while other children tell him what to do:

*Children:* Take two steps.
*Child:* (moves two units in the positive direction) That's two.
*Children:* Take three more.
*Child:* (moves three more units in the same direction) Three more.

Aide brings out that two and three more makes five.

*Children:* Go back one step.
*Child:* That is one less.

The aide brings out that one less than five is four.

The game continues until each child has added and subtracted. The aide concludes the activity by suggesting that the children can play the

A LINE WITH NUMBERS.

game on their way home from school by using the spaces marked off in the sidewalk. With more experienced children either a Classroom Aide or a Playground Aide can help them link their addition and subtraction experience in space with what they do in playing hopscotch.

When playing the addition and subtraction game in space, the aide makes a point of drawing the chalk line segment sometimes in one location, sometimes in another, and sometimes on paper. In this way the aide helps the children realize that they can set up such a reference line at any time and in any place. Later the children will find it easy to set up a simple arithmetic problem using digits from 1 through 10 or 15 as a first step toward solving a more complicated problem. The concepts of mensuration (measurement) and of transposition will be more readily understandable to children who have moved themselves through space in adding and subtracting small numbers. This basic experience that each child can have is usually possible only when an aide is at hand.

### Linking Addition with Childhood Experience

An aide reinforces with a few children at a time what the teacher has previously presented to a larger group. Many children need additional experience. Often the teacher will ask an aide to reinforce through experience what has yet to be learned completely by some of the children. Here is a delightful poem using additional concepts. An aide can use it with children who are in the process of mastering addition with digits from 1 through 10.

TEN LITTLE FROGS

One little frog thinks, "What shall I do?"
Along comes his friend. Now that makes two.

Say the frogs to each other, "Let's see.
If we have *one more*. Then that will make three."

The third frog comes and brings *one more*.
So now we count that there are four.

The four frogs take a swim and then a dive.
Up pops *one more* to make the count five.

Five little frogs in quite a fix.
They can't play games 'til there are six.

"Let me be six!" says little green frog.
His friend yells, "I'm seven!" and jumps a log.

In hops *one more* frog. Say, isn't that great!
*One more* after seven. Now that makes eight.

They all shout out, "The water is fine!"
So in jumps *one more*. Now there are nine.

Nine little frogs. *One more* will make ten.
He'll bring the towels. They'll tell him when.
—Barbara McBride

When the teacher has guided the children into thinking about the numbers from six through ten, the aide can help them think in terms of "How many?" with answers in that range:

*When you join the set of five fingers on your left hand with the set of five fingers on your right hand, how many fingers are there in the new set?*

*When the three children at this table join the two children who are at the big table, how many sets of crayons will we need for them?*

*Two girls are absent today, and one boy is also absent, how many are absent all together?*

With more experienced children, the aide asks:

*It is now nine o'clock. What time will it be one hour later?*

### Linking Subtraction with Childhood Experience

The aide who has a child helping him set or clear a table has an excellent opportunity to help the child link addition or subtraction to the experience. In setting the table, a child is constantly adding *one more* piece of flatwear or *one more* dish. "Add a fork here," an aide may suggest. "That will be the third piece of flatwear. It will complete the set at that place." In clearing the table, the aide guides the child to see that when a glass is removed, the set of glasses on the table is *one less* in number.

When a child is helping an aide serve milk to the children at a table, the aide may be able to guide the child to observe that the number of milk cartons on the serving tray is the same number as the number of places at the table. The two sets match. Then as the child serves each of the seated children at the table, each serving reduces the number of cartons on the tray by one at the same time that it adds one more to the number of cartons on the table. In serving milk at a table seating four children, an aide may point out:

"We have a set of four children at the table, and we have a set of four milk cartons on the serving tray. There is one milk carton for each child. The set of children and the set of cartons match."

On another day, the aide may explain further: "As we serve you, we are going to *remove* milk cartons from the set of four milk cartons on the tray. We *remove* one carton to serve Sue, and have three cartons left to serve others. Now we *remove* one more carton to serve Tim, and have two cartons left to serve others. Now we *remove* one more carton to serve Mary, and have one carton left to serve Sam. When we remove Sam's carton from the tray, the set of cartons is *zero*."

On a third day, an aide can guide the children to observe the increase in the set of cartons on the table and to see that removing one carton from the tray set adds one more carton to the set of cartons on the table. Thus the children experience a basic concept in conservation. The total mass is constant although part or even all of it may change in form.

### Ordinal Numbers

When the children are well established in working with number concepts, they will feel the need to use ordinal as well as cardinal numbers. Their teacher guides them in thinking about numerical order and talks with them about first, second, third, and other ordinal numbers. At this point, an aide helps small groups of children as well as individuals in using the ordinal numbers. Experience with the series of ordinal numbers is especially important when children seem overly concerned about being first. "Me first!" is the cue to guiding children into appreciating second, third, and other places as well.

A sorting box such as that illustrated here is invaluable to an aide in helping children use ordinal numbers. It can be made with ten sectional boxes arranged in two rows:

A SORTING BOX FOR MAKING LINKAGES.

When the children work with counting, numerals from 1 through 5 are used in one row. When they work with counting up to ten, numerals from 1 through 10 are used. But when children understand the concept of *zero*, the Sorting Box can be arranged starting with zero:

| 1 | 2 | 3 | 4 | 5 |
|---|---|---|---|---|
| 6 | 7 | 8 | 9 | 10 |

| 0 | 1 | 2 | 3 | 4 |
|---|---|---|---|---|
| 5 | 6 | 7 | 8 | 9 |

In introducing the sorting-box experience to the children, an aide can reinforce their concepts of ordinal numbers. The aide lets the children place a sequence of felt numerals 1 through 5 in the top row of the sorting box. Then he invites a child to choose an object cut-out, perhaps a tree, and put it in the *first* box, the box that is below the box with the numeral 1.

| 1 | 2 | 3 | 4 | 5 |
|---|---|---|---|---|
|  |  |  |  |  |

"Which box did you put the tree in?" the aide asks to reinforce the concept of *first*. The aide continues to guide the children to choose an object for the *second* box, the *third* box, and so on until the sorting box is filled.

Then the aide and the children can play the game of "What Is Missing?" The children close their eyes while the aide removes the object from one of the boxes. "Which is the box that has something missing?" the aide asks. "Is it the first box? The second box?" and so on until the empty box is identified correctly. "What was in the (*third*) box?" the aide asks, and a child responds by mentioning both the object and the box.

On subsequent days when sorting boxes are used for practice with ordinal numbers, one of the children can take the part of the aide while the aide acts as an interested listener. Each child should have a turn when he is willing to do so. If the child demurs, the aide calmly says, "You may have your turn another time," and thus helps the child learn to expect such performance of himself.

When the children are used to having their teacher use a pocket chart, the aide can use one to review shape concepts with a small group of children at the same time that he gives them opportunity for a meaningful experience with ordinal numbers. For example, the aide may use a set of disks having circular edges to represent "circles," a set of squares, and a set of rectangles. The aide places the squares in the first row of the pocket chart, the circles in the second row, and the rectangles in the third row. After the children identify each of the shapes, the aide asks, "Mary, will you please remove a shape from the *first* row, and tell us the name of the shape?" A few minutes later, when the chart is being cleared of the shapes, the aide asks, "Larry, will you please remove a square, and tell me in which row you find it? Is it in the *first* row, the *second* row, or the *third* row?" Through this process, the aide guides the children to use ordinal numbers as a means of locating an object, and to use the terms aloud to describe the location of the object.

On other days, the aide provides further practice with ordinal terms by using the pocket chart and various sets, each having a Key Card, a matching card, and two other cards. The aide places the Key Card at the left of the pocket chart and the three other cards in the row to its right. He describes the cards as *the first, the second,* and *the third* card. Then he says, for instance, "Look at the Key Card. (Hand under the Key Card.) Now, who will *remove* the card that is exactly like our Key Card?" "Thank you. The (*second*) card was like the Key Card." In this way, the aide helps the children to functionally use the ordinal numbers, and lays a basis for developing fast reactions on scholastic aptitude and other achievement tests the children will take in later years.

### Writing Numerals

When teacher and children have worked with numerals to the point at which the children are ready to write numerals themselves, an aide can guide their practice as they work in a small group. This song can be sung quietly to the tune of "The Mulberry Bush" as they work.

WRITING NUMERALS

1. One stroke down and we make a 1.
   One stroke down and we make a 1.
   One stroke down and we make a 1.
   We make the numeral 1.

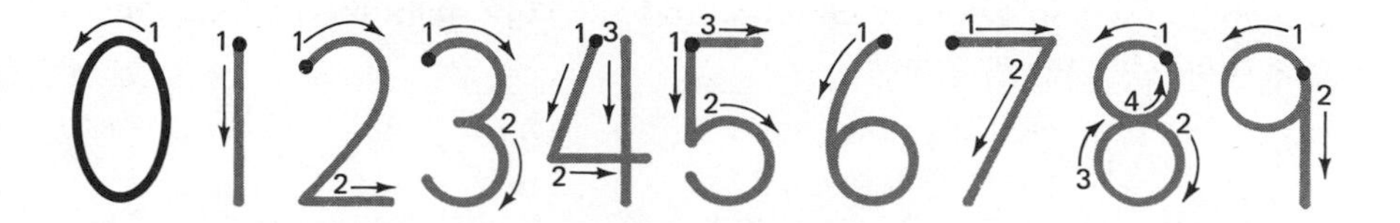

MANUSCRIPT WRITING GUIDE SHEET: NUMERALS.

2. Half around, down, and then across
   (Repeat, as in verse 1)
   We make the numeral 2.

3. Half around, and half again
   We make the numeral 3.

4. Top, down and over, top down again
   We make the numeral 4.

5. Top down, then around, and put on a hat
   We make the numeral 5.

6. All the way down and then around
   We make the numeral 6.

7. Straight line over and down we go
   To make the numeral 7.

8. Here we go loopitty, loopitty, loop
   To make the numeral 8.

9. All the way 'round and then come down
   To make the numeral 9.

10. One stroke down. Then make an egg.
    We make the numeral 10.

—Anonymous

When the teacher is guiding the children in writing numerals, she can have the aide duplicate a letter with a set of the numerals for the children to take home. If the child's family knows how the child is learning to write numerals at school, the family members can encourage his practice with that method instead of trying to teach another method they know.

#### Reading Number Words

When the teacher notices children who are interested in written words, she can ask the aide to use the flannel board, a set of objects, a set of numeral cut-outs, and a set of corresponding number-word cut-outs to help the children link numerals to sets, sets to number words, and numerals to number words. The aide can guide the children in placing the numerals in sequence in a column at the left of the flannel board, the corresponding sets in a second column, and the corresponding number words in a third column, as follows:

| | | |
|---|---|---|
| 1 | * | one |
| 2 | ** | two |
| 3 | *** | three |

The cues that the aide gives the children to help them link together the number of objects, the corresponding numeral, and the written form of the number will probably include, "Look at the numeral and then select the number of stars that shows how many the numeral means," and, "Find the word that tells how many are in the set of stars." When the children put the numerals, objects, and words away, they read each numeral and its number word.

### Sorting Money

When money is collected for milk or for some other purpose, an aide can work with the children on a committee to make sure that the money collected corresponds to the amount expected. Members of the committee have practice in counting, working with cardinal numbers, sorting and grouping coins, and learning coinage equivalents. When the committee of experienced children makes its report to the class and writes the record of the transactions on the chalk board, then all of the experienced children in the class have an opportunity to read and verify the addition.

The aide arranges for each child to bring his money to the sorting table in turn, and has the child's transaction recorded. The committee members use a sorting box or a series of containers, one for pennies, one for nickels, one for dimes, and one for quarters. Each container is labeled with the name of the coin and its value, for instance: 5¢, nickel. A child who is sorter distributes the coins among the boxes appropriately. Other children group each kind of coin in stacks of five: five pennies, five nickels, and so on. When all the money has been collected and the transactions recorded, the experienced sorters and counters complete their responsibilities by counting the number of stacks and writing the values on the board:

| | |
|---|---|
| 15 pennies | $ .15 |
| 10 nickels | .50 |
| 5 dimes | .50 |
| 1 quarter | .25 |
| Total | $1.40 |

If each of twenty-eight children paid 5¢, the total amount of money collected should equal $1.40. The committee reports its findings to the teacher who decides whether or not it is appropriate to make the report to the class and to enlarge on the accounting procedure.

### Dramatic Play of Marketing

The teacher often enlists the cooperation of an aide to set up a grocery store so that the children can have experience in buying and selling and in the number transactions that marketing involves. The aide uses a felt-tip pen to mark prices in large numerals on the empty cans and cartons that the children bring from home. If play money is not available, the aide may be asked to make some to equip a cash register and the purses of the shoppers. With this play money, the children match their script with the marks on the packages they purchase. When working with experienced shoppers, the aide will probably make a poster showing each kind of coin and its value in the event that a cashier or a customer needs to verify his mental arithmetic.

If shelves and counters are not already set up, an aide can work with the children to measure the boards and the space to make sure that they match. Such a building project can involve an excellent discussion that uses quantitative words such as *big, little; large, small; narrow, wide; high, low;* and so on.

The grocery store experience should be made available to each child. To make sure that no child is omitted in playing the role of clerk, and that each child has the chance to play the role of shopper, the aide keeps a record of participation, a copy for the teacher, and a continuing record for himself.

To help make the shopping an enjoyable experience, the aide often takes the role of shopper himself. To provide the children with speech patterns that will enlarge their shopping experience, the aide can occasionally role-play a part such as the role of the shopper who wants to exchange one purchase for another equivalent purchase.

**Measurement**

Besides the simulated grocery store, children can have other activities that involve the use of number concepts in actual measurement. One measurement activity that is a part of most early childhood years is that of finding out and recording the height and weight of each child. The teacher has the responsibility of preparing the children to enjoy and learn from the measurement activity, but with an aide to help the teacher can make a routine procedure into an interesting experience. One imaginative teacher created the record form shown and had an aide make it out in duplicate with one form for the child's folder at school and the other form sent home for the family records. The delightful picture was something for each child to color if he wished.

The aide helped the children read their height and weight, link their measurement report with the readings on the measuring devices in the room, and make comparisons with each other. "I am taller than you." "Yes, but I weigh less than you do."

By having previous records on hand, an aide can talk with each child about how he is growing. "Last year you were twenty-eight inches tall, but

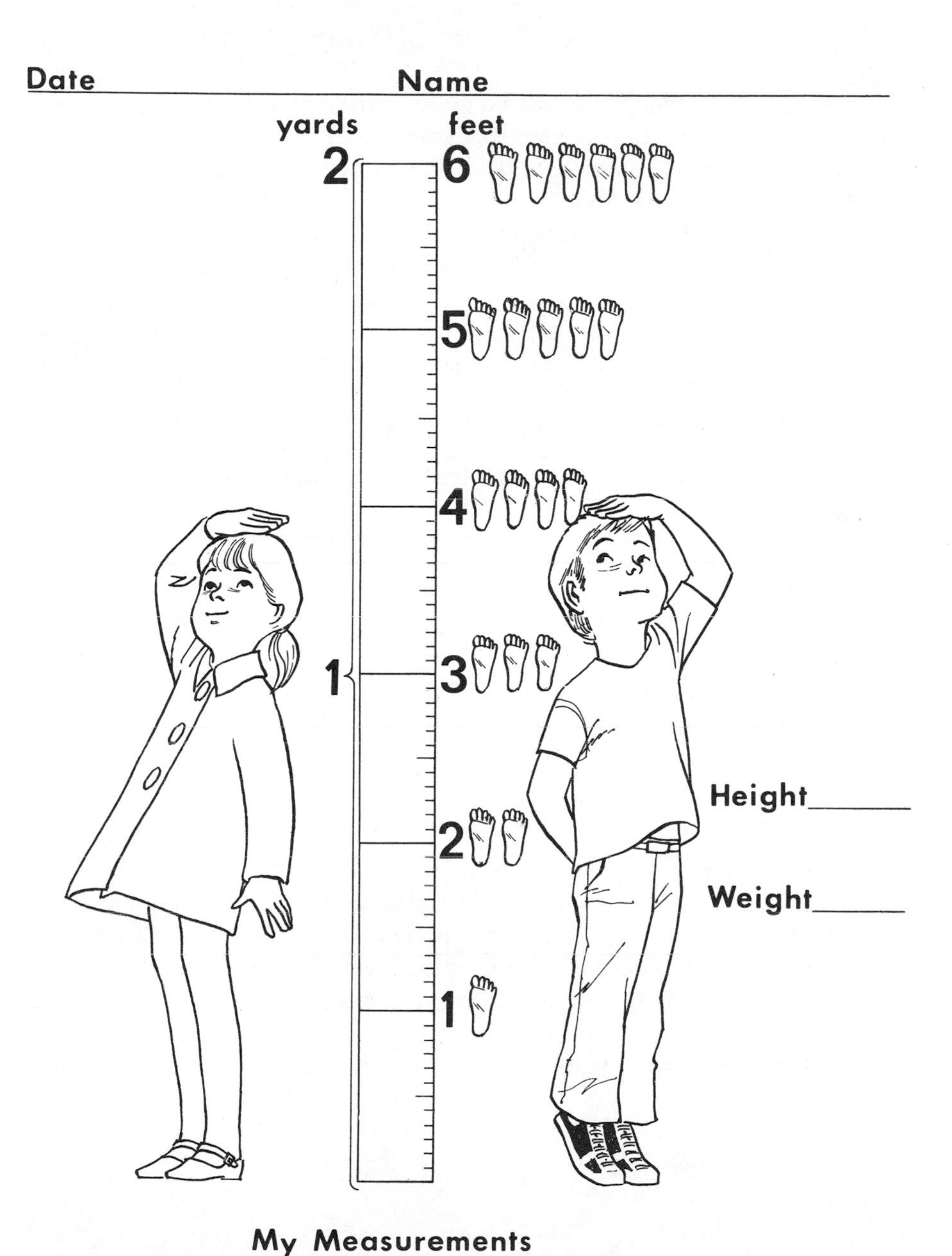


My Measurements

A MATHEMATICAL EXPERIENCE.

this year you are two inches taller," an aide may say. "You certainly are growing!"

An aide can guide children who are experienced in beginning measurement to other activities suggested by their teacher. The aide makes it possible for the teacher to provide individual children with additional practice or new experience as needed.

An aide can also watch for opportunities to help children build linkages that are basic to measurement. As shown in the chart entitled "Examples of Linkages Basic to Measurement," these linkages include linking together in all possible combinations experience with sets of objects, number concepts, written numerals, and written words for cardinal and ordinal numbers.

EXAMPLES OF
LINKAGES BASIC TO MEASUREMENT

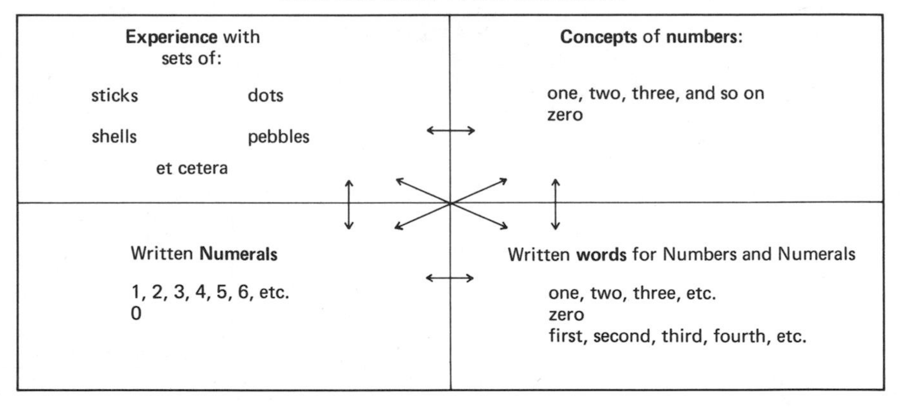


When a child collects such objects as pebbles, blocks, or stamps, he can be encouraged to group them in meaningful sets. Depending upon the extent of his previous quantitative experience, the child can also be encouraged to count the items in each set as well as the sets themselves. A more experienced child can also record the numbers he has determined, perhaps in numerals and perhaps also in words. Thus, with the help of an aide, the child is laying a foundation for his future experience with measurement.

# TOWARD AND INTO READING

When early man communicated with his tribesmen through petroglyphs as well as spoken words, parents, grandparents, and other members of the tribe were probably concerned that the children learn to read the petroglyphs, and as a result they spent hours getting the children ready for this important responsibility.

Today parents, grandparents, and other people in the life of a child are eager for the child to learn to read, to learn to translate into meaningful messages the symbols through which the history of the society as well as the trivia of the day are communicated. As taxpayers they are concerned with providing schools where the children will learn under the guidance of skillful teachers. But as parents they are more personally involved with their children's important developmental tasks of learning to read and reading to learn. The parents eagerly reinforce what their children learn under the expert tutelage of dedicated teachers and aides.

Teachers know that learning to read is facilitated by a wealth of additional linkages—words heard linked to words said; words recalled linked to words that were an integral part of an experience; words linked to representations of situations or events; words linked to words that are similar, or perhaps different; written words linked to words said, and to words heard; words linked to actions. (See chart on page 152.) Teachers who recognize the limited school time that can be devoted to learning experiences are glad to have paraprofessionals at school as well as volunteer aides out of school to reinforce and extend the linkages that a child has learned. Aides, like teachers, play important roles in helping children develop interest in, enthusiasm about, and appreciation of the usefulness of written communications; skill in perceptual and conceptual activities that will carry the children forward in time into learning to read; and a wealth of concepts, facts, and generalizations that will be most useful to the children now and in the future as they widen their world through reading.

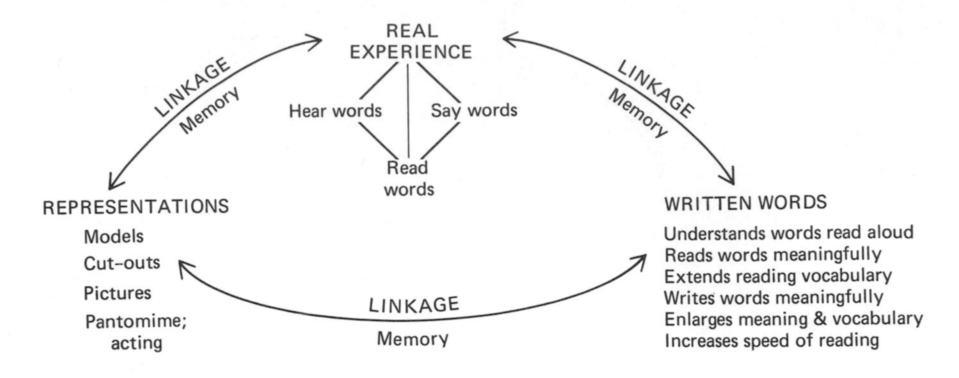


LINKAGES BASIC TO LEARNING TO READ.

## LINKING WORDS WITH CONCEPTUAL EXPERIENCE

One of the most important aspects of a child's life is that of linking to his activities words that he hears and says. A teacher, an aide, a parent, or anyone else who relates to a child serves as an effective linkage agent when he calls the child's attention to some part of a pleasant experience by giving the child a name for it and encouraging him to talk about it. A child can play in a colorful garden without learning the name of a single color, but a child who comes to a garden with a helpful aide can learn at least one more color each time he comes to the garden.

In learning a language, a young child makes a direct linkage between what he is aware of through his senses and the word that he hears and says. He links words with sensory inputs. If the child has linked a Spanish word for red to the red rose in the garden, he nevertheless also needs to hear and say the English word, *red*, in the garden. To be learned readily, languages should be functional. The direct linking of words to experience in each of two languages not only facilitates linking the words together but also facilitates the meaningful use of the words in everyday communication.

When a child is not interested in working with words in a classroom situation, he is communicating his need for more meaningful experience. Visual aids such as models, pictures, or pantomime may provide sufficient cues to stimulate his interest. But if they do not, the aide and the child's teacher should confer about providing the child with firsthand experience in which the aide helps the child make direct linkages between experience and the words that he hears and uses.

### Similarity and Difference in Linkages

One of the early-learned tools of learning is the ability to perceive both similarity and difference. An aide is invaluable in providing for individual or small groups of children the additional practice that enables learners to master these concepts. Whenever a teacher has pointed out similarities and differences, an aide can provide activities such as the following:

*Simple Classification*

The aide mixes two sets of objects and asks the children to separate them: a set of squares and a set of triangles in the same color; two sets of flannel board cut-outs; a set of dark-blue disks and a set of light-blue disks of the same diameter; two kinds of cookies with one of each kind to be put on the plate of each child.

As the child carries out a sorting operation, the aide talks with him about what he is doing. The aide may say, "These are alike (pointing to the first set), and these are alike (pointing to the second set), but the two sets are different from each other." He encourages the children to use such words as *alike* and *different*.

*Auditory Discrimination*

When children are experienced in hearing the beginning sounds of their own and others' names and are learning to hear the endings of words as well, an aide can help them think about similarities and differences in the names of their friends. For instance, an aide had the following conversation with several children in a class that included Annette and Lynette:

> *Aide:* Have you noticed that two children have similar names: Annette and Lynette? How else are these two girls alike?
> *Children:* They have long hair.
> *Aide:* Good. They both have long hair. What else is the same about them?
> *Children:* They both have brown eyes.
> *Aide:* Yes, they both have brown eyes and both have long hair. What is different about the two girls?
> *Children:* Lynette has dark hair. Annette has light hair.
> *Aide:* Yes.
> *Children:* Lynette is short. Annette is tall.
> *Aide:* Yes, Lynette is shorter than Annette. Have you noticed what part of their names are alike?
> *Children:* The end.
> *Aide:* Yes. The last of their names are alike. Annette and Lynette are words that rhyme—and girls we enjoy.

## LINKING SOUNDS HEARD AND SPOKEN

When a teacher is guiding children to link the sounds they hear with the sounds they say, an aide can help provide them with additional practice.

Whereas the teacher is broadening the experience of the group, she depends on the aide to reinforce the basic linkages that have already been introduced. The aide does this by providing games and other pleasant activities that the children enjoy at the same time they learn from doing them.

### Alphabet Sounds

After the teacher guides the children to link a special sound and the corresponding letter of the alphabet, the aide reinforces these linkages by giving individual and small groups of children further practice with them. For instance, if the teacher has introduced the speech sound of *T* as the clock sound, the aide can reinforce the linking of saying *T* to hearing the speech sound of it. A child can hold a small desk clock to his ear as he says with the aide the following verses:

THE SOUND THE CLOCK MAKES

We have a new desk clock
At school to hear each day.
We hold it closely to an ear
And we can hear it say,
T, t, t, t, t, t, t, t, t.

Now let your tongue touch just its tip
To roof of mouth, behind the teeth and lip,
To make the very sound we hear,
The sound the clock makes loud and clear:
T, t, t, t, t, t, t, t, t!

Using specific activities suggested by the teacher, the aide can also help children link the speech sound of *T* to mathematical concepts about counting by tens: twenty, thirty, forty, fifty, sixty, seventy, eighty, ninety, and one hundred.

The game of the Pocket Apron is one that an aide can first play with the children and then let them play by themselves. The aide procures or makes an apron out of a sturdy material such as denim. He selects a practical neutral color such as light blue, and then adds seven large pockets of different colors such as red, yellow, orange, blue, green, purple, and pink.

If the aide is using the Pocket Apron to help children hear and say the speech sound *th*, the aide collects objects or pictures of objects whose initial, medial, or final sound incorporates the *th* speech sound:

| | |
|---|---|
| *th*imble | too*th* brush |
| *th*ree | tee*th* |
| *th*read | fea*th*er |
| *th*ermometer | |

Then the aide may proceed in this way:

1. Have children identify each object.

   *Aide:* (holding up the thimble) Let's all say what this is. "*Th*imble."

2. *Aide:* Stephen, you may choose an object. . . . Put it here on the table. . . . Tell us what it is.

3. When all objects are displayed the aide continues:

   *Aide:* Look carefully at each object and all say what it is. Let's start with the *th*imble.

   The aide selects each object in turn starting with the object that is at the children's left.

4. The aide explains the way the game is played, perhaps as follows:

   *Aide:* Now remember where each object is placed. I am going to choose someone to be "It." "It" will hide (e.g., behind the piano). Then I'll point to one of you to select an object to hide in one of the apron pockets. When "It" comes out, he will look to see what is not *th*ere on the table. Then he will tell us in which color pocket he *th*inks the missing object has been hidden.

5. The game proceeds, with the aide trying to have each child hear and say the words distinctly, and to use complete sentences.

   *Aide:* What do you *th*ink is not *th*ere?
   *It:* The thimble.
   *Aide:* The *th*imble is not *th*ere. Which pocket do you *th*ink the *th*imble is in?
   *It:* (Points to the purple pocket.)
   *Aide:* Yes, the thimble is in the purple pocket. Let's say it together. "The thimble is in the purple pocket."

A child who learns to play the game using complete sentences is ready to wear the apron and take the role of the aide another day.

When such delightful games have been enjoyed by the children to the point of acquiring mastery of linkages between hearing and saying sounds with precision, an aide can help the teacher identify the children who need to perfect their identification of one or more sounds. An aide can work with each child individually in an activity that is fun but that is also a survey of a group of sounds to be identified correctly as a basis for subsequent linkages. The aide has a child count a series of twelve small blocks or wooden beads to show his mastery of simple letter sounds. If the aide observes and records the sounds that the child needs to perfect, the aide can report the results of such a survey to the teacher, perhaps using forms such as the two shown here. The teacher will then make suggestions

Child's Name____________ Aide____________ Date_____

SURVEY OF SOUNDS IN NAMES OF NUMBERS

Activity: Child counts twelve similar small blocks (or wooden beads) arranged in a line. Examiner says smilingly, "Please count the blocks. Start here (pointing to the first block at the child's left)." Examiner makes check marks to show "sounds pronounced accurately."

| Name of Number | Sound Expected | Sound Pronounced Accurately |
|---|---|---|
| One | w n | |
| Two | t | |
| Three | th r | |
| Four | f r | |
| Five | f v | |
| Six | s ks | |
| Seven | s v n | |
| Eight | t | |
| Nine | n | |
| Ten | t | |
| Eleven | l v n | |
| Twelve | w l v | |

about what guidance an aide may give selected individuals working in small groups.

**Rhyming Words**

A child who is listening for rhyming sounds at the ends of words becomes increasingly aware of the words themselves. The child's auditory perception and his ability to speak clearly develop when an aide reinforces the guidance of the teacher in helping children link together words that rhyme.

For a small group of children who need additional experience with rhyming words an aide can provide activities such as those on page 158.

Child's Name__________ Aide__________ Date_____

## SURVEY OF SOUNDS PRONOUNCED

Activity: From an attractive box, a child selects first one and then another object until he has chosen each of them. Each time the dialogue is as follows:

Examiner: What will you choose?
Child: I'll choose a ______.

| Answer Expected | Sound Expected | Sound Pronounced Accurately | Object Identified Accurately |
|---|---|---|---|
| ball | b l | ______ ______ | ______ |
| doll | d | ______ | ______ |
| fork | f | ______ | ______ |
| gum | g | ______ | ______ |
| house | h | ______ | ______ |
| jack | j | ______ | ______ |
| kite | k | ______ | ______ |
| lamp | l | ______ | ______ |
| mouse | m | ______ | ______ |
| nail | n | ______ | ______ |
| pencil | p | ______ | ______ |
| ring | r ng | ______ ______ | ______ |
| soap | s | ______ | ______ |
| telephone | t | ______ | ______ |
| valentine | v | ______ | ______ |
| wagon | w | ______ | ______ |
| yellow yarn | y | ______ | ______ |
| zipper | z | ______ | ______ |
| whistle | wh | ______ | ______ |
| bathtub | th (voiceless) | ______ | ______ |
| feather | th (voiced) | ______ | ______ |

*Linking "Words That Rhyme" with Examples*

The aide who is familiar with nursery rhymes can help children in hearing the rhymes.

*Aide:* I am going to say a nursery rhyme. Listen for the words that rhyme, the words that sound alike on the last sound we hear.

Little Bo-Peep
Lost her sheep

What words sounded alike at the end of the word?
*Children:* Peep and sheep.
*Aide:* Good!

When children are familiar with words that rhyme in short verses, they enjoy having an aide give them a sentence to complete:

Hickory dickory dock
The mouse ran up the ___.

*Linking Together Words That Rhyme in a Song*

When the teacher has introduced a song with simple rhyming words such as "A Hunting We Will Go," the aide can give small groups of the children additional practice, one group at a time.[1] He can use picture cards to call attention to the words that rhyme when each rhyming word is sung, for instance, a picture of a fox and then a picture of a box.

*Linking Rhyming Words Together Through Their Pictures*

Using a set of picture cards for pairs of matching or rhyming words, an aide can have a child or a small group of children first identify the object by linking a word with what is pictured on the cards: fox, box; coat, boat; mouse, house; fish, dish. Then from a display of eight cards perhaps on a chalk board, the aide asks a child to select two pictures of things that have rhyming names. Another child selects a pair, and so on, until all the pairs have been arranged. Each time a rhyming pair is formed, the children say the names of the paired objects pictured.

*Linking Rhyming Words Together Through Miniature Models*

An aide can help a child or a small group of children to hear and use rhyming words that are names of objects if he has a collection of them in miniature, augmented by other miniature models the names of which have the same beginning sounds. By working with the models, the children have

[1] Rose Marie Grentzer and Margaret V. Hood, *Birchard Music Series, Kindergarten* (Sacramento, Calif.: California State Publishing Co., 1960), p. 60.

pleasant tactile, kinesthetic, and visual experiences to facilitate their linking the rhyming words together. A set of miniature models that are available commercially includes such objects as: shell, bell; fork, cork; tire, wire; star, car; sock, block; man, fan; key, bee; moon, spoon. Through a discussion of each miniature model, an aide guides the children to formulate a simple concept of each object. Then the aide guides the children in linking rhyming words together through the fun of activities such as the following:

The aide places squares of different colored construction paper in front of the children. Then he uses the top of the model storage box as a display place for three object models, two of which have names that rhyme. As the aide places a man at the child's left, a fan next to the man, and a house next to the fan, the children name the objects with the aide.

*Aide:* Jane, find two objects whose names rhyme. . . . Place them on the light-blue square.

If Jane selects the man and the house, the aide may say, "Man. House. Do those sound alike at the last sound we hear? Do their names rhyme? Are their ending sounds alike?"

If Jane selects the man and the fan, the aide may say, "Good. *Man* and *fan* have the same ending sounds. They are rhyming words."

The activity continues until pairs of object models are on each of the colored squares. If time permits, the children in the following activity can return one of each pair of object models to the box in which they are kept.

*Aide:* Look at the objects on the dark-blue square. The names of the objects rhyme. What are they?
*Child:* Wire, tire.
*Aide:* Fine. Let's put one of them back in the box.

The aide can ask a more experienced child, "Please bring something whose name rhymes with mouse," and expect to have the house put back with the mouse. If a child has difficulty in finding an object whose name rhymes with mouse, the aide can provide a meaningful clue: "The word that rhymes with mouse is the name of the place where you live." The clue provides another linkage through concepts. In the course of the activities, the aide makes certain that each child has the opportunity to be praised for successfully completing what he was asked to do.

## FROM IDENTITY TO READING AND WRITING

As a child begins to use sounds meaningfully, he is also moving toward a sense of his own identity. His own name is one of the words that will be of great importance to him. When the child's life space is expanded to include a preschool group, he finds his name used very often. In fact, when a child makes a picture an aide usually says the child's name as the aide writes it in the corner of the picture.

In the process of marking a young child's paper for later identification, an aide has an excellent opportunity to help the child learn to first recognize his initial, and then to reproduce it later. Barbara, who is proud of her name, links it to the letter *B*; Tom links his name to *T*, and so on. By meaningful repetition, done pleasantly and patiently, the aide helps a child to establish a very useful linkage.

A young child who has linked his name and initial together can go on to make linkages between the names and initials of beloved people in his family and in his school group. "My name is Sue, and my letter looks like this: *S*," is followed by, "That's Pete, and that's his letter: *P*." Sometime later, Sue will be able to write names on valentines that she gives to her classmates. A sense of identity and friendships can thus lead into reading and writing when an aide is available to help a teacher.

*Linking the Beginning Letter of a Child's Name and Its Sound*

A child who links the beginning sound of his own name to its initial can link beginning sounds of words to the initial letter of the word. A teacher asks an aide to facilitate the formation of the linkages by working first with an individual child, perhaps Paul.

The aide who was to help Paul link the initial sound and letter of a word cut pictures of various objects that begin with the letter *P* from discarded magazines—for instance, a purse, a penny, a pencil. The aide put a square of adhesive material on the back of each picture so that it would stick to a flannel board, and then put the collection of these pictures in an attractive box together with an assortment of other pictures.

The next day the aide said to Paul, "Paul, here are pictures of things that have the same beginning sound as your name. Pick them out from the other pictures and put them on the flannel board." The aide put a card with the word [Paul] on the flannel board and then said, "Here is your name as the key word. Find a picture of something that begins with the same sound as your name does."

As Paul made his selections, he and the aide tested each one by saying, for example, "Paul—*p*ig," and "Paul—*p*enny."

Another day the aide had a collection of miniature models from which Paul could select objects with names beginning with the same sound as his name: a purse, a pig, a pan, a pencil, paper, a picture, a pail. Each object that Paul selected was tested in the same way as before—"Paul—*p*urse."

One day Paul found a large pink pocket made from construction paper and fastened to a flannel board. The aide had labeled it Paul's Pocket, and was ready to help Paul as he filled it with pictures of objects beginning with the same sound as his name. Paul searched through old magazines to find suitable pictures to tear or cut out for his pocket. The aide encouraged him and helped him listen to the beginning sound for each object. "Paul—*p*et," said Paul testing the name of what he had found.

When the aide reported to Paul's teacher that Paul had a pocket full of tested pictures, the teacher suggested that Paul show what he had been doing to a small group of children. The aide encouraged each of these children to create a similar collection of pictures of objects with names beginning with the same sound as their own name. In a few days Paul's Pocket was one of a row of similar "pockets" shaped and labeled as follows:

1. Barbara's Basket.
2. Carl's Car.
3. Charles's Chest.
4. Lucy's Locket.
5. Susan's Sun.

When each set of pictures had several tested items, the aide encouraged each of the children to make a booklet of his pictures to take home. When a child was ready to take his booklet home, he asked the aide to help him test each picture once more against his name and his big initial on the front of the booklet. At that time, the aide shared this responsibility with children who had linked their own initial with other words having the same beginning sound. Soon these children were extending their linkage of sound and symbol by helping other children in the ways that the aide had helped them.

### Linking Beginning Sound and Symbol

As soon as a child is aware of the linkage between his initial and the initial sound of his name, an aide can reinforce the teacher-guided experiences that help the child link a symbol to a meaningful sound. For instance, an aide can help the child link the sound of a consonant to the capital and small forms of the corresponding letter of the alphabet; or the sound of a number to its numeral; or a one-syllable word to its printed form. The aide is an important linkage agent and an invaluable supplement to the teacher who guides children as they develop the foundations of reading.

With the leadership of an aide, a small group of children can make a display about the clock sound for the benefit of the entire class. The display probably will include a capital *T* and a small *t*; a picture of a friend whose name is Tom; a top; a toy turtle; pictures that may have been cut out from old magazines to show various objects whose name begins with *T*, and an alphabet book opened to the page for the letter *T*. As the children work with the display, the aide comments and asks questions so that the children are led to frequently use the speech sound of *T* in their conversation.

The activities that the aide enjoyed with Paul and then with the other children working in small groups continue to be useful. As the teacher identifies a linkage that one or more children need to develop, she asks the aide to give them the practice they need. For instance, if Ann and Mark have not yet mastered the linkage between the letter *P* and its speech sound, the aide will use with them the flannel board pictures, the collection of miniature models, and a pink pocket in a series of activities much as he did with Paul.

The aide who has anticipated the letter-linkage needs of children has a series of sound boxes, one for each consonant speech sound. A sound box contains a collection such as the one that one aide had for the speech sound of the letter *B:* a ball, a baby (doll), a brown bear, a boat, a bee, a blue book, a butterfly, and a basket. The aide is prepared to initiate a learning activity by placing objects on the top of the box—a bear, a ball, and a tire—and saying clearly, "This is a bear. This is a ball. This is a tire . . . bear, ball, tire. Who would like to choose something with a name that begins with the same sound as *bell* (or Bob)?" When a child says, "bear," the aide adds, "Tell us what you will choose by saying, 'I'll choose the bear.' " This suggestion helps to advance the children toward a meaningful concept of a sentence and toward using complete sentences.

When the teacher is helping the children to make an experience chart, she often notices one or more children who are not yet linking sound and letter with confidence. With an aide to help her, the teacher can easily make certain that these children gain needed practice through activities that involve the use of the linkage they are in the process of learning.

If the teacher thinks that a child needs help in linking the letter *M, m* to its speech sound, the aide can help the child think about *M, m* in relation to various objects. For instance, the aide can show him picture cards such as those that are commercially available. Using as a key card the card that pictures *milk*, the aide can make sure that the child identifies its beginning sound, and then goes on to test the beginning sound of objects pictured on other cards until the child finds those that match the key card.

When the aide makes a delightful game for several children out of the hunt for *M, m* linked words, the children may want to draw a picture of what they think of in connection with *M*. The drawing and subsequent displaying and labeling of the pictures can involve much use of the *M, m* linkage as the children and the aide discuss what they are doing.

On page 163 is a useful list to help an aide to select or prepare pictures or objects to be linked to key words.

As the aide works with a small group of children, he is alert to guide

| CONSONANT | SUGGESTED KEY WORDS |
|---|---|
| B, b | box, bee, bear, ball, boy, boat, bat |
| D, d | duck, doll, dog |
| F, f | fish, fork, fan |
| G, g | girl, goose, gum |
| H, h | hat, hen, house |
| J, j | jar, jam, jack |
| K, k | key, kite |
| L, l | lamp, leaf, lamb, lion |
| M, m | moon, milk, mouse, mitten |
| N, n | nut, nest, nail |
| P, p | pig, pail, pan, penny, paper |
| R, r | rope, ring, rose, rabbit |
| S, s | sun, soap, sack |
| T, t | top, tie, tent, table |
| V, v | valentine, velvet, vine |
| W, w | wagon, watch |

the children to think of each activity as a pleasant one. Thinking about key words he will be using with the children, the aide thinks of related activities that will be fun for the children:

*B, b*—Read *The B Book* by Phyllis McGinley.[2]

*P, p*—To the tune of "The Muffin Man," sing or say, "Do You Know the Popcorn Man?" Children can pretend they are popcorn popping as they fit this action into the rhythm of the music.

**Words and Their Symbols**

Several activities of aides can help a child to make a direct linkage between an object and its name, or a friend and his name, for instance:

1. Helping a child label what he has brought.
2. Relating a numeral and the corresponding number written in manuscript.
3. Writing in manuscript a brief caption for a picture the child made.
4. Printing a brief title for a story or verse dictated by the child.
5. Helping a child address an envelope for a drawing or a valentine for a friend.
6. Relating word and picture of outdoor signs on a study trip.
7. Linking a printed street name with its pronunciation on a walk.
8. Linking traffic signals in writing with those in colored lights on a walk.

[2] Phyllis McGinley, *The B Book* (New York: The Macmillan Company, 1968).

When such personally meaningful linkages are featured, relatively few repetitions lead to a mastery of them by the child.

*Riddles Reinforce Linkage of Sound and Symbol*

When children are interested in riddles, an aide can facilitate their linking a key word such as *fish* with other words having the same beginning sound through the medium of a riddle. For instance:

> *Aide:* I have a riddle for you. I'm thinking of a word that begins with *F*. It has the same sound that begins *fish.* (Places an F, f card and a fish picture card on the flannel board.) It is a number.

Children guess both four and five. (Aide places each numeral on the flannel board.)

The aide continues with another riddle, by saying, "I'm thinking of another word that begins with *F*. It has the same sound that begins *fish.* We have five of them on each hand." (Fingers)

Other riddles of this kind include familiar descriptions such as:

> We have two of them. (Feet)
> It is something we use at the table. (Fork)
> Cows and horses live there. (Farm)
> It is a baby deer. (Fawn)

In making up such riddles for different key words, the aide is careful to use descriptions of objects and situations that are an integral part of the everyday life of the children he is with. One aide made up the following riddle:

> *Aide:* I am thinking of a word that begins with S. It has the same sound that begins *Sally*. It is the name of a day in the week. (Saturday, Sunday)

Then the aide went on to several other riddles of the same kind:

> We like it for lunch. (Soup, salad, sandwich)
> We use it when we wash our hands. (Soap)
> We see it each day. It looks round and yellow. (Sun)

Helping a child make such linkages is possible when aide and child have built a mutual appreciation for each other, and are not under pressure or tension.

*Helping Children Write Their Names*

As children become aware of name writing, they begin to attempt such writing. An aide as well as a teacher needs to be able to help a child. Sometimes a child is working near one adult, sometimes another. It is important for the child to have a single pattern in his planned learning experiences

MANUSCRIPT WRITING GUIDE SHEET: LETTERS.

and, therefore, for all the adults to use the same form and method of writing his name.[3]

In one school, a manuscript guide sheet such as the one shown was made available to each of the adults participating in the guidance of learn-

[3] Such manuscript guides are commercially available.

ing. This sheet was also sent to the home of each family so that a child might have guidance at home that is similar to that given to him at school. The letter that an aide duplicated for the teacher to send home to parents is presented.

Dear Parents:

Please save for future reference this copy of directions for forming manuscript letters.

Some of the children are ready and eager to learn to write their name. At school we are encouraging them in using manuscript letters, both capitals and lower case.

It is helpful if parents know how we are teaching so that the child is not confused by having different directions at home. Remember that only the first letter is a capital; the remaining letters are small, for example: John.

As they write the letters the children also learn the names of the letters in the alphabet.

We hope you will find this copy useful.

Sincerely yours,

(Mrs.) Mary H. ________
Teacher

Approved:
John S________, Principal

## OTHER LINKING OF WORDS WITH EXPERIENCE

As the teacher skillfully guides children into reading, she can suggest many activities to an aide to be carried out with individuals or with small groups of children to give them enjoyment and additional practice with words. The aide can then guide the children to reinforce the linkages between words and features of their real experience so that they extend their concepts and build their vocabulary. Each day an aide asks the teacher for suggestions, and each day the teacher makes suggestions for activities that help children link together words that are similar, opposite, or otherwise related in meaning.

### Linking Opposites

Words that are opposite in meaning can be readily understood by children who first work with manipulative materials. To develop an understanding of such position opposites as "inside" and "outside," an aide can present a miniature object such as a toy dog, in relation to a box, perhaps as follows:

> *Aide:* Jane, please put the dog *inside* the box. (Jane does so.) Thank you. Now, Jane, put the dog *outside* the box.

As Jane moves the dog to the outside of the box, the aide continues by pointing out that *inside* and *outside* are opposite in meaning. Then the aide develops other opposite concepts as the children pantomime them and talk about what they are doing. These opposites include:

1. In—out.
2. On—off.
3. Near—far.
4. Over—under.
5. High—low.
6. Above—below.
7. Top—bottom.
8. Front—back.

As the aide guides the children, he develops their skill in enjoying their activity at their pace, thus increasing the pleasantness of their experience and their interest in words and concepts.

### Other Teacher Suggestions

The teacher can develop with a larger group of children an activity that would also be valuable for the children to do individually or in a small group at whatever pace is comfortable for them. Having an aide makes it possible for the teacher to provide this additional experience for the children. Experiences that a teacher may ask an aide to provide include:

1. Listening to a child tell about an experience he has had and encouraging him to express his thoughts in sequence by asking such questions as: "What happened first?" "What happened next?" "How did it end?"
2. Helping a child use and enjoy picture books.
3. Helping a child to select a library book.

4. Encouraging a child to add new concepts and new words to his vocabulary.

When the teacher introduces a child who has been living in another country to the class, she will ask the aide to work with him as one of a small group of children. The aide can help the children get further acquainted with each other. He can find out how the children in the other country greet each other at school, and encourage the children to learn greetings in different languages. An aide can do a great deal to help children appreciate both their own language and culture and that of others. Such appreciation enriches their lives at the moment and carries over into travel and other interests in later years.

In general, a teacher encourages an aide to observe in detail what she does to guide the learning of the children. The aide begins by reinforcing such essential elements as those shown in the chart on page 152 entitled "Linkages Basic to Learning to Read." With increasing experience, an aide becomes able to guide more and more aspects of child learning. Throughout this learning process, the teacher and the aide establish and maintain good rapport. They keep in close touch with each other.

# FLANNEL-BOARD POEMS, SONGS, AND STORIES

An aide continuously collects, adapts, and creates poems, songs, and stories to use with children. He knows poems and songs to enhance every learning situation, and he knows stories that he can use to help children develop awareness of a facet of their environment as yet unnoticed, stories to reinforce what their teacher has presented, and stories to help them relate what they have learned to new situations. All of his flannel-board materials are carefully chosen to be entertaining, to guide the learning of the children, and to lead the children into discussion and other activities.

To have his poems, songs, and stories easy to use whenever he needs them, an aide arranges them in a file, each in a separate folder. He may arrange them in alphabetical order by title, by subject, or by the use he expects to make of them to guide learning. He may decide to color code the folders, using a different color for each story or poem. A pocket on the inside of the cover holds the cut-outs arranged in the order of their use.

The songs, poems, and stories presented in this chapter constitute a basic collection of material that will get an aide started in his work. They can be selected from and adapted for use with children of different levels of maturity and experience. They can be adapted for use at different seasons of the year. They can be shortened to make the most of a few minutes, or lengthened to profitably occupy children who will be rejoining a group or going home at an expected time.

Above all, songs and stories are materials for an aide to use to help children experience the fun of learning. Universally, a child or an adult likes to hear them. Listening to a poem or story can lead a child to learn activities in a delightful manner. The wise aide develops skills in telling stories, watching the response of each child and using such feedback to improve his storytelling. He makes a point of continuously enlarging his storehouse of stories, songs, and poems to guide learning, and regularly adds another poem, song, or story to those he already knows.

### Conferring with the Teacher

An aide begins by using songs, poems, and stories to entertain the children and establish rapport with them. The aide progresses to the guidance of their learning through the telling of stories. In doing so he supplements the teacher who has the primary responsibility of guiding pupil learning. It is important that the teacher and her aide coordinate their activities so that pupil learning will progress smoothly and without confusion about what is expected.

An aide regularly confers with the teacher to ask whether his plans will be appropriate for guiding the learning of children he has been helping. The aide also reports regularly on the accomplishment of the children and asks whether the children should continue to work with him. The teacher may feel that other children now have more need for reinforcement in learning what she has presented and would thus like the aide to work with them to guide such learning.

When a teacher has presented a flannel-board story, song, or poem, she will encourage an aide to retell it with the children who wanted to hear it again; to guide the creative activity of children who were inspired to carry the story over into new variations or familiar games; or to carefully guide the children who need more practice in the kind of thinking that the story, song, or poem involved. This chapter suggests stories and poems that an aide should be prepared to reteach, or to initiate with a few children who need further guidance to achieve an expected objective. They are stories, songs, and poems especially useful in helping children progress in preschool and primary grades.

Each story is prepared in advance to use with a flannel board. The aide makes or obtains a set of flannel-board objects, each of which is intrinsically interesting for a child to handle, look at, and work with. The aide thinks through his own pantomime with the flannel-board objects so that it will enhance the telling of the story. He anticipates the response of each child and plans how to guide the child's learning. All of his planning is in terms of what he expects a child to be able to do by the end of the story.

## STORYTELLING

Through the ages storytelling has been a delightful way to pass on cultural heritage to the young. The children love to hear what has happened to others, or what has been imagined about their experiences. A story is intrinsically interesting, and so is the storytelling situation. Each child moves toward the beloved person who is sharing his thoughts with them. Each has the pleasure of being part of a group enjoying a favorite pastime.

To the aide comes the limelight role of storyteller. He prepares for his role carefully. He puts in sequence the flannel-board cut-outs that will emphasize the few major concepts of the story, and will give at least some of the children the opportunity to identify with the storyteller role. The aide puts the cut-outs out of sight and sets the stage for his performance. If he needs the security of notes or books, the aide plans their use so that they do not come between him and the children. He thinks about how to place illustrative pictures at the eye-level of the children, and how to help the children be comfortable and ready to listen to something fascinating. If the aide is preparing to work with experienced listeners, he gives particular attention to an interesting introduction. He wants to help the children learn to appreciate and to do storytelling themselves at school for the other children, and at home for their families.

Flannel-board storytelling is especially welcome for preschool and primary schoolchildren because it combines the fun of imaginative participation with the fun of physical participation. The appropriate cut-out is selected from among other cut-outs, and is placed on the flannel board in an appropriate place. Furthermore, his aide and his peers watch each child act out his role in helping with the story. The child learns by his action, and the satisfying action helps him prepare for more thinking and more action.

Every storyteller and song leader develops his unique style by trying out a song or story with a group and noticing the responses of the group members. An aide selects a poem, song, or story that lends itself to flannel-board presentation because it mentions a few objects and characters easily represented by a few cut-outs. The aide then explores placing the cut-outs on the flannel board so that they enhance the presentation and never interfere with it. The more use an aide makes of a flannel board, the more proficient he becomes in guiding learning through its use, and the more at ease he becomes in working with the learners, helping them develop in the affective (feeling), conative (doing), and cognitive (thinking) domains.

Each aide tries out different emphases and tones of voice with the children. He discards those that do not help the children learn and retains and improves those that the children enjoy. Good use of a flannel board in guiding learning is a happy experience for everyone concerned and a springboard to creative activities.

Here are suggestions that most flannel-board users have found helpful:

1. Use a good size flannel board of a suitable background color (e.g., two feet by three feet in soft green or sky blue).
2. Make large cut-outs for the objects or characters essential to the

concept or relationship to be learned by the children, not cut-outs of every character or every object in the story. Pellon or felt and construction paper cut-outs are marked with crayon or felt-tip pens to show essential detail the children observe. The construction paper cut-outs require a square of sandpaper, felt, or other adhesive to help them adhere to the flannel board.

3. In telling a story, saying a poem, or singing a song, give your complete attention to those who are listening. Avoid any interruption or any potential distraction, such as having to glance down at a paper or a cut-out. Practice with the cut-outs in advance so that the story, poem, or song is well memorized and the placing of cut-outs is done firmly, easily, and casually.
4. Place the flannel board so that each child has a good view of it. Have the cut-outs arranged in a pile in order of use and placed out of sight in a box or in your lap.
5. Develop a technique for placing cut-outs on the flannel board so that their placement guides the eyes of children from left to right and from the top to the bottom as in reading (e.g., sit on the side of the board at the children's left and place cut-outs on it with the left hand).

**From Listening to Telling**

After listening to a story they have enjoyed hearing over and over again, children like to tell the story too. A flannel-board story that has been introduced by the teacher and retold by the aides can be left in its folder next to the flannel board for the children to use. When an aide notices a child working with the flannel-board cut-outs, he encourages another child to hear the story while the first child tells it. The aide may be a listener too, and in that role he can encourage creativity by reminding the storyteller, "It's your story. You're telling it the way you want to." If the storyteller wants to tell the story as he heard it, the aide can ask a question whenever the storyteller needs a cue to remember what happened next.

Telling a story at school can lead to retelling the story at home. If a child asks to take a story home, an aide can encourage him to select or create cut-outs to use on an upholstered chair or davenport or other rough textured material, and a folder like his in which to carry the cut-outs home. After the child has created his cut-outs, he can use them on an individual flannel board at school, to be sure that he has all the pieces he needs for telling his story. Then he can put the pieces in his folder and assume a new role in his family—storyteller.

More experienced children can include printed words among their flannel board cut-outs. An aide encourages them to print words to label the important cut-outs in their story. The aide also encourages them to label their folder, first with their own name, and then with the name of the story or any aspect of it that they think is important.

## POEM: A GAY LITTLE CLOWN

To introduce children to storytelling with the flannel board, the aide can use a short poem that introduces a single character. A poem of this type that is well within the area of interest of young children is entitled "A Gay Little Clown."

1. Formulate objectives:
   a. A child becomes aware of the primary and secondary colors and brown and black.
   b. A child creates original flannel board cut-outs with which he tells the poem.
   c. A child clearly pronounces the speech sound of *L*.
   d. A more experienced child labels each balloon with the printed name of its color.
2. Prepare cut-outs for use on a flannel board:
   a. A clown
   b. Eight balloons, each of a different color and each with a string attached

| red | yellow | blue | brown |
|---|---|---|---|
| orange | green | purple | black |

   c. Put the clown at the bottom left corner of the flannel board. Arrange other cut-outs.
   d. Tell the poem.

A Gay Little Clown

This gay little clown has pretty balloons,
Balloons of many colors.
He has
One that is blue, blue as the sky, or blue as the sea
(put on blue balloon);
One that is green, green as the grass, and green as a tree
(put on green one);
One that is yellow, bright as the sun
(put on yellow balloon);
One that is purple, like a plum
(put on purple balloon);
One that is orange, like the fruit, round, juicy, and sweet
(put on orange one);

One that is red, like some apples we eat
(put on red one);
One that is brown, like the trunk of a tree
(put on brown balloon);
And one that is black, like the old witch's hat
(put on black balloon).

### Additional Learning Activities

"Which color balloon would you choose?" is a question an aide asks the children in the small group to help them associate the name of a color with a familiar object of that color. If Alice responds to the question by choosing the blue balloon after saying the word, *blue*, she then stands to one side while the game continues through a selection of all the colors.

If Alice does not select the blue balloon, the aide asks the group of children, "Is that a blue balloon?" Then Alice chooses someone from the group to help her find the blue balloon. Later the aide provides a further opportunity for Alice to associate the word *blue* with objects of that color, and makes sure that Alice has succeeded in making such linkages accurately.

Putting the balloons back in the hands of the clown gives further opportunity to help each child in a group link the name of a color with familiar objects of that color. "If you have the blue balloon will you please return it to the flannel board?" the aide asks. As the child does so, the aide asks, "Can you tell us something else that is usually blue in color?" Or he may ask, "Do you see something blue here in our room?" or, "Who is wearing something that is blue?" From the responses of the children, the aide infers which children need additional experience with naming colors of familiar objects, and talks later with the teacher about how to provide such experience.

When a child uses a work period for making his own clown and balloon cut-outs, an aide has an opportunity to obtain feedback about the child's color-recognition skill. The aide asks, "Do you have a balloon of each color?" If one balloon is missing, he asks, "Which color balloon do you *not* have yet?" By comparing the balloons that he has with those that the clown has on the flannel board, the child can find out for himself which color balloon he should add to his clown's balloons. The aide is careful not to supply information but to encourage the child to discover for himself the other color of balloon for his clown to have. The aide then praises the child for his success. The aide points out the child's accomplishment and helps him appreciate it.

With children who need additional practice with matching names of colors and objects of that color, an aide can play the game of "What Color Is Missing?" by using a set of real balloons, each of a different color, or a set of simulated balloons cut from construction paper of different colors.

The children in the group all close their eyes while one child quickly removes a balloon and hides it. They open their eyes when the aide says, "Open your eyes to see which color balloon is missing." The aide rewards successful naming of the color with praise, "Good! You have sharp eyes."

With children experienced in naming primary and secondary colors, an aide can add tones and tints to the color of the balloons, for instance, pink, lavender, light green, maroon.

The aide can also use the clown and his balloons to help children learn numbers: adding a balloon and increasing the number that the clown has; removing a balloon and decreasing the number that he has.

An aide also encourages the children to use their own clown and balloon cut-outs in creative storytelling. He notices the child who thinks of his clown as selling balloons and saying, "Who will buy my red balloon, red as an apple?" The aide enjoys with the child the delightful concept he has formulated, and later mentions it to the teacher. The child also enjoys the broadening of comparisons as he hears, "Brown as sticks," "Brown as a teddy bear," "Black as a pencil lead," and so on. His appreciative smile is real encouragement for creativity.

When an aide works with children interested in printed words, he prints the names of the colors in one-half inch sizes, and backs each printed name with a square of sandpaper or other adhesive. He arranges these color words along the left-hand edge of the flannel board that has the clown with his balloons. Then as he says the poem, the aide invites a volunteer to put the word *blue* next to the blue balloon, and so on through the word *black* next to the black balloon.

Especially when an aide works with a child who is learning to hear and speak the sound of the letter *L*, he is careful to pronounce the word *balloon* so that the child has a clear pattern to imitate. He may ask him, "What color balloon did you choose?" and expect him to say in reply both the name of the color and the word *balloon*. In a similar way the aide can help each child to pronounce color words clearly.

## STORY: THE LITTLE ELF WHO LISTENED

When the teacher introduces the concept of listening and when she reminds the children to listen quietly, the well-prepared aide can use the story entitled, "The Little Elf Who Listened," to help certain children suggested by the teacher, perhaps children who need to think frequently about using voices which are just right for the situation they are in. If the teacher uses the story with the entire group of children, she probably will ask the aide to tell the same story to children who were absent as well as to children who want to hear the story again. At any time during the year, the teacher may ask the aide to tell the story to children who need a reminder about using appropriate voices.

1. Formulate objectives:
   a. The child will notice when voices are too loud, too soft, or just right.
   b. The child will have his tone of voice soft and quiet when he is indoors.
2. Prepare cut-outs for the flannel board:
   a. A large elf almost as tall as the height of the flannel board but without ears.
   b. Three pairs of ears: one large pair, one middle-sized pair, and one small pair.
   c. Tell the story.

THE LITTLE ELF WHO LISTENED

Do you know what an elf is? No one ever saw an elf, but we can pretend that it is a little boy about the size of a squirrel. (Put elf at left side of flannel board.)

WHAT EARS DOES THE ELF NEED NOW?

This elf I am going to tell you about lived at the edge of a big woods. He played with noisy, chattering chipmunks, with bushy-tailed squirrels, and with hopping rabbits. These animals were his good friends.

Now this elf had something very special. His fairy godmother had given him *three pairs* of listening ears! That was six ears, wasn't it? He had a pair of big ears (put at top right). A pair of middle-sized ears (put at center right). And a pair of tiny ears (put below other pairs). When the little elf wore his *big* ears (put big ears on elf), he could hear the faintest sounds in the woods: leaves falling from trees, the wind whispering to flowers, or the water rippling over stones in the little stream. He could hear dogs barking far, far away. The little elf wore his big ears to tell his friends the squirrels, the chipmunks, and the rabbits, about dogs out hunting so that his friends could run and hide. They were very thankful. (Remove large ears.)

The little elf wore his *tiny* ears (put tiny ears on elf) when the storms came and the wind blew loudly, and when the thunder roared and crashed. The little animals who had only one pair of ears apiece, were frightened by the loud noises, but their friend, the elf, told them that the wind and the thunder were important to have. Rain usually comes with wind and thunder, and rain is needed to help plants grow. (Remove tiny ears.)

Most of the time the little elf wore his *middle-sized* ears. (Put ears on elf.) He liked them best of all. He listened to all the middle-sized sounds with them. Not the very loud and not the very soft sounds, but the sounds for every day.

One morning some children came to the woods to pick flowers. "What shall we do with our flowers?" a little girl asked.

A boy called Billy said, "Let's take them to school."

"Let's," the little girl agreed. "We can show them to the other children."

The little elf listened and wished that he could go to school. He wanted to see and hear what the children did with what they brought. He told his friends the chipmunks, the squirrels, and the rabbits about his wish.

But they said, "No. An elf can't go to school. School is for children."

But the little elf decided he would go to school anyway. So the next morning he crept out of his warm bed of leaves under a toadstool, and skipped down the road toward school.

Soon he came to a big building. Girls and boys were playing out on the playground. A red, white, and blue flag waved high on a pole, so the little elf knew he was really at school. Just then he heard a bell ring and watched the children line up and go inside. Quietly the little elf slipped inside too.

*You* were the boys and girls playing outside. You are the children that the little elf followed. He is here in this room right now. You can't see him because no one can see an elf. But he is here and he will see what a good time we have. And he will listen to the voices we use.

Which pair of ears do you think he will use?

—His tiny ears, because you talk so loud that you sound like a thunderstorm? or his

—Big ears, because you talk too low, as if you were afraid of your own voice? or his

—Middle-sized ears, because you are talking in quiet, soft, inside voices?

Remember, the little elf likes his middle-sized ears best!

—Anonymous

## STORY: SCAT-THE-CAT

An aide can use this cat story to help children associate a color with its name, either spoken or in print; or to help children develop the speech sounds of *S* and *T*. But it is especially useful in helping a child who may feel different from people around him and who thus needs to remember the importance of being himself.

1. Formulate objectives:
   a. The child appreciates the importance of being comfortable with what he is.
   b. The child associates the name of a color with familiar objects in that color.
   c. The child makes more clearly the speech sounds of *S* and *T* as he tells his story with cut-outs.
2. Prepare cut-outs for the flannel board:
   a. Five cats, identical in shape but each of a different color (e.g., black, green, blue, yellow, and red).
   b. Tell the story.

### SCAT-THE-CAT

Once upon a time there was a little black cat whose name was Scat-the-Cat. (Put black cat at left of flannel board.) One day he looked around and saw that all his brothers and sisters were black too. He thought he would like to be some other color. He said, (Aide sits straight and proud.)

I'm Scat-the-Cat. (Thumbs in armpits.)
I'm sassy and fat. (Point finger and then shape a fat figure with both hands.)
And I can change my color (Shake finger.)
Just like that! (Snap fingers briskly.)

All of a sudden, at the snap of his fingers, he was a *green* cat. (Put green cat at the right of the black cat.) Green like the leaves and green like the grass. He went out to play with his friends and what do you think happened? His friends did not see him because he was just the same color as the grass and the trees. He was so disappointed. He didn't think it was any fun at all to be a green cat. So he said, (Gestures as before.) (Children say the poem with the aide.)

I'm Scat-the-Cat.
I'm sassy and fat.
And I can change my color
Just like that!

And then what color was he? (Put blue cat at the right of the green cat.) Yes, he was *blue* all over. Blue like the water; blue like the sky. He was so proud of his pretty new color that he decided he would take a walk and let everyone admire it.

But do you know what happened? He came to a little pond of water. He leaned away over to look at himself in the water. Kerplop! Splash! Into the pond he went! Right down into the deep blue water, and back up to the surface. Poor little Scat-the-Cat had not learned how to swim yet. He was frightened. He called for help. He called so loudly that his friends heard him. They ran to the pond and looked down into the blue water. They could not see him because he was blue like the water.

It just happened that his friend, Timothy Turtle, came swimming by. He told Scat-the-Cat to climb on his back. Then Timothy Turtle carried him safely back to shore. Scat-the-Cat was so grateful. He thanked his friend over and over again for saving his life. Right there he decided never again to take a chance like that! He thought he had been blue long enough, so he said: (Gestures as before.) (Children and aide say poem.)

I'm Scat-the-Cat.
I'm sassy and fat.
And I can change my color
Just like that!

And what color was he then? (Put yellow cat to the right of the blue cat.) Yes, he was *yellow,* like the sun. He was very proud of his new color. He decided that he would take a walk through the jungle.

Whom do you suppose he met in the jungle? He met his Cousin Leo, the Lion. Leo, the Lion, looked at Scat-the-Cat and said, "What are you doing in that yellow coat? I'm the only animal in this jungle that is supposed to wear yellow!" Leo, the Lion, growled so loudly and so fiercely that Scat-the-Cat was frightened, so frightened that he ran all the way home.

As soon as he was able to catch his breath, he said: (Children and aide say poem with gestures.)

I'm Scat-the-Cat.
I'm sassy and fat.
And I can change my color
Just like that!

And what color was he then? (Put red cat to the right of the yellow cat.) Yes, he was *red* like an apple. He decided he would go out and play with his brothers and sisters and all his nice friends.

What do you suppose happened? When his friends and his brothers and his sisters saw him, they all stopped playing and just stared at him. Then they started laughing and making fun of him. "Ha, ha, ha!" they said. "Whoever heard of a red cat?" Do you think they were very polite cats? No, they were not. No one played with him. They all ran away to play and left poor little Scat-the-Cat sitting there all by himself.

He felt sad. Soon he started thinking. He decided he didn't want to be a *red* cat any more. (Take red cat off.) Nor a yellow cat. (Take off yellow cat.)

And he didn't want to be a *blue* cat any more because he might not be lucky enough to have his friend Timothy Turtle come swimming by again. (Take off blue cat.)

He didn't want to be a *green* cat because then he would be like the grass and trees, and none of his friends would see him. (Take the green cat off.)

But do you know what he thought? He thought he would rather be just himself, a pretty black cat like all his brothers and sisters, and have lots of friends to play with.

So after that, Scat-the-Cat was always happy being himself, a black cat.

—Anonymous

### Suggestions for Telling the Story

With children who are becoming acquainted with a flannel board and with colors, the aide uses only the first and the last of the story of Scat-the-

Cat, and talks only about the black cat who tried to be a green cat. With more experienced children, the aide can add as many of the color changes as will enable the children to know well one more color than they previously knew.

To help experienced children to transfer their learning of colors to other color situations, the aide varies the order in which the colored cats appear, and also varies the color of the hero, Scat-the-Cat. If Scat-the-Cat was a black cat, the next time he may be a gray cat. Another telling of this story might make him a white cat. Such variations emphasize the role of the storyteller in making the story what he wants it to be. The children like to take on the decision-making power of the storyteller by suggesting the color that Scat-the-Cat decided to be next.

The participation of the children in the story depends on what they are learning. Children who have been noticing colors of objects welcome the opportunity to mention, for instance, "green like our plants," "blue like my dress," "yellow like Tom's shirt," "red like a radish." Children who are working with color words like to select the printed word for the color mentioned and to put it on or under the cat of that color.

All of the children enjoy saying the poem with the aide, carefully putting the final *T* sound on the end of "Scat," "cat," "fat," and "that"; and clearly pronouncing "Scat" and "sassy." They like to say it clearly the way the aide does.

After enjoying the story, the children like to make a set of cut-outs to use on their individual flannel boards. Out of half a sheet of construction paper, each child creates cats of green, blue, yellow, and red, as well as a cat that is black or gray or white as he chooses to make it. The child completes each cat by pasting a piece of adhesive material on the back of it, perhaps a piece of sandpaper or flannel. When the child has his cut-outs ready to use on his flannel board, he tells his story to a friend or two, and makes sure that he is ready to tell it at home. With the help of an aide, the child staples together two pieces of construction paper to make a folder with which to carry home his cut-outs intact. He tells his story of Scat-the-Cat to his family by using the cut-outs on a rough textured material (e.g., upholstery of a chair or couch).

More experienced children working with Scat-the-Cat like to use numeral cut-outs for counting the cats, and later, printed cut-outs such as the title, "Scat-the-Cat."

## SONG: HOW MANY PEOPLE LIVE AT OUR HOUSE?

Early in the school term young children link their new experience at school to the home experience they have had and are continuing to have. A song with the flannel board can help them do that at the same time that it helps them build new tools for learning such as the concept of "How Many?" One of the songs that a teacher finds useful in helping children link home with school is adapted from a song entitled, "How Many People Live at Your House?" written by Lucille F. Wood and Louise Binder Scott.[1] As soon as the teacher has presented the song to the children, an aide can help small groups of the children to work with it more fully.

1. Formulate objectives:
   a. The child talks about the members of his family.
   b. The child counts the members of his family.
   c. The child formulates a concept of *family* that will fit his own and other families.
   d. The child develops his concept of *growing up* into adult family roles (e.g., father, uncle, grandfather).
2. Prepare cut-outs for flannel board selecting from flannel of different skintone colors:
   One mother    Two boys
   One father    Two girls

FUN WITH FAMILY CUT-OUTS REINFORCES *FAMILY* CONCEPTUALIZATION.

[1] "How Many People Live at Your House?" reprinted by permission from *Singing Fun* by Lucille F. Wood and Louise Binder Scott. Copyright © 1954 by McGraw-Hill, Inc.

a. With more experienced children, add numerals within their experience.
b. Later count the extended as well as the immediate family, using numerals.

3. Sing or say the words; placing the appropriate cut-outs:

How Many People Live at Our House? [2]

How many people live at our house?
How many people live at our house?
One, my father; two, my mother;
Three, my sister; four, my brother.
There's one more, now let me see!
Oh, yes, of course, it must be me!
How many people live at our house?
How many people live at your house?
—Louise Binder Scott

**Suggestions for Using the Song**

By using one skin-tone color at one time and another tone at another time an aide can help the children realize that a family can have various skin tones, and can help them in becoming acquainted with people throughout their community and the world.

Talking about family often leads the children into expressing their feeling with other media, perhaps with paint at the easel, or with scissors and paste at the cut-and-paste table. It may lead to typing a simple page for the children to take home to their family. Here is one such statement prepared by an aide at the request of the teacher:

FAMILIES

The world is made of boys and girls, and grown-ups in families.

Little girls who grow up are mothers, aunts, and grandmas. Little boys who grow up are fathers, uncles, and grandpas.

All of these make families. Oh, aren't you glad you're part of these?

The statement was followed by a picture the child drew of his own family with the caption "Here Is My Family."

## STORY: THE LIFE OF A PUMPKIN

In October when teachers and other people talk with children about pumpkins and Jack-o'-Lanterns, an aide helps to guide the children to learn

[2] Ibid.

about how plants grow. The aide knows the life story of the pumpkin well and is prepared to tell it to one or more children who were absent when the teacher told it to the large group of children, or to tell it to other children as they reinforce what they have learned and go on to learn more of the sequence of plant growth for a pumpkin.

1. Formulate objectives for the children to achieve as you tell the story. These will include one or more of the following:
   a. The child will save pumpkin seeds to grow a pumpkin the following year, or to feed to birds.
   b. The child will eat pumpkin seeds.
   c. The child will accurately use similar and contrasting words, such as *tiny* and *small,* and *thin* and *fat.*
   d. The child will notice aspects of plant growth, especially changes in size and color.
   e. The child will tell in order the observable sequence of the growth of a pumpkin.
   f. The child will develop and use such concepts as:
      1) Some birds eat seeds.
      2) Farmers plant pumpkin seeds and grow pumpkins to sell.
      3) The market has pumpkins to sell.
2. Prepare cut-outs for the flannel board:
   a. A pumpkin seed. (Use a real seed if possible.)
   b. Brown earth.
   c. Green pumpkin leaves.
   d. Yellow buds, bell-shaped.
   e. Yellow flowers.
   f. Long, brown, thin vines with curled ends—tendrils.
   g. A tiny green pumpkin about the size of a pea.
   h. A larger green pumpkin about the size of an apple.
   i. A still larger yellow pumpkin.
   j. A big orange pumpkin.
   k. A Jack-o'-Lantern.
3. Tell the story thinking of the flannel board divided into four quadrants:

   1, 2,
   3, 4.

THE LIFE OF A PUMPKIN

A pumpkin seed looks like this. (Put the seed at the bottom left of quadrant 1.)

Last year I found this seed inside a pumpkin. It was one of many seeds in a soft, sticky mass we call "pulp." I dried it off and kept it to show to you.

A PUMPKIN GROWS ON A FLANNEL BOARD.

A farmer does the same thing with some of the pumpkins he grows. He takes out the seeds, dries them, and then keeps them in a cool, dry place all winter. In the spring, he plants the seeds in the soft, brown earth. (Put the earth cut-out over the seed.) The sun shines down to warm the earth around the little seed. The rain brings it water to drink, and very soon it begins to grow. It sprouts right up through the earth until we begin to see the little plant it grows into.

The sun and the rain help the seed grow and grow until long, thin vines crawl along the ground. (Put on the vine cut-out.) The vine has little, curled ringlets called tendrils that reach out and cling to a fence or a wall. Soon the vine begins to climb up, up off the ground.

Pretty green leaves grow on the vine. (Put on leaves.)

Then little yellow, bell-shaped buds appear. (Put bud on vine.)

Soon a bud opens into a pretty yellow flower that bees and other insects like to visit. (Put yellow flowers on vine.)

When the flower wilts and its petals fall off, we can see a tiny green pumpkin about the size of a pea. (Put the pea-size pumpkin in place of one of the flowers.)

The tiny green pumpkin grows and grows until it is about the size of an apple. (In quadrant 2 place a vine cut-out with the apple-size pumpkin hanging from it.)

The sun shines warmly and the rain falls helping the little green pumpkin to keep on growing. Soon it is a little larger, plump and fat, and yellow. (In quadrant 3 place a vine with the large yellow pumpkin hanging from it.)

The sun and the moisture help the little pumpkin to grow, grow, grow! Its color gets brighter and before long the farmer has a big, fat, orange pumpkin! (In quadrant 4 place a vine with the big orange pumpkin hanging from it.)

The farmer gathered the big, fat, orange pumpkin and other pumpkins he had grown like it. He put them in his truck and took them into town to sell to the vegetable man at the market. Our teacher bought one of them in the vegetable department of the market near where she lives, and brought it to school to make a Jack-o'-Lantern. (Display it.)

### Leading into Other Learning Activities

The aide can guide the children into a discussion of the Jack-o'-Lantern activity, or he may talk with them about what a mother can do with a pumpkin that she buys at the market, and thus move into a discussion of desserts such as pumpkin pies, pumpkin pudding, and pumpkin ice cream.

In telling the story another day, an aide can use pumpkin seeds to show the children how to enjoy eating them. That day he may continue the story by saying:

> Sometimes the farmer has more pumpkins than the store needs for its customers. When this happens, the farmer cuts the pumpkins into pieces and feeds them to his cows, pigs, and chickens, which is a special treat for them. Birds fly down to get a share of the seeds. People in town also like to eat pumpkin seeds. They buy them at the market in little bags like salted peanuts. I bought a bag of pumpkin seeds today.

As the children enjoy eating the nuts, the aide helps them learn how to peel off the thin shell on the outside and eat the sweet little nut that is inside.[3] They talk about drying and eating the seeds from the Jack-o'-Lantern, and about how good the pumpkin seeds are that the birds also eat. The children sometimes like to hear or talk about another story entitled *Pumpkinseeds*.[4]

Each time that the aide tells the story, he helps the children review

[3] Roast in oven at 350 degrees. Add butter and salt to taste.
[4] Stephen A. Yezback, *Pumpkinseeds* (Indianapolis, Ind.: The Bobbs-Merrill Co., Inc., 1969).

the sequence of plant growth by asking them appropriate questions in sequence:

*Where do the seeds come from?*
*What does the farmer do with the seeds?*
*What helps the seeds to grow into a plant?*
*What comes up through the ground first?*
*Then what happens?*

Early in October, if the teacher agrees, an aide creates a bulletin board that shows the sequence of events pictured with the flannel board. He may arrange the four events in sequence from left to right across the bulletin board, and add a fifth event: the Jack-o'-Lantern. The children will enjoy the display all through the mouth of October if the teacher or aide calls their attention to it from time to time. The bulletin board or the completed flannel board can be used with more experienced children who want to tell the story of the life of a pumpkin using the sequence of cues pictured.

With three or four children at a time, an aide can extend the enjoyment of the story by helping them learn a song entitled, "In a Pumpkin Patch." [5] Out of construction paper, an aide cuts a small green pumpkin, a medium-sized yellow pumpkin, and a large orange pumpkin. He pastes each of these on a sheet of twelve-inch by eighteen-inch black construction paper. He then cuts a hole in the center of each pumpkin for a child to put his face in. The three masks can be held by their wearers while they sit and say or sing their part of the song.

## SONG: A HALLOWEEN SONG

A story can lead into a song, and a song can lead into other songs and stories. Both song and story can lead into creative learning activities with reminders of previous experience, with various art media, and with more words and songs. At Halloween time an aide has an excellent opportunity to help individual and small groups of children to have a richer learning experience if he has songs and poems as well as activities and stories at his fingertips. Here is a song adapted from one entitled, "This Is Halloween," a song that helps young children to understand a simple number sequence as well as the lore of a holiday. Placing cut-outs on the flannel board reinforces their learning of the number sequence through physical and visual activity accompanying the hearing and saying of the words. Thus the song enables the aide to provide a multisensory learning experience that involves visual, kinesthetic, tactile, as well as auditory senses.

[5] Lucille F. Wood and Louise Binder Scott, *Singing Fun* (New York: McGraw-Hill Book Co., 1954), p. 9.

1. Formulate objectives:
   a. A child reviews the sequence and concepts of numbers from one through five.
   b. A child links skeletons, witches, goblins, pumpkins, and other children to Halloween.
   c. A child sings a song musically and in sequence both at school and at home.
2. Prepare cut-outs for principal words of the song for flannel-board use:
   a. One skelton
   b. Two witches
   c. Three goblins
   d. Four pumpkins
   e. Five children
3. Guide children in learning the song: (Starting at the top of the flannel or felt board, place the rows of figures in keeping with each stanza of the song.)

THIS IS HALLOWEEN [6]

One little skeleton (put one skeleton at top) hopping up and down,
Hopping up and down, hopping up and down;
One little skeleton hopping up and down
For this is Halloween!

Continue with one or more of the following stanzas according to the experience of the children:

Two little witches flying through the air
(put on two witches in a second row)

Three little goblins skipping down the street
(put three goblins in third row)

Four little pumpkins walking in a row
(put four pumpkins in fourth row)

Five little children playing trick or treat
(put five child figures in last row).

The aide repeats the words of the song as he follows the flannel-board sequence with his hand. As the children gain experience with the song they replace the aide at the flannel board, leaving the aide free to enhance the song by playing it on an instrument such as an autoharp or a piano. More mature children are soon eager to create their own flannel-board figures.

[6] From *Sing a Song* by Roberta McLaughlin and Lucille F. Wood. Copyright © 1969 Bowmar Publishing Corp., Glendale, California. Used by permission.

With the guidance of the aide, each child individually places his figures on a flannel board as he sings the song easily and musically. The number in each set of cut-outs gives the child the cues that he needs to recall the stanzas of the song in sequence. The opportunity for a satisfying time in front of his peers and realistic praise from an appreciative aide encourage the child to put his cut-outs into an envelope with a copy of the song to take home to his family.

## STORY: THE BOY WHO HAD TO DECIDE

Here is a story that can be used at Easter time. It helps children to enjoy coloring Easter eggs and to appreciate colors either by matching them or by abstracting the concept of its color from a familiar object.

1. Formulate objectives:
   a. The child is able to abstract from familiar objects the concepts of their colors.
   b. The child is able to match one flannel-board object with another of the same color.
   c. The child becomes interested in coloring Easter eggs.
2. Prepare cut-outs for the flannel board:
   a. Objects: green trees, orange carrots, blue waves, yellow ducks, red fire truck, brown cow, bunch of purple grapes, nine eggs (four-and-one-half to five inches long). One egg of each of the following colors:
      white orange
      red purple
      green blue
      brown yellow
      all of the eight colors
   b. Optional: An Easter rabbit holding a paintbrush (seven to twelve inches tall).
3. Arrange flannel-board objects in the sequence in which they are to be used in telling the story and place the pile of them in an envelope attached to the story folder.
4. Tell the story. (Have the pile of flannel-board objects handy and out of sight of the children, e.g., in your lap.)

To begin, place a white egg at the top of the flannel board. Scatter the monocolored eggs at random at the bottom right. As the story unfolds, place the other flannel-board objects (e.g., trees, carrots . . .) down the left side of the flannel board.

After Benedict in the story asks, "If I wanted my egg the same color, what color would it be?" invite one child in the group to find the egg of the same color (e.g., green) and place it next to the object (e.g., tree). The aide may say, "Mary, will you find that colored egg? Find the egg that is the same color as the trees."

If any child selects an egg of a color he likes rather than the matching color, the aide asks the children, "Is that the matching color?" The aide then asks the child, "Would you like to ask someone to find the egg he thinks is the same color as the (e.g., ocean)?" At no point should the aide say, "You're wrong," or "You made a mistake."

If a child loses interest, or time for storytelling is at an end, the aide should say with Benedict, "Oh, dear, oh, dear," and conclude the story.

### THE BOY WHO HAD TO DECIDE

Once upon a time there was a little boy named Benedict who didn't know what color he wanted his egg to be for Easter. (Put white egg at top of flannel board.)

He said, "I've always liked the color of trees. (Put trees at left.) If I wanted my egg the same color, what color would it be?" (A child puts on a green egg.)

"But then I like the color of carrots," Benedict said. (Put on carrots under trees.) "Perhaps I should have my egg that color." (Another child puts on an orange egg.)

"Of course, the color of water is very pretty too." (Put on waves.) "I wonder how my egg would look if it were the color of the ocean?" (Child puts on blue egg.)

Then Benedict thought of ducks in the meadow. (Put on ducks.) He decided then and there to have his egg be the same color as the ducks. (Child puts on yellow egg.)

But at that moment a big red fire truck drove by. (Put on fire truck.) Benedict said, "That's the color for me! I'll make my egg the color of that fire truck!" (Child puts red egg on.)

A moment later, Benedict saw a brown cow standing near a grape vine. (Put on cow and grapes.) Then he tried to decide whether to use the color of the cow (child puts on brown egg), or the color of the grapes. (Child puts on purple egg.)

"Oh, dear, oh, dear," said Benedict. "I must make up my mind. All those colors are so pretty!"

Just then who should appear but the Easter Rabbit. (Put on Easter Rabbit.) "Don't worry, Benedict," said he. "I know what to do!" (Remove white egg and put many-colored egg in its place.) And what he did made Benedict very happy.

Do you know what he did?

—Anonymous

### Using the Story

In planning the use of the Benedict story, a classroom aide can talk with the teacher to determine the colors the children have studied and can decide with her how to lengthen, shorten, or otherwise adapt the story to make it especially appropriate for the children the aide is to help. The teacher may make suggestions to the aide such as the following:

1. Reinforce the learning of colors by having Benedict consider only those colors the children have already studied (e.g., the three primary colors).
2. Introduce one more color to prepare slow learners for what the teacher will soon be presenting (e.g., add one secondary color to the primary colors that Benedict considers).
3. To find out whether children may be color blind, observe a child who has difficulty in learning to match colors, and mention his behavior to the teacher so that she can refer the child to the school nurse. The child may need a medical examination.
4. To find out if a child is able to say the names of colors, ask him, "What color is the egg that Mary is putting next to the tree?" before describing what Mary did, "Mary has put the green egg next to the green tree."
5. When some children are ready to work with printed words for each color, arrange a column of the printed words along one edge of the flannel board and select the appropriate one to place next to the flannel-board object and matching colored egg. Later each child will be able to make the selection himself.

### Adapting the Story

In the spring, the story "The Boy Who Had to Decide" can be used in connection with coloring eggs either for Easter or for an Egg tree, or to introduce a friendly adviser who may be a parent or someone else, in place of the Easter Rabbit. In December, by omitting all references to Easter, the story can be used with children coloring ornaments for a Christmas tree. Then make changes in the felt cut-outs and in the words of the story (i.e., "ball" for "egg"). Santa Claus can replace the Easter Rabbit.

## STORY: THE FIRST TEDDY BEAR

1. Formulate objectives:
   a. The child reinforces his concepts of colors: brown, tan, black, red.

b. The child is able to consider several alternative choices.
c. The child is able to make a selection of what is suitable.
d. The child appreciates the fact that the teddy bear had to be his unique self.

2. Prepare cut-outs for the flannel board:
   a. Brown furry body (e.g., from brown construction paper, with fur simulated by crayon)
   b. Two brown furry legs
   c. Two brown furry arms
   d. Four paws
   e. One head of a Scotty dog
   f. One head of a horse
   g. One head of an elephant
   h. One head of a rooster
   i. One head of a pig
   j. One brown furry head with two black eyes, one black shiny nose, and a cherry-colored mouth, but without ears
   k. One pair of brown furry ears
3. Tell the story so that the children can see its drama unfold:

THE FIRST TEDDY BEAR

Once upon a time, there was a Great Toy Maker who created all kinds of toys to please boys and girls. Each day he worked on a new toy. As the toy was finished, it gave him great joy.

One day, as he sat at his work bench, he picked up some soft brown fur. "This would make a lovely toy," he said. So he made a fat chubby body of soft brown fur. (Put body on the flannel board.)

Next, he made two long, brown, furry legs. (Add the legs to the body on the flannel board.)

Then the Toy Maker made two short, furry, brown arms. (Put the arms on the figure taking form on the flannel board.)

Lastly, he added a little tan paw to each arm and leg. (Add the paws to the arms.)

Then the Toy Maker stepped back to see what he had made. Something was missing. "Of course, the head!" he said. And the Toy Maker thought: "What sort of head should he give this toy?

He finally thought out loud.

"Perhaps one like I used on the Scotty dog would do." So he put it on the fat, furry body. (Put the Scotty head on the flannel board figure.)

As he stood back to look at his toy, he shook his head, "No, that Scotty's head won't do at all!"

He tried a horse's head on the furry body. (Put the horse's head on the figure.)

He still wasn't satisfied.

Next, he tried an elephant's head. (Put the elephant's head on the figure.)

He knew, as he stepped back and considered the toy, that the elephant's head wouldn't do either. It just didn't look right on that fat, brown, furry body.

Then he tried a rooster's head. (Put the rooster's head on the figure.)

And a pig's head. (Put the pig's head on the figure.)

Then he said, "It is very plain to see that this new toy must have his own special head."

So he made a large furry, brown ball, and on this he put:

—a black, shiny nose,

—two black eyes and,

—a round, cherry-red mouth.

Last of all, he added:

—two brown, furry ears!

"Now, I think that will be all!" said the Toy Maker.

As he stepped back to look at his newest toy, he smiled; then broke into a laugh! He laughed and laughed, until the tears spilled out of his eyes and fell down over his cheeks. This was a happy day for the Great Toy Maker, for he had just made the very first Teddy Bear!

—Anonymous

### Encouraging Creative Activity

With children getting acquainted with flannel-board stories, the aide can use the head of only the Scotty dog. Children more experienced in identifying animals by their appearance like to review familiar animals and add a new one.

If what experienced children need is available, they construct cut-outs to make their own teddy bear flannel-board story. An aide, therefore, prepares piles of construction paper for them, perhaps as follows:

nine-inch brown squares (to cut the body)
four-inch by seven-inch brown pieces (to cut legs)
four-inch by six-inch brown pieces (to cut arms)
seven-inch brown squares (to cut the head)
three-inch tan squares (to cut paws)
three-inch by four-inch brown pieces (to cut ears)

By using crayons, the children can simulate fur or draw in other details.

For children who want to create different heads, an aide can prepare nine-inch squares of colored construction paper (e.g., gray, tan, red, flesh-colored).

An aide also provides piles of flannel strips to cut into lengths to paste on the back of each cut-out.

The aide talks with the children about what materials to choose on an individual basis. If a child asks, "What do I need?" the aide helps him think back to the story. If a child seeks help in deciding what to use, the aide encourages the child to make his own choice. The aide does not tell the child what to select. He discusses with the child the sizes that he needs for what he will cut out, but the aide leaves to the child the decisions about what to choose. When the child makes his choice, the aide encourages him to go on with his project. At no point does the aide expect the child to conform to models of what to make, but rather expects the child to express the concepts that he has in mind at that time. The aide appreciates whatever the child makes, commends whatever he accomplishes, and helps him enjoy making it.

## SELECTING MORE FLANNEL-BOARD SONGS, STORIES, POEMS

Each year an aide adds to his collection of songs, stories, and poems to use with a flannel board. Such materials must be intrinsically interesting to the children, or they are not worth using because they may dull the fascination of the flannel board for the children. They should also be instructive because time in school or out of school should be used to good advantage for the children.

Here are some objectives that an aide has in mind when he selects another song, story, or poem for flannel-board presentation:

1. A child becomes aware of an important item represented by a cut-out (e.g., a pumpkin vine).
2. A child becomes aware of the place relationship of two objects (e.g., apples on a tree; a sweater on a boy).
3. A child notices the parts of an object in relation to each other and to the whole (e.g., lunch can be a sandwich and a glass of milk).
4. A child compares two objects or concepts (e.g., a black cat with a white cat; three children with three pairs of mittens).
5. A child sings a song or says a poem in sequence using flannel board cues.
6. A child links together cut-out object and a printed word.
7. A child arranges letters and numerals meaningfully in relation to object cut-outs.

No limit exists for a collection of flannel-board songs, stories, and poems.[7] An aide, however, discards less instructive material as he finds material that guides a child's learning more effectively. And he uses flannel board material as one of several ways of guiding learning rather than the only way. Thus the aide encourages the children to have an added edge of pleasant emotion when the flannel board is used with a song, poem, or story to guide their thinking.

[7] Sources of songs, stories, and poems include:

Carlson, Bernice Wells. *Listen and Help Tell the Story*. New York: Abingdon Press, 1965.

Grayson, Marion F. *Let's Do Fingerplays*. Washington, D.C.: Robert C. Luce Inc., 1962.

McLaughlin, Roberta, and Lucille Wood. *Sing a Song*. Glendale, California: Bowmar Publishing Corporation, 1969.

Scott, Louise Binder, and J. J. Thompson. *Talking Time*. New York: McGraw-Hill Book Co., 1966

Wood, Lucille F., and Louise Binder Scott. *Singing Fun*. St. Louis: Webster Publishing Co., 1954.

———. *More Singing Fun*. St. Louis: Webster Publishing Co., 1961.

# FROM AIDE TO PARENT AND TEACHER

Many aides to teachers become competent parents who effectively guide the development of their own children and simultaneously contribute to the development of their children's playmates. Other aides are quite content to become increasingly competent as aides without thinking of such responsibility as a stepping-stone to greater responsibilities. But in large part those who are aides come to see their responsibility as a foundation stone in the sequence of steps leading to becoming a teacher; and then possibly a director of a preschool group or a principal of a school that has several groups of young children, both preschool- and school-age; or possibly a professorial supervisor of those wishing to become teachers of young children or directors of schools for them. A position as an aide is an end in itself and is also potentially a means to other ends.

Whether an aide sees a professional future beyond his immediate position or not, he will want to build the marketable skills that an aide position involves and become increasingly comfortable with the responsibilities that an aide has. He can build these competencies at his own rate. As he does so, he has more and more to contribute to the development of the children with whom he works. With each new marketable skill that he develops—the ability to guide playground activities, or the ability to tell a children's story—an aide has more personal satisfaction as he uses the skill with young children.

## DEVELOPING COMPETENCE AS AN AIDE [1]

### The Starting Point

In arranging to serve as an aide, a person finds out what early childhood programs are set up in his community. The counseling office of a high

[1] Vivian Edmiston Todd and Helen Heffernan, *The Years Before School* (New York:

school or a community college probably can provide information about how to apply for volunteer positions as an aide, and the office of the superintendent of schools can advise him how to apply for employment as an aide. Experience as a volunteer aide is usually excellent preparation for employment as an aide. Sometimes community and other colleges offer courses that include experience as an aide as an integral part of the course. Such courses may be offered in departments of education, psychology, home economics, or other behavioral sciences and applied fields.

Most application procedures include an interview. This gives the applicant an opportunity to see realistically what it will be like to serve as an aide. He talks with the teacher with whom he will be working, and with others on the team that guides the children and administers the program for them. He then decides whether he wishes to join the team as an aide.

Meanwhile the team will be attempting to determine whether the aide that they must depend on is this applicant or another one. When they offer a position to a prospective aide, their offer means that they have confidence that the prospect will develop into the person needed to round out the team.

### In Costume

Everyone working with young children wears clothing that washes and dries readily. Learning involves trial and error, and spilling is incidental to learning such fascinating things as how to obtain a drink, how to control a garden hose, or how to wash one's hands.

Since picking up a child can be necessary or desirable at any time, an aide or a teacher is careful to avoid wearing a clasp or pin that might scratch a child. Of course any item that is easily broken is also not worn. In general, a person working with young children wears comfortable clothing requiring a minimum amount of care.

### What to Learn First

An aide usually begins as an observer because he must focus his attention on learning the names of the children, the location of the supplies and equipment, and the patterns of activities that the teacher has developed with the children. As soon as the aide has these items clearly in his mind, he can begin to actively help the teacher in whatever ways the teacher suggests.

How does each child learn most readily—and in what situations? An aide can carefully observe a particular child, noticing the child's interests and skills in learning and how the teacher guides his learning. The aide can then ask the teacher if he can work with that child from time to time

---

The Macmillan Co., 1970). Pages 621–658 deal with "Participation in Teaching Preschool Groups."

during the next few days. In this way an aide can enter into a rewarding relationship with a child.

Here is a list of five questions for the beginning aide, with additional subquestions to be kept in mind as soon as the aide is ready for them:

1. Can I call each child by name?
   a. Do I interact with each child each day?
   b. What is each child especially interested in?
   c. How does each child learn most readily? (How can he use this skill in the group?)
   d. What additional learning would be especially useful for him? (How can I encourage his learning it?)
2. Can I get each piece of equipment and each supply item as it is needed?
   a. How is each item useful to children in their learning of skills, concepts, and basic beliefs?
   b. What factors are associated with the location of each item? (e.g., storage of an item near where it will be used.)
3. What is the pattern of activities within a school day? (How does an aide fit into them?)
   a. What variations in the pattern occur frequently?
   b. At what transition points are children likely to be fatigued? Thirsty? Hungry? (What help can I give a child who is fatigued? Thirsty? Hungry?)
   c. What are the cues about when a child is fatigued? Thirsty? Hungry?
   d. What stress situations do individual children encounter? (How can an aide help each of them manage himself in the situation?)
4. What are the learning goals that the teacher has for the children?
   a. How does an adult guide their learning?
   b. What cues does the child need?
5. What am I comfortable in doing as an aide?
   a. What additional experience do I need to broaden my zone of comfort?
   b. How can I arrange the additional experience?

### Working with Individuals

Often a teacher wishes that she could spend more time with an individual child but realizes that the rest of the children can also profit from additional teacher time and attention. But the teacher who is fortunate to have an aide can ask him to make a mini-case study of an individual child, attempting to find out how that child learns and what kind and amount of inputs the child needs to facilitate his learning.

AIDE AND TEACHER ENJOY GUIDING LEARNING.

A teacher would also often like to help a child who has been absent. The teacher can plan with an aide how to provide the essential experiences that the other children have had while the absentee has been away from the group.

When a child has unsolved problems or insecurities, he may need more adult attention than the teacher can easily provide. Again an aide can be invaluable in reassuring the child and providing whatever support is needed. The aide can make learning fun for the child.

In each of these situations, the aide works as he is guided by the teacher. From time to time the aide provides the teacher with feedback about the progress the child is making, and obtains additional suggestions about how to further help the child.

### Working with Small Groups

An aide can soon feel as comfortable in working with two or three children as he can with an individual child. At the suggestion of the teacher, the aide may have several children who need additional experience to master some important concept or acquire some desirable skill.

In working with two or three children, an aide makes sure that each child has a turn to be prominent in the activity of the group. The aide expects the children to work together cooperatively, probably sharing equipment and supplies, and taking turns as needed. The aide also makes sure that each child feels that his efforts are really appreciated by the group. Later with the teacher the aide discusses situations involving noncooperation. He needs to know how to use such feedback to help children learn to share and to take turns.

The successful aide is the one who really enjoys the group activity and sees that it is fun for each child.

### Working with the Entire Class

When an aide is learning how the entire group functions under the guidance of its teacher, he is an observer who participates in some quiet way. Perhaps he keeps records for the group, or perhaps he prepares materials the children will use later. As he works the aide also observes what the teacher does and says, and what the children do and say in response. In his own mind, an aide thinks about himself in the role of teacher.

When an aide takes over the responsibility for the class in an emergency or in advancing to new skills, he must first have the class understand what is to be done. The aide may say, "We'll go on with what we are doing." If the aide does not tell the children what is expected of them, some of them will become active in different ways in their attempt to find out what is expected. The reassuring command from the aide tells them both what to do and what he as their temporary leader expects. The calm assurance of the aide is a stimulus to calm assurance on the part of the children.

A more experienced aide may be asked to take the responsibility for the class for an entire group activity. In this manner, the aide's experience in working with children in a small group is enlarged. But basically the aide is guiding the learning of children according to the same principles, independent of the size of the group. He soon feels comfortable working with larger numbers of children, and with the help of the teacher he adds the additional tactics and strategies that are needed.

## SEEING AND REINFORCING PATTERNS IN LEARNING

An aide advances toward becoming a teacher through carefully observing, thinking about, and trying to do essentially what the teacher does to guide the learning of the children. At first the aide observes each activity as a separate learning project. Soon he notices that certain kinds of activities recur frequently and usually in somewhat the same situations. Presently the observant aide begins to see patterns in what the teacher does. When the aide discusses his observations with the teacher, the teacher helps him understand the basic learning and child development theory that underlie each pattern. His increased understanding of each learning-teaching pattern enables the aide to use it when a suitable occasion arises.

The observant aide, who has been watching a good teacher guide child learning, probably notices such child-learning patterns as moving eyes from left to right across the page of a book, and looking to the left before stepping off a curb, then looking to the right.

The aide can see the advantage in having children always work from left to right, perhaps because the teacher has pointed out to him the general rule of placing material on the flannel board so that the left side is used first, or the general rule of holding a picture book so that the children look first at the left-hand page and then to the right. The aide then consciously develops ways of working so that the material he places on the bulletin board, a flannel board, or a chalk board will be read by the children from left to right.

When he discusses his purposes and activities with the teacher, the aide becomes aware of the desirability of children consciously learning and using the concepts of *left* and *right.* A child who distinguishes his right hand can quickly learn to link the word *right* with right-hand movements and with eye movements from left to right. The aide then experiments with helping children build linkages between moving their right hand and using the word, *right.* Here are some of the activities the aide may use to facilitate linkages and obtain feedback about child learning of the concept *right.*

### Guiding Thinking, Doing, and Feeling

When an aide is at hand, a child arriving at school has not only a friendly greeting from the aide but also comments about the *right* tied in with the removal of his coat sleeves and footwear. "Can you tie the lace on your *right* shoe?" the aide may ask if the right one needs tieing. Or the aide may say, "Out comes your *right* arm," when the right coat sleeve is removed. Such comments about *right* are gradually linked to the appropriate motions of the right arm or foot through repetition in a functional situation. *Left* is learned subsequently.

Putting on or taking off footwear can occasion the linking of *left* and *right* together to make a *pair.* If an aide sees that a clothespin is used for each pair of rubbers, he can soon guide the children into linking this new word to previously learned concepts of *left* and *right.*

The aide can also help them learn one-to-one correspondence of objects as they learn both *right* and *left.*

### A Rhyme on Occasion

When an aide has a few minutes with a group before it joins another group, he can use those few minutes to teach a finger play, a verse from a song, or a poem. Here is a favorite verse for an aide's collection to guide children to learn the concepts of *left* and *right:*

My Right Hand

This is my right hand. (Extend it.)
I raise it up high. (Raise it.)
This is my left hand. (Extend it.)
I will touch the sky. (Raise it.)
Right hand, left hand. (Show each.)
Whirl them around. (Do it.)
Right hand, left hand. (Show each.)
Pound, pound, pound. (Do it.)
—Anonymous

### In the Playhouse

An aide can guide the setting of the table in the playhouse so that the children learn to place the knife and spoon on the right of the plate and the fork on the left. If the aide prepares a large picture or drawing of a place setting, it can soon guide children to link some new words to their earlier learned concepts of *left* and *right*.

### A Story

In facing a group of children to teach them about left and right, an aide, like a teacher, is careful to use the hand or foot opposite the one he is saying. In this way the children react to the aide's pantomime as they do to their own movements when they see them in a mirror. The following story is told with gestures in this way.

MR. LEFT AND MR. RIGHT

This is Mr. Left. (Hold up left thumb.)

This is Mr. Right. (Hold up right thumb.)

Mr. Left lives in a house (make a fist for the house) at the top of a hill. He opens the door (fingers out) and goes inside (thumb goes into opened fist). He closes the door (fingers close).

Mr. Right lives in another house (other fist) at the top of another hill. He opens the door (fingers out) and goes inside (thumb into opened fist). He closes the door (fingers close).

One day Mr. Left opened his door and came out of his house (thumb comes out of fist). He closed the door and said, "It's such a nice day. I think I'll go for a walk and visit my friend, Mr. Right."

Mr. Left walked down the hill, and up a hill, down another hill, and up a hill. (Pantomime the up and down walk.) He came to Mr. Right's house. He knocked on the door (left fist knocks on right fist), waited a few seconds, and knocked again. "I guess Mr. Right is not home. I'll come back another day."

Mr. Left went back down the hill, up the other hill, down the hill, and up the hill to his own house. He opened the door, went inside, and closed the door.

(Repeat for Mr. Right).

Another day they decided to visit each other.

They opened their doors, stepped outside and closed their doors.

They both walked down the hill and up the hill until they met.

"How do you do, Mr. Right," said Mr. Left.

"How do you do, Mr. Left," said Mr. Right.

They talked and talked and talked (wiggle thumbs). When the sun was low in the west, they each waved "Good-bye." Then each went down the hill, and up the hill back to his own house. They popped into their houses, and were out of sight. (Pantomime with thumbs. End with thumbs inside fists.)

### Other Activities

The teacher may suggest other activities through which an aide can help the children reinforce their concepts of *left* and *right*, for instance:

A child makes a hand print by dipping his palm into finger paint and pressing it on a piece of construction paper of a color that contrasts with the color of the paint. Depending on the word experience of the child, the aide will encourage the child to label the finger print *left* or *right* or will label it with him. For Valentine's Day double hearts folded like a book can open to show a left hand and a right hand, perhaps red hand prints on white hearts, or white prints on red hearts.

An aide can read to a small group of children a book such as *Good Day—Which Way?* by Charlotte Steiner that emphasizes the concepts of *left* and *right*.[2]

An aide can lead a group of children in the singing game of "Looby-Loo." Putting a colorful bracelet on the right arm will help the children be aware that it is in use.

With a child or a small group of children, an aide can review an experience chart showing the words of a familiar song or a familiar poem. The aide can say, "Now I will shine a light on our chart. You follow the light with your eyes." Then the aide focuses his flashlight on the beginning of the sentence on the experience chart, reminding the children that "they start at the left and go to the right." The aide turns the flashlight off at the end of the line and turns it on for the beginning of the next line.

## FROM AIDE TO PARENT

Whether he is a prospective parent or an actual one, an aide has an invaluable experience that prepares him for being a better parent than he

[2] Charlotte Steiner, *Good Day—Which Way?* (New York: Alfred A Knopf, Inc., 1960). Osmond Molarsky, *Right Thumb, Left Thumb* (Reading, Mass.: Addison-Wesley Publishing Co., Inc., 1969).

would otherwise be. As he works with teachers who have studied the learning process and ways of guiding it effectively, an aide develops concepts that are as applicable to guiding children in a family as they are to guiding children in a school. The aide who has become comfortable in his role is prepared to develop comfortable relationships with his own children. Furthermore, his interest in reading and studying about how children learn and develop should motivate the aide to read about how a parent, as well as other aides, facilitates this learning process. The parent who has been a skillful aide to teachers working with children continues to be a skillful aide to the teachers of his own children.

By working with children as an aide, a parent or a prospective parent becomes proficient in observing how children learn and how this learning process is facilitated. A young child who shows his awareness of a new object by breaking it can be guided to use better ways of getting acquainted

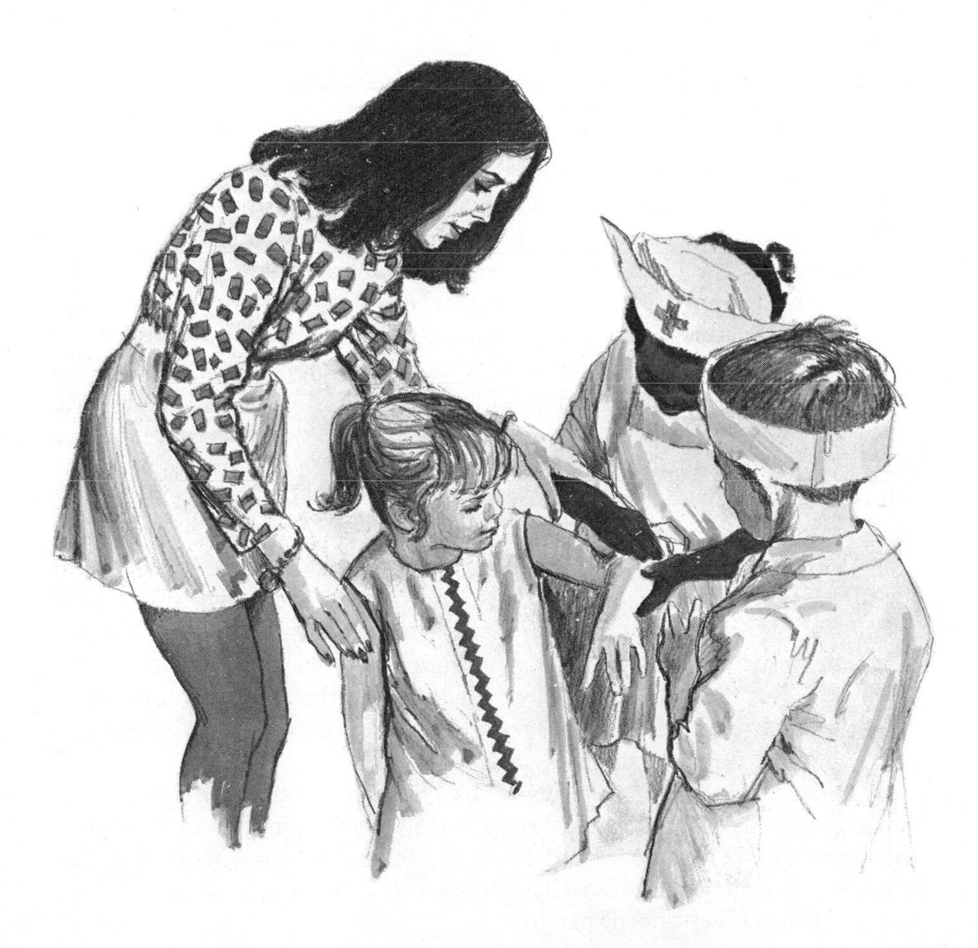

AN AIDE TODAY; A PARENT TOMORROW.

with objects. The aide who has observed and participated in the guidance of the child's relearning is better able to accept behavior of children simply as feedback about what they have learned up to that point. Such an aide is more ready to work with his children as their guide rather than as their evaluator or rejector. This aide will probably be a more proficient and happy parent.

An experienced aide will see various opportunities to carry over tactics from the school situation he has experienced into the home situation. For example, the aide who has helped small groups of children in role playing the immunization procedure can help his own children and their friends in similar role playing. One child can have the role of doctor; another, the role of nurse; and the third, the role of patient. The "doctor" learns to explain that "It may hurt," and then plays giving the shot by pressing on the arm of the "patient." The "patient" learns to interpret this pressure as evidence that he will now be well rather than as evidence that he is being hurt badly and should yell or scream. The "nurse" also learns her pantomimes for helping the "doctor" and the "patient."

### Self-Development of an Aide

As an aide moves toward becoming a proficient parent, his self-development is readily observable in his interaction with other people. Working with others necessitates having the other persons as the focus of his attention. A self-centered aide is a person who has not yet learned to think primarily in terms of the children with whom he is working.

As an aide feels increasingly comfortable with each young child, he is able to guide the child into a wider range of activities and concepts. A comfortable relationship with a child is the first step in helping him learn. The child has confidence in the aide and is willing to try what he suggests. The success of the young child in coping with his world increases the self-confidence of the child, the confidence of the child in the aide, and also the self-confidence of the aide.

With an enlarging zone of comfort, an aide increases the frequency of his interactions with the child. If these occur at the points at which a child is completing one activity and is making a transition to a new activity, the aide will probably be successful in guiding the child into a satisfying experience. The increased frequency of successes for the child is accompanied by satisfaction both for him and for the aide. Furthermore, an initial success will make for more success in the future.

The aide who thinks in terms of the children and their teacher can become a warm person, a person who openly enjoys the children and supports their activities. The aide who is characterized by a warm personality can become a parent who is also characterized as a warm person who is successful in the chosen role of parent.

## THE EXPERIENCE ROUTE TO TEACHING

Serving as an aide can be a first step in discovering the joy of professionally guiding the learning of young children. Laboratory experience as an aide can be supplemented by college-course work that combines the aide activity with the theory of child development and learning in a larger framework of "teaching." This integration of practice and theory prepares a prospective teacher well. Many successful teachers have become teachers by going from experiences as aides and tutors to substitute teaching and to full responsibility as teachers. When combined with studies in liberal arts and sciences, and in professional education, the experience route to teaching is excellent: It keeps the focus of attention on the young child as a learner.

The pattern of professional courses that a prospective teacher follows differs from state to state and from college to college. However, some characteristics are found in most programs for teachers:

| EXPERIENCE WITH CHILDREN | COURSE WORK INCLUDES SUCH TOPICS AS: |
|---|---|
| Part-time aide or tutor | Basic concepts in Education or Behavioral Science |
| | How children develop |
| Full-time aide | How children learn |
| Student teacher | Programs for guiding children's learning |
| Substitute teacher | Methods and materials for children's learning experiences (e.g., in reading, mathemetics, art . . .) |
| | How to guide learning |
| | Diagnosis of what needs to be learned |
| Full-time teacher | Philosophy of education |
| | Research about education of young children |
| Supervisor | Direction and supervision of teaching |
| Administrative intern | Administration of a school of young children |
| Administrator | Problems in administration |

### Abilities of an Aide

Both the course work and the directed experience that an aide has prepare him for increasing responsibility as an aide. As he develops in his ability to guide the learning of children, the aide's competence is easily recognized by what he is able to do. No set list of abilities is all-inclusive, nor is every aide able to develop all skills on any list if the teacher whom he assists limits the area in which the aide can show responsibility. Nevertheless a list of expected behaviors for an aide will include the following:

**ABILITIES AN AIDE DEVELOPS**

| MINIMUM | OPTIMUM |
|---|---|
| Is eager to be helpful to the teacher. | Anticipates what is needed and provides it. |
| Knows the name of each child. | Knows how each child learns. |
| Knows the location of equipment and supplies. | Has needed equipment and supplies at hand when children are to use them. |
| Works as directed by the teacher in guiding one or more children. | Needs minimal cues about how to work with one or more children as teacher suggests. |
| Provides teacher with feedback on what children can do, as requested. | Takes initiative in supplying teacher with feedback and asking about what help to give next. |
| Helps teacher with group management as requested (i.e., record keeping). | Improves on record keeping, simplifying it, and thinking of uses for record information. |
| Develops excellent rapport with one or more children. | Has excellent rapport with every student and can take responsibility for the group in an emergency. |
| Does outside reading as requested. | Enrolls in related courses. |
| Knows the teacher's objectives. | Guides children in keeping with teacher's objectives. |
| Carries out a planned activity with a few students. | Has a growing file of lesson plans with materials needed for each. |

### Abilities of a Teacher [3]

By the time an aide has completed his liberal education with the professional studies required of a prospective teacher, he has enlarged his abilities a great deal. The aide's competence in guiding the learning of children has developed to the point where he can guide the development of each child in an entire class. The teacher can do this himself, and can make effective use of aides in supplementing what she does personally. Furthermore, the teacher can so guide the learning activities of her class that the group fits easily into the overall structure of whatever school system it is in.

Some of the specific abilities that a teacher develops are as follows:

1. Plans sequences of learning experiences to guide optimum development of children.

[3] Vivian Edmiston Todd and Helen Heffernan, *The Years Before School* (New York: The Macmillan Co., 1970).

2. Plans in such a way as to obtain feedback about what each child is learning to do.
3. Anticipates and minimizes the learning problems of each child.
4. Guides the learning of individual children within the setting of the large group, or of small groups.
5. Uses feedback to diagnose what each child needs to learn next.
6. Makes learning fun for everyone, including himself.
7. Keeps records as needed by the school system, by parents, and by himself.
8. Plans and directs the assistance of aides.
9. Arranges with fellow teachers to supplement his teaching as needed.
10. Interacts with parents so that they reinforce classroom learning of their children.
11. Continues to develop in service, taking additional college courses, reading government publications and current books and articles about child development and teaching young children.
12. Takes responsibility in his profession, attending professional conferences and visiting demonstration schools each year.
13. Recommends equipment and supplies to meet the children's needs.

## A SUBSTITUTE TEACHER

The experienced aide who is completing college studies for being credentialed as a teacher of young children is eager to gain experience on a part-time basis. When state law permits, the aide makes himself available as a substitute teacher. So does the teacher of young children whose family responsibilities have increased to the point of interfering with full-time employment. Another person who is often available as a substitute is the teacher who has retired from full-time teaching, has had a year or two of travel and other activities, and feels the need for further involvement with young children. Such people are a boon to the teacher who needs a capable person in her place when she attends a professional conference, or interprets the school to people in the community, or becomes ill.

When the teacher knows in advance that she will be away from her group of children, she arranges with the substitute teacher what the children will do in her absence. However, when the teacher has an emergency situation that requires her absence from her group, she counts on the substitute teacher to be prepared to guide the children in constructive learning activities throughout their usual day. The well-prepared substitute can easily do this. She goes to her files and selects material to help the group of children to develop concepts of significance to them and skills appropriate to their level of development. She plans to use with all the children materials she first used as an aide working with one or two children. For a kindergarten, she may select the following four sets of materials:

1. To reinforce concepts of shape, size, and color; and to provide an opportunity for language development, the substitute has cut-outs of different shapes and sizes made from construction paper in primary and secondary colors. She plans to use them as described previously (pages 96 and 123).

2. To help children listen carefully to words and notice similarities and differences, the substitute has objects or miniature models with which to carry on rhyming word games. (See page 158.)

When all of the rhyming-word pairs are on diamond-shaped papers, the substitute can guide the children to play "What Pair Is Missing?" making sure that each child says the rhyming names as often as possible.

3. To provide an opportunity for the children to reinforce their number concepts, the substitute uses felt numerals, sets of felt objects, and cards having the names of the numbers printed on them. With a flannel board, these cut-outs can be used in various combinations, as described in Chapter 6 on page 146.

With additional cut-outs, the sustitute can teach the children a simple poem such as "Five Baby Sea Turtles" (see Chapter 9, page 213). This will give them practice in using cardinal numbers from 1 through 5. For practice with ordinal numbers, the substitute may want to use "Twelve Little Rabbits" as adapted here.

TWELVE LITTLE RABBITS [4]

Four little rabbits on a big, big farm
Put an ear to the ground to catch the sound.

The first little rabbit heard a cow moo,
The second little rabbit heard a horse neigh,
The third little rabbit heard a dove coo,
The fourth little rabbit heard a mule bray.

Four other little rabbits on the big, big, farm
With little pink eyes looked to see what flies.

The fifth little rabbit saw a chickadee,
The sixth little rabbit saw a black crow,
The seventh little rabbit saw a bumblebee,
The eighth little rabbit saw a scarecrow.

[4] Adapted from "Five Little Rabbits," reprinted by permission from *Talking Time*, Second Ed., by Louise Binder Scott and J. J. Thompson. Copyright © 1966 by McGraw-Hill, Inc.

Four other little rabbits on the big, big farm
Left their cozy lair and sniffed the air.

The ninth little rabbit smelled a cabbage green,
The tenth little rabbit smelled the growing wheat,
The eleventh little rabbit smelled the earth so clean,
The twelfth little rabbit smelled a carrot sweet.

All twelve little rabbits on the big, big farm
Were hungry for lunch, so they started to munch.

(Children tell what the rabbits ate.)
—Louise Binder Scott

With younger children, this poem may be shortened and adapted to teach ordinal number concepts of *first* through *fourth*. An aide can omit "other" in the first line of the two-line verses and replace "twelve" with "four" in the last verse. In each of the four-line verses, he can mention "the *first* little rabbit," and the *second, third,* and *fourth.*

4. To encourage the children to be creative with shapes, the substitute may talk with them about houses, perhaps showing them pictures of houses, and then suggesting that they think about their own house. At the cut-and-paste table, each child has a piece of paper, and each group has an assortment of triangles, rectangles, and squares cut from construction paper of different colors. "Will these help you make a picture of your house?"

If aides are available to help the less mature children, the substitute encourages each child to print his home address on his house.

## GUIDING THE PROFESSIONAL DEVELOPMENT OF AN AIDE

One of the privileges of the teaching profession is to advise aides who are interested in joining its ranks and are potentially successful teachers. The teachers who are assisted by aides are fortunate not only in being able to teach children more fully and more easily because of an aide's help but also because they are able to serve as examples and guides for the aides as they move into the teaching profession.

### Self-Confidence

In addition to personal satisfaction, perhaps the major index that a teacher has of her success in guiding an aide is the self-confidence of everyone involved:

1. Self-confidence of the children in using new concepts and skills.
2. Self-confidence of the aide in helping children learn.

3. Self-confidence of the teacher herself in guiding the learning of children, aides, and herself.

The teacher helps the aide to consciously use the criterion of self-confidence. For instance, if an aide passes out pencils for the children to use and then thinks that it is best not to use the pencils at that time, the aide may want to take the pencils back. But the aide should realize that the children will have more self-confidence if he proceeds with a modification of his first plan and lets them use the pencils that they have in their hands.

It may help the self-confidence of the aide temporarily if he gives arbitrary orders to the children, but doing so will make for dependency rather than self-confidence on the part of the children. The aide will become self-confident if he helps the children understand what is desirable to do, together with the reasons for doing it that way. In discussing an incident with the aide, the teacher helps the aide understand that no adult should build his own self-confidence at the expense of those with whom he works.

### Files for Teaching

One of the major ways in which a teacher helps the children, herself, and her aides is by encouraging the aides in developing files of materials to use with the children. The teacher has collected and created over the years those materials that enable her to guide the development of the children. The teacher defines goals that she expects the children to achieve as well as changes in their behavior that are feasible for the children to achieve within the school term. For each of these goals, the teacher selects or designs strategies and tactics that she can use to guide the children. She plans daily lessons in which the children's activities are fun for the children and are at the same time means for furthering their development as planned. The teacher's files are a basic factor that give her confidence in her ability to do this day after day.

The files of the teacher serve as an example of one way in which to collect material and organize it for use with the children. Some teachers like to use manila and other colored file folders arranged alphabetically in a file drawer. Other teachers like to have a collection of boxes neatly labeled and stacked on cupboard shelves ready to be taken down and opened up with the children. Such boxes contain flannel-board cut-outs, duplicated copies of poems and stories, suggestions for study trips and creative activities, materials the children will need to work with, and even the picture books that will help to make important concepts vivid in the minds of the children. In short, each teacher organizes the teaching materials she collects in whatever way seems to her to facilitate easy retrieval of what is needed by the children.

When a child brought his pet turtle to school, one teacher encouraged an aide to receive the turtle and to build a file of materials to use in this situation. The librarian in the professional library for teachers in the school system and the librarian in the Boys and Girls Department of the local public library helped the aide to locate suitable material. While guiding the child and his friends into learning experiences about the turtle the aide selected especially useful material for his file as follows:

1. Pet Care Information
   a. Food
      1) Raw hamburger.
      2) Shredded raw fish.
      3) Bits of lettuce, tomatoes, and fruits.
      4) Feed the turtle once a day all that he will eat in thirty minutes.
   b. Care
      1) Put in a terrarium, with a dish of water for swimming.
      2) Clean the terrarium and change water daily.
      3) Allow two hours a day of direct sunlight.[5]
2. Finger Play Poem

THE LITTLE TURTLE,[6] BY VACHEL LINDSAY

3. Flannel-Board Poem

FIVE BABY SEA TURTLES

One baby sea turtle hatched so new.
*One more* was hatched, so that makes two.

Two baby sea turtles swimming out to sea.
*One more* swam beside them, so that makes three.

Three baby sea turtles on the ocean floor.
They met *one more,* so that makes four.

Four baby sea turtles learning how to dive.
*One more* joined their class, so that makes five.

Count the baby sea turtles glad to be alive;
One, two, three, four, five.

—Barbara McBride

[5] The American Humane Association, *Turtle* (Denver, Colorado: The American Humane Association, [n.d.]).
[6] May Hill Arbuthnot (ed.), *Time for Poetry* (New York: The Macmillan Co., 1961), p. 63.

4. Poem

THE SATISFIED TURTLE

I like it very well
Inside my cozy shell.

If it rains outside,
Indoors I hide.

If the sun's too hot.
My house is not.

My shell
Is swell.
—Anonymous

5. Books and Articles
   a. Science picture book showing turtles hatching from eggs: Mel Crawford. *The Turtle Book*. New York: The Golden Press, 1965.
   b. Story picture book about helping a turtle on his back turn over: Alice Vaught Davis. *Timothy Turtle*. New York: Harcourt Brace Jovanovich Inc., 1940.
   c. Story picture book about a dead pet: Edith G. Stull. *My Turtle Died Today*. New York: Holt, Rinehart and Winston, Inc., 1964.
   d. Newspaper article telling about local people who have pet turtles.

### Beginning a Library of Children's Books

When an aide in a Day Care Center in Los Angeles wished to begin a collection of books to read to young children, he discussed with the teacher how to best use the money he had for that purpose. He had in mind a collection for future teaching situations in the Los Angeles area. The teacher referred him to a librarian who specialized in books for boys and girls. The librarian had in her files a list of recommended children's books for the preceding year.[7] The aide recognized on the list books to which the children responded well. He also noted books that seemed especially appropriate in urban communities. At that point the aide realized that he was using the following criteria for books that he should purchase:

1. Recommended by a librarian for children's books.
2. Of interest to the children worked with.

[7] Virginia Haviland, Lois B. Watt, et al., "Children's Books 1970" (Washington, D.C.: Library of Congress, 1971).

3. Useful for preschool children in an urban community in Southern California today.

The list of 1970 books that the Los Angeles aide prepared for his beginning collection with notes was as follows:

Alexander, Martha G. *Bobo's Dream.* New York: The Dial Press, Inc. 1970. An aide listens while a child reads the pictures from a book or a projection screen.

Borten, Helen. *Do You Know What I Know?* New York: Abelard-Schuman, Limited, 1970. "How do I find out? By using my eyes and my ears, my tongue and my nose, my fingers and toes, and the skin that I'm in."

Eckert, Horst. *Dear Snowman.* New York: World Publishing Company, 1970. Introduces Johnny, the Snowman created by the author who is the artist H. Eckert Janosch.

Lobel, Arnold. *Frog and Toad Are Friends.* New York: Harper & Row, Publishers, Inc., 1970. Simple words and pictures recount humorous adventures of two friends.

When the aide discussed his list with the librarian, the librarian asked the aide if he had considered the black families with whom he might be working in the Los Angeles preschool groups. The librarian suggested that the aide check his list with that published in 1971 by the New York Public Library, "The Black Experience in Children's Books." The aide was delighted to find *Bobo's Dream* on the list of the New York Public Library as well as on his own.

When the teacher reviewed his list, the aide received two other suggestions—a book to help a child enjoy the addition of a new baby to his family, and a book or two by a well-known local author. The aide added to his list of books for preschool children in the Los Angeles area the following:

Politi, Leo. *Emmet.* New York: Charles Scribner's Sons, 1971. A troublemaker dog becomes a hero when a local market is set on fire.

Politi, Leo. *Rosa.* New York: Charles Scribner's Sons, 1965. Lonely Rosa welcomes a baby sister.

Talking with colleagues about his list enabled the aide to realize that each person has individual criteria that make his book selection unique in some respects, but that everyone should select some books that have been favorites of preschool children over the years. His last selection of books was from a Children's Book and Record Library, as follows:

*Caps for Sale* by E. Slobodkina
*Harold and the Purple Crayon* by Crockett Johnson
*Curious George Rides a Bike* by H. A. Rey
*The Golden Treasury of Mother Goose*

At the same time he began a collection of records for children with "Sounds of the City."

### Obtaining Feedback

Another way in which the professional person helps the aide become a capable teacher is by encouraging him to use the scientific method of guiding children:

1. Plan an activity through which children may have fun developing a skill and concept that they need. Prepare or obtain materials they will need.
2. Guide the children in carrying out the activity, and note their success and their problems in doing it.
3. Use this feedback to plan their next experience facilitating or reinforcing their learning, or going ahead.

When the aide reinforces the concept of *one more* by using the verse about "Five Baby Sea Turtles," he is pleased with the immediate feedback of the children's enjoyment of the flannel-board verse. But he hears better feedback when a child asks for "one more cookie," and thus uses the concept of "one more" in a different situation. The aide's recognition of the child's question as feedback needed by the teacher, and his reporting it to the teacher, enable the teacher to guide the learning of the children more effectively.

# INDEX

## A

## I



## L



## M



## N



## O



## P

## R



## S



## T

## V



## W



## Z